Strategies for Teaching Students with Disabilities in Inclusive Classrooms

A Case Method Approach

Joseph R. Boyle

Rutgers, The State University of New Jersey

Mary C. Provost

College of Charleston

Boston   Columbus   Indianapolis   New York   San Francisco   Upper Saddle River
Amsterdam   Cape Town   Dubai   London   Madrid   Milan   Munich   Paris   Montreal   Toronto
Delhi   Mexico City   São Paulo   Sydney   Hong Kong   Seoul   Singapore   Taipei   Tokyo

Vice President and Editorial Director: Jeffery W. Johnston
Executive Editor and Publisher: Stephen D. Dragin
Editorial Assistant: Jamie Bushell
Vice President, Director of Marketing: Margaret Waples
Marketing Manager: Erica DeLuca
Senior Managing Editor: Pamela D. Bennett
Production Manager: Laura Messerly
Senior Art Director: Jayne Conte
Cover Designer: Bruce Kenselaar
Cover Art: Fotolia
Full-Service Project Management: Munesh Kumar/Aptara®, Inc.
Composition: Aptara®, Inc.
Printer/Binder: R.R. Donnelley & Sons
Cover Printer: R.R. Donnelley & Sons
Text Font: Times

Credits and acknowledgments for materials borrowed from other sources and reproduced, with permission, in this textbook appear on the appropriate page within the text.

Every effort has been made to provide accurate and current Internet information in this book. However, the Internet and information posted on it are constantly changing, so it is inevitable that some of the Internet addresses listed in this textbook will change.

Library of Congress Cataloging-in-Publication Data
Boyle, Joseph.
   Strategies for teaching students with disabilities in inclusive classrooms : a case method approach / Joseph Boyle, Mary C. Provost.
      p. cm.
   ISBN-13: 978-0-13-183777-5
   ISBN-10: 0-13-183777-X
   1. Inclusive education—United States.   2. Curriculum planning—United States.   3. Classroom management—United States.   4. Children with disabilities—Education—United States.   I. Provost, Mary C.   II. Title.
   LC1201.B7 2012
   371.90973—dc23

                                                                                                    2011018214

10 9 8 7 6 5 4 3 2 1

PEARSON

ISBN 10:   0-13-183777-X
ISBN 13: 978-0-13-183777-5

This book is dedicated to the late Floyd G. Hudson, advisor and expert, whose influence on inclusive education carries on in the lives of others.

JRB

This book is dedicated to my family, colleagues, educators, and students who support the education of individuals with and without disabilities. Without these people this book would not have been possible.

MCP

PREFACE

Welcome to the first edition of *Strategies for Teaching Students with Disabilities in Inclusive Classrooms: A Case Method Approach*. Teaching students with disabilities in general education classes poses a challenge for both special education and general education teachers. Often, teachers are not certain about how to modify teaching assignments for students with disabilities, or are not familiar with teaching methods to help students learn the content or skills. Moreover, general education teachers often indicate that they would like more support and training at meeting the academic needs of students with disabilities in their classes. And so, we designed a text that can help teachers learn about students with disabilities and some possible methods to help them learn. Through the use of cases, we hope that the reader will be brought one step closer to reality.

The teacher's role in educating students with diverse learning needs is crucial in today's classroom. We often meet teachers who have diverse learners in their classroom and these students have a wide range of skills. As teachers move through the curriculum to keep pace with the *average student*, often students with learning problems fall behind and, if not provided with supports or remediation, may simply lose interest in the class and move one step closer to failing. Effective teachers not only meet the needs of average students, but also attend to the needs of students who are falling behind. In many inclusive classrooms, the general education teacher works with a special education teacher, and together these teachers meet the needs of at-risk students and students with disabilities. Through the techniques and cases presented in this text, we hope that teachers can better meet the needs of all students in inclusive classrooms.

When used in the college classroom, this text is a practical textbook that can be used by undergraduate and graduate students, as well as teachers who are new to special education or inclusive teaching. The design of the book is based on our beliefs that college students and new teachers learn best when research is linked to practice through application of knowledge. In doing so, we developed both *content chapters*, as well as *case chapters,* whereby the reader would apply content to actual cases. The *content chapters* serve as an *overview* in different domains (e.g., inclusion, reading, mathematics, content-areas), and it is assumed that the reader has had previous exposure to each domain through other classes or supplemental class readings. The *case chapters* that follow each content chapter focus on one or more aspects of teaching in inclusive classrooms. These cases vary from special education law to working collaboratively in the classroom to improving the academic achievement or classroom behaviors of students with disabilities in inclusive classrooms. Using information from courses and content chapters, the reader will examine each case, problem solve to resolve different aspects of the case, and then make recommendations about how to deal with the pertinent or core issues of each case.

Having written a number of casebooks before, we found that the best approach toward writing a useful text is to use a variety of writing styles for the cases. In other words, some of the cases will be more *clinical* in nature, providing much more detail about test results and classroom observations, and some of the cases will be written in a *flexible narrative style*, containing much more dialogue which describes the relationship between the student and others in his/her environment. Still other cases will seek to use a combination of these two styles. Despite the style, each is meant to prompt thoughtful discussion and problem solving.

We feel that there are a number of unique uses for this book in college classes, such as special education or inclusive teaching courses. First, the primary use of this text will be for students enrolled in undergraduate or graduate *inclusion* or *collaboration* courses. These courses are generally designed to teach college students about models of inclusion, how to work effectively with other teachers and professionals, instructional techniques or strategies for teaching students with mild disabilities, management of students within the inclusive classroom, and monitoring student progress within inclusive settings. The text is designed to help students apply knowledge directly from their classes. The cases could also be used by the instructor to generate discussions about the complexity involved in teaching students with learning or behavioral problems within inclusive settings. Because the cases vary in their nature and content, they can be used in a variety of ways. For instance, class discussions could center around a topic-of-the-week, whether it is an issue involving co-teaching or with providing better support for students within inclusive settings.

Second, this text can be used as a supplement to a traditional special education methods course, particularly one that links teaching methods with collaboration. Most methods textbooks lack cases or case application, or use shorter vignettes which often provide only a *surface-learning* approach. Students in these types of courses typically learn many techniques, but fail to apply the techniques to actual students or simulated students (i.e., cases). The cases developed for this text try to move the reader one step closer to reality. Using methods and techniques from their classes, students can directly apply these techniques to the cases.

Third, this text can be used in a general education teaching course. Used in this type of course, students can apply their content knowledge from the course (e.g., literacy, science, social studies) to students with disabilities and, in the process, use differentiated instruction or assessment to describe how to teach students in inclusive settings. Moreover, it is hoped that using the cases from the book will prompt discussion about teaching students with disabilities within the general education or inclusive classroom. Often non-special education majors (e.g., preservice general education teachers) feel unprepared to teach students with disabilities in the general education classrooms, particularly content-area classes. Practice through cases could better prepare students and teachers to deal with the complexities that come with teaching students with disabilities.

As the saying goes, "If the only tool in your toolbox is a hammer, then everything looks like a nail." Hopefully, this text will provide you with several tools that can address a variety of teaching challenges and issues in the classroom.

We hope you enjoy learning the content and applying the techniques and strategies to the cases!

NEW! CourseSmart eTEXTBOOK AVAILABLE

CourseSmart is an exciting new choice for students looking to save money. As an alternative to purchasing the printed textbook, students can purchase an electronic version of the same content. With a CourseSmart eTextbook, students can search the text, make notes online, print out reading assignments that incorporate lecture notes, and bookmark important passages for later review. For more information, or to purchase access to the CourseSmart eTextbook, visit www. coursesmart.com.

ACKNOWLEDGMENTS

We want to thank the following reviewers for their valuable input and feedback in the development of this text: Elizabeth Alteri, Radford University; Kimberly Baumgardner, National Board Certified Teacher Educational Specialist, ESC-20, San Antonio, TX; Gail Peterson Craig, University of Wisconsin – Superior; Karen Kusiak, Colby College; Marilyn Lovett, George Mason University; Kathleen McCoy, Arizona State University; Shaila Rao, Western Michigan University; Craig Rice, Middle Tennessee State University; Maria Stetter, Roosevelt University; Shannon Taylor, University of Nevado Reno; and Mary Kay Zubel, Kansas State University.

BRIEF CONTENTS

CONTENTS

Using Cases in Special Education and Inclusion Courses

In this chapter, we describe cases and discuss how they can be used in college classrooms to expand the reader's knowledge of persons with disabilities in inclusion settings. We first define cases and then discuss how we developed them. Next, we describe the case questions, purpose of the questions, and different types of questions. We then delve into how to analyze a case. We also describe cases used in other fields and how they can be used in special education. Finally, we report on what others have found using case method teaching as part of a teacher training program.

WHAT ARE CASES?

Cases are short narratives used by instructors to help students understand some of the issues and problems that individuals with disabilities encounter in their daily lives. The cases presented in this book are meant to reflect common characteristics and issues associated with working in inclusive classrooms. Furthermore, we have designed the cases to cover a range of grades K–12. Although some events may seem overstated, the incidents come from students we have known over the years through our experiences as teachers and faculty in public and private schools. However, we use fictitious names for both students and places to protect the confidentiality of those individuals. Each case contains student and other technical information (e.g., testing information, drug information) derived from student data. The cases are meant to be used as tools by the reader to better understand both the complexities in the lives of students with disabilities and the issues commonly associated with inclusive schools and classrooms.

CASE QUESTIONS

The questions that follow each case can be used by the reader in several ways. First, the questions help the reader better understand the issue(s) related to working with a student or several students. Second, the questions are designed to help the reader more fully comprehend how inclusive schools view students with disabilities. Third, the questions are centered on issues that students with disabilities experience or that teachers deal with while working in an inclusive classroom. Fourth, some questions focus on applying knowledge and skills learned from classes, such as behavior management, collaboration/consultation, transition, academic problems, and others.

These issues were chosen because they represent skills or information that teachers, parents, and other service personnel can use as they work with students with disabilities. For example, knowledge of behavior management techniques, how to improve collaboration or co-teaching, and how to use effective instructional methods for working with students with disabilities represent basic teacher training skills. We also include issues that relate to the student's or teacher's background so that the reader can more fully understand the perspective of the student or teacher. We hope that the issues and problems incorporated into these cases will invoke the reader to reflect more deeply on how best to approach a situation or address an academic or behavior issue occurring in an inclusive classroom.

BACKGROUND ON CASE METHOD TEACHING

Case studies and cases have been used for some time in a number of disciplines—medicine, nursing, law, and business being the most notable (Hudson & Buckley, 2004; Kagan, 1993; Kim, Utke, & Hupp, 2005). In medicine, college students learn general principles as part of their knowledge base and then apply that knowledge to cases. For example, during the premedical and preclinical phases of their education, the typical medical student is instructed in general principles that help to guide the decision-making process (Shulman, 1986). Once these principles are acquired and demonstrated through exams and projects, students receive opportunities to demonstrate their knowledge during supervised residency and clinical trials. Similarly, cases have been used in nursing to help students make decisions and apply their knowledge, all while in a controlled paper-and-pencil environment (Jones & Sheridan, 1999).

In law school college students reason facts from previous court cases and apply precedents to their own case. Learning the knowledge base of law requires repeated opportunities to practice the general principles of law and to generalize laws and principles to new and different cases (Shulman, 1986).

Likewise in business, cases are used to help college students tackle the complex issues of business management. Using cases of fictional businesses, students have to manage the business while the instructor changes variables in the environment so that students can practice applying knowledge of business to simulated examples. For example, as changes occur, such as periods of high unemployment, tight fiscal spending, and recession, business students decide what appropriate actions to take to ward off business failure (i.e., what products to sell, how high (or low) to set prices, or whether to sell off excess inventory). Following the use of these "paper" cases, it may be possible to use field-based projects so that students can apply their knowledge to "living cases" (Richardson & Ginter, 1998).

In education, some professionals have argued that similar methods should be used in teacher training programs. Fenstermacher (1986) feels that educating a teacher involves more than just teaching a set of skills and competencies; instead, teacher training programs should encourage students to generalize principles from research in order to make better educational decisions. Similarly, we feel that case method teaching can greatly enhance the knowledge base of future teachers, providing them with important reasoning and decision-making skills. By doing so, college students can learn to apply the principles and theory derived from their courses to make sound decisions. Some educators feel that cases "bring to life" much of the factual knowledge that students have learned throughout their education and that this process enables students to begin to "think like teachers" (Harrington & Garrison, 1992). Others argue that cases develop higher order thinking skills in students and using these higher order skills often results in learning that continues long after discussion of the case has ended (Kim, Utke, & Hupp, 2005; Kuntz & Hessler, 1998).

CASE METHOD TEACHING

Case method teaching is a method that allows the reader to "connect" theory with practice, particularly when problems from cases are explored in an environment of "shared inquiry" (Harrington & Garrison, 1992). In this environment, the reader can work with others to discuss their perspective of the problem or issue, come up with some collaborative solutions, and look for ways to apply multiple solutions to a problem.

Case method teaching involves a number of components and steps (Martin, Glatthorn, Winters, & Saif, 1989; Wassermann, 1994a, 1994b). First, cases such as the ones presented in this book should be explored one case at a time. In doing so, the reader can focus on the important issues or concepts of each case. To assist you, we have limited the number of variables used in each case to prevent students from losing sight of the important theme of each case. Second, the cases were written at different levels of difficulty. The cases can thus be used with a variety of courses or at specific junctures in a course (e.g., serving as a review of a certain concept, such as "inclusion"). Third, the questions included with each case are meant to help the reader understand or elaborate on the issues and problems from the case. The questions are framed to engage the reader in multiple levels of thinking, from low-level factual skills to more complex problem-solving skills. Many of the low-level (factual) questions require that the reader state only minimal information derived directly from the cases, whereas other questions require the reader to think through their responses and support them with specific details. Fourth, like the saying goes, "two heads are better than one," the reader is encouraged to work with others to problem solve the issues surrounding the cases. In addition, by using small-group discussion, students can deliberate and discuss different aspects of the case. Of course, the small groups must be arranged so that students feel free to express their opinions in front of other students and not feel intimidated by the process. Prior to using a case, it may be helpful to learn and discuss different aspects of collaboration and problem solving. Taken from special education, collaborative problem solving is meant to include partnership-building skills, communication skills, knowledge about effective teaching practices, and knowledge about how to problem solve (Robinson, 1991). Having taught collaboration to students before, we feel that these techniques help students better understand group dynamics or at least make them sensitive to the fact that their interactions with fellow students have both positive and negative influences.

USING PROBLEM SOLVING WITH CASES

In this text, we strongly urge the use of collaborative problem solving (CPS) for addressing case issues and problems (Knackendoffel, 1996).

Most problem-solving frameworks, including CPS, involve the following steps:

1. Define the problem by using objective and measurable terms.
2. Identify possible solutions, allowing for many different solutions.
3. Vote on and select the best solution or solutions.
4. Develop an implementation plan with specific steps for carrying it out.
5. Develop criteria for success, making it objective and measurable.

PROBLEM SOLVING WITH OUR EXAMPLE CASE: COCO HAVLIN

Coco Havlin was born in Mexico and came to the United States 4 years ago. Coco is currently in sixth grade attending Terger High School in California. Terger has a culturally diverse population that includes many Hispanic Americans, African Americans, and Asian Americans. Terger is located in an economically depressed area of southern California, and gangs have a large influence on the community, as well as local schools. The average drop-out rate before 10th grade for Terger is about 50%, although the school has made strides to steadily reduce this rate over the past several years.

Despite her language barrier, Coco has learned to speak English quite well since moving to the United States. She was identified last year as having a learning disability through the school's Response to Intervention (RTI) identification and eligibility process. For Coco, it was her fifth-grade teacher, Sally Ballow, who felt that Coco's learning problems were the result of a true disability, not just an economic or language disadvantage. Last year, in the beginning of fifth grade, Sally Ballow noticed that Coco had great difficulty reading even some of the easiest books in her classroom. Sally set up a leveled reading system using books that she had purchased through the years and arranged them from easy first-grade to more difficult sixth-grade reading books. Sally noticed that when she asked Coco to read a first- or second-grade book, she often tripped over words, mispronounced some words, or skipped reading more difficult words. As a follow-up, when she would ask Coco questions about the story, Coco had no idea what she had just read. Even though Sally used effective teaching techniques such as direct instruction, Coco still struggled even after much help. Sally also used prompts, cues, and effective pacing in her class to get students to pay attention and to think and expand upon what was just read, but Coco would learn only from listening to others read and discuss the stories that they read.

Once Sally pointed out Coco's problem to the special education director and collaborative teacher, Coco was identified as at risk while she made her way into the next tier. In Tier 2, the resource teacher, Mark Reison, who was already collaborating in Sally's room and also noticed Coco's problems, was asked to make observations and write up a report on Coco's learning issues. As part of Tier 2, Mark would help co-teach several classes and pull at-risk students aside during language arts to work with them on their reading skills in small groups. Once students like Coco were identified, Mark would continue to work on reading skills in small groups and keep track of their progress. He used a variety of methods such as vocabulary instruction and repeated readings. Over the next 10 weeks, Mark taught and monitored progress, and even though other students made slow, steady progress, Coco continued to struggle and simply lacked any comprehension skills to be able to keep up with the others in the group. During the 11th week, Dr. Larry Anderson, the school psychologist, came by to observe and eventually test Coco for learning problems. Shortly after testing was completed, Dr. Anderson and the other eligibility team members determined that Coco met the definition for specific learning disabilities and placed her in Mark's resource room on a permanent basis.

Although Mark has tried other techniques such as pronunciation of vocabulary words and extra readings, Coco still struggles to comprehend what she reads.

1. From the case, what skill(s) would you target for remediation? What skill(s) would you target for further assessment?
2. In the classroom, choose a skill area and decide what modifications and supports could be used to help Coco.
3. How would you monitor progress on the skill(s)? Describe how and when you would monitor progress.

Identifying the Problem

1. *From the case, what skill(s) would you target for remediation? Or, what skill(s) would you target for further assessment?*

    In terms of Coco's learning problems, it might be useful for Mark to find out which specific skills Coco is having problems with. He could do this through a number of different methods. For example, he could use an informal reading inventory and other reading measures to identify Coco's specific skill deficits in reading. These measures should be able to answer the following questions: Does she have problems with word attack? Can she pronounce most sightwords? Does she need training in phonological awareness? Does Coco have problems with comprehension monitoring? Is it a problem with fluency?

2. *In the classroom, choose a skill area and decide what modifications and supports could be used to help Coco.*

    From the assessment, if word attack were identified as a skill deficit, we would advise teaching Coco the *Word Identification Strategy* (Lenz & Hughes, 1990). Essentially, Coco would use the strategy to be able to break apart words so that she could pronounce them (see the chapter on teaching basic skills in reading for specific steps). Each step would prompt her into some action with the unknown word. The initial step would prompt Coco to use context clues to determine the unknown word. The next few steps would prompt her to remove parts of the word to shorten it to its stem. Another step would prompt Coco to use syllabication rules to try to pronounce the stem. Finally, the last two steps would prompt her to check with someone or try the dictionary to help pronounce the word. Of course, there are other methods that teachers could use to increase Coco's reading fluency.

3. *How would you monitor progress on the skill(s)? Describe how and when you would monitor progress.*

    There are a number of different methods to monitor progress, such as having Coco read vocabulary words or sightwords prior to reading a story and then keeping track of her miscues, or using a running record to keep track of miscues, or the teacher could keep track of miscues and fluency (or rate) to see how many words per minute the student could read. Whatever measurement system is used, the teacher should change or modify the teaching method based on the child's performance (via recording data) during reading.

SUPPORT FOR CASE METHOD TEACHING

The case method teaching technique has a record of success in other professional programs (Wassermann, 1994a). For example, Cruickshank and Broadbent (1968) found that students who use cases (i.e., simulated experiences) during preservice training experience fewer problems in the actual classroom. A number of other leading educators also report similar benefits from using cases in college courses (Shulman, 1986; Wassermann, 1994a). For example, when used with preservice teachers, a case method approach (that included discussion) is believed to be responsible for teachers' increasing sensitivity toward culturally diverse students. Through case discussions, Dana and Floyd (1993) found that teachers are able to examine and understand their beliefs, subjectivity, and biases for culturally diverse students in learning environments.

    From our experience using cases in our courses, we have found that students become more aware of the personal issues related to having a disability. Rather than just studying unrelated facts and figures about students with disabilities, the student can now apply their tacit knowledge base of special ·education to simulated experiences. Or, as summed up by Harrington and Garrison (1992), case method teaching allows students "opportunities to generate *better* solutions and to see the possibilities by viewing connections between theory and practice through normative lenses" (p. 271).

USING CASES IN COURSES

The cases in this book are designed to present a broad overview of individuals with disabilities from numerous categorical areas. Moreover, we designed the cases so that they could be used to supplement learning after reading about the different categorical areas or during instruction to further elaborate on new knowledge about teaching. The cases are meant to complement instruction in a variety of classes such as a survey course about disabilities, a characteristics course, a methods course, a behavior management course, or a parenting course.

In conclusion, case method teaching has been used, in one form or another, for more than 50 years (Kagan, 1993), yet it is probably one of the most underused methods in teacher training programs. If effectively carried out, case method teaching can offer students the opportunity to examine how their beliefs interact with their knowledge of education and help them understand effective teaching principles (Wassermann, 1994a). Often students can describe a specific technique or method, but are unable to explain why they are applying the technique because they are unable to *connect* theory with practice. Because a firm understanding of effective teaching principles is needed for special education teachers and others working with students with disabilities, case method teaching appears to be a valuable tool to allow students to practice what they have learned. More specifically, case method teaching can serve as an effective tool to use during the stage between acquiring knowledge and actually using that knowledge in the classroom.

References

Cruickshank, D. R., & Broadbent, F. (1968). *The simulation and analysis of problems of beginning teachers* (Final report, Project No. 5-0798). Washington, DC: Department of Health, Education, and Welfare. (ERIC Document Reproduction Service No. ED 024637)

Dana, N., & Floyd, D. (1993, February). *Preparing preservice teachers for the multicultural classroom: A report on the case study approach*. Paper presented at the annual meeting of the Association of Teacher Educators.

Fenstermacher, G. D. (1986). Philosophy of research on teaching: Three aspects. In M. C. Wittrock (Ed.), *Handbook of research on teaching* (3rd ed., pp. 37–49). New York: Macmillan Publishing Company.

Harrington, H. L., & Garrison, J. W. (1992). Cases as shared inquiry: A dialogical model of teacher preparation. *American Educational Research Journal, 29*(4), 715–735.

Hudson, J., & Buckley, P. (2004). An evaluation of case-based teaching: Evidence for continuing benefit and realization of aims. Teaching with problems and cases. *Advances in Physiology Education, 28*, 15–22.

Jones, D. C., & Sheridan, M. E. (1999). A case study approach: Developing critical thinking skills in novice pediatric nurses. *Journal of Continuing Education in Nursing, 30*(2), 75–78.

Kagan, D. M. (1993). Contexts for the use of classroom cases. *American Educational Research Journal, 30*(4), 703–723.

Kim, O., Utke, B., & Hupp, S. (2005). Comparing the use of case studies and application questions in preparing special education professionals. *Teacher Education and Special Education, 28*, 104–113.

Knackendoffel, E. A. (1996). Collaborative teaming in the secondary school. In D. D. Deshler, E.S. Ellis, & B. K. Lenz (Eds.), *Teaching adolescents with learning disabilities: Strategies and method* (2nd ed., pp. 579–616). Denver, CO: Love Publishing Company.

Kuntz, S., & Hessler, A. (1998, January). *Bridging the gap between theory and practice: Fostering active learning through the case method*. Paper presented at the annual meeting of the Association of American Colleges and Universities.

Lenz, B. K., & Hughes, C. A. (1990). A word identification strategy for adolescents with learning disabilities. *Journal of Learning Disabilities, 23*(3), 149–158, 163.

Martin, D. S., Glatthorn, A., Winters, M., & Saif, P. (1989). *Curriculum leadership: Case studies for program practitioners.* Alexandria, VA: Association for Supervision and Curriculum Development.

Richardson, W. D., & Ginter, P. M. (1998). Using living cases to teach the strategic planning process. *Journal of Education for Business, 73*(5), 269–273.

Robinson, S. M. (1991). Collaborative consultation. In B. Y. L. Wong (Ed.), *Learning about learning disabilities.* San Diego, CA: Academic Press.

Shulman, L. S. (1986). Paradigms and research programs in the study of teaching: A contemporary perspective. In M. C. Wittrock (Ed.), *Handbook of research on teaching* (3rd ed., pp. 3–36). New York: Macmillan Publishing Company.

Wassermann, S. (1994a). Using cases to study teaching. *Phi Delta Kappan, 75*(8), 602–611.

Wassermann, S. (1994b). *Introduction to case method teaching: A guide to the galaxy.* New York: Teachers College Press.

2

Special Education Law and Inclusion

INDIVIDUALS WITH DISABILITIES EDUCATION ACT (IDEA) 2004

The Individuals with Disabilities Education Act (IDEA) 2004 was designed by Congress to protect the rights of students with disabilities. In 1975, Congress passed the Education for All Handicapped Children Act (PL 94-142), and it became effective in 1977. After several amendments, PL 94-142 eventually was renamed IDEA 2004. Perhaps the most influential law of its time, IDEA was designed to address past injustices and to provide a well-defined set of rights for students with disabilities. Accordingly, the purpose of IDEA is

> (A) to ensure that all children with disabilities have available to them a free appropriate public education that emphasizes special education and related services designed to meet their unique needs and prepare them for further education, employment, and independent living; (B) to ensure that the rights of children with disabilities and parents of such children are protected; and (C) to assist States, localities, educational service agencies, and Federal agencies to provide for the education of all children with disabilities. (Sec. 601)

Moreover, IDEA provides a unique structure in that for states to receive federal funding, states must submit an annual program plan to the U.S. Secretary of Education that describes how they will comply with IDEA (Turnbull, 1993). In each state's plan, they must describe how they will provide services and what procedural safeguards will be in place to protect the rights of students with disabilities (Rothstein, 1995). This annual plan then assures that states will comply with the regulations under IDEA in order to receive further federal funding.

The framework of IDEA has been described in a number of ways (Raymond, 2008; Rothstein, 1995; Turnbull & Turnbull, 2003); yet, it remains difficult to organize the statute around specific themes because of the interrelatedness of each theme. Our approach is to use a combination of past approaches so that the statute can be examined in depth, yet also discussed within an organized "whole." Hence, we examine IDEA around themes of

1. Child find and zero reject
2. Evaluation, classification, and placement
3. Appropriate education and the individualized education program

4. The least restrictive environment

5. Parent participation

6. Due process

7. Confidentiality and privacy

Throughout these themes, we will discuss the definitions for eligibility and the common terms used in IDEA.

Eligibility

In order for a student to qualify for services, he or she must first be found eligible. In general, only students who have a disability and absolutely need special education should receive it. Accordingly, under IDEA an individual's disability must interfere in their learning to such an extent that they "*need* special education and related services" (Sec. 300.7). For some students (in certain situations), their disability may not interfere with their learning. For example, a student with a physical disability may not need special education services to learn math skills; however, the same student may need adapted physical education for proper motor skill development. However, you will find that many categories are defined so that in order for the student to qualify, the disability must interfere with learning or that it "adversely affects a child's educational performance."

The disability categories include mental retardation, hearing impairments or deafness, speech or language impairments, visual impairments or blindness, serious emotional disturbance, orthopedic impairments, autism, traumatic brain injury, other health impairments, specific learning disabilities, deaf-blindness, or multiple disabilities. Each of the following disability areas is defined in Section 300.7 as:

1. *Autism* means a developmental disability significantly affecting verbal and nonverbal communication and social interaction, generally evident before age three, that adversely affects a child's educational performance. Other characteristics often associated with autism are engagement in repetitive activities and stereotyped movements, resistance to environmental change or change in daily routines, and unusual responses to sensory experiences. The term does not apply if a child's educational performance is adversely affected primarily because the child has a serious emotional disturbance.

2. *Deaf-blindness* means concomitant hearing and visual impairments, the combination of which causes such severe communication and other developmental and educational problems that they cannot be accommodated in special education programs solely for children with deafness or children with blindness.

3. *Deafness* means a hearing impairment that is so severe that the child is impaired in processing linguistic information through hearing, with or without amplification, that adversely affects a child's educational performance.

4. *Hearing impairment* means an impairment in hearing, whether permanent or fluctuating, that adversely affects a child's educational performance but that is not included under the definition of deafness in this section.

5. *Mental retardation** means significantly subaverage general intellectual functioning existing concurrently with deficits in adaptive behavior and manifested during the developmental period that adversely affects a child's educational performance.

---

*In 2010, President Barack Obama signed into law Rosa's Law, which strikes references to the term *mental retardation* and replaces it with *intellectual disabilities* in all federal laws.

6. *Multiple disabilities* means concomitant impairments (such as mental retardation-blindness, mental retardation-orthopedic impairment, etc.), the combination of which causes such severe educational problems that they cannot be accommodated in special education programs solely for one of the impairments. The term does not include deaf-blindness.

7. *Orthopedic impairment* means a severe orthopedic impairment that adversely affects a child's educational performance. The term includes impairments caused by a congenital anomaly (e.g., clubfoot, absence of some member, etc.), impairments caused by disease (e.g., poliomyelitis, bone tuberculosis, etc.), and impairments from other causes (e.g., cerebral palsy, amputations, and fractures or burns that cause contractures).

8. *Other health impairment* means having limited strength, vitality, or alertness, including a heightened alertness to environmental stimuli, that results in limited alertness with respect to the educational environment, that is due to chronic or acute health problems such as asthma, attention deficit disorder or attention deficit hyperactivity disorder, diabetes, epilepsy, a heart condition, hemophilia, lead poisoning, leukemia, nephritis, rheumatic fever, and sickle cell anemia; and adversely affects a child's educational performance.

9. *Serious emotional disturbance* is defined as follows:
  (i) The term means a condition exhibiting one or more of the following characteristics over a long period of time and to a marked degree that adversely affects a child's educational performance.
    (A) An inability to learn that cannot be explained by intellectual, sensory, or health factors;
    (B) An inability to build or maintain satisfactory interpersonal relationships with peers and teachers;
    (C) Inappropriate types of behavior or feelings under normal circumstances;
    (D) A general pervasive mood of unhappiness or depression; or
    (E) A tendency to develop physical symptoms or fears associated with personal or school problems.
  (ii) The term includes schizophrenia. The term does not apply to children who are socially maladjusted, unless it is determined that they have a serious emotional disturbance.

10. *Specific learning disability* means a disorder in one or more of the basic psychological processes involved in understanding or using language, spoken or written, that may manifest itself in an imperfect ability to listen, think, speak, read, write, spell, or do mathematical calculations. The term includes such conditions as perceptual disabilities, brain injury, minimal brain dysfunction, dyslexia, and developmental aphasia. The term does not apply to children who have learning problems that are primarily the result of visual, hearing, or motor disabilities, of mental retardation, or emotional disturbance, or of environmental, cultural, or economic disadvantage.

11. *Speech or language impairment* means a communication disorder such as stuttering, impaired articulation, a language impairment, or a voice impairment that adversely affects a child's educational performance.

12. *Traumatic brain injury* means an acquired injury to the brain caused by an external physical force, resulting in total or partial functional disability or psychosocial impairment, or both, that adversely affects a child's educational performance. The term applies to open or closed head injuries resulting in impairments in one or more areas, such as cognition; language; memory; attention; reasoning; abstract thinking; judgment; problem-solving; sensory, perceptual, and motor abilities; psychosocial behavior; physical functions; information processing; and speech.

The term does not apply to brain injuries that are congenital or degenerative, or brain injuries induced by birth trauma.

13. *Visual impairment including blindness* means impairment in vision that, even with correction, adversely affects a child's educational performance. The term includes both partial sight and blindness.

Child Find and Zero Reject

The child find portion of IDEA grew out of the need to locate and identify children who are eligible for special education services but might be overlooked by a school district. These procedures should ensure "that all children residing within the jurisdiction of the local educational agency (LEA; e.g., school districts, private schools, or intermediate units) who have disabilities, regardless of the severity of their disability, and who are in need of special education and related services, are identified, located, and evaluated, including a practical method for determining which children are currently receiving needed special education and related services and which children are not currently receiving needed special education and related services" (Sec. 300.220).

Each state must also develop a plan that includes the policies and procedures that the state will undertake to ensure that "all children with disabilities, regardless of the severity of their disability, and who are in need of special education and related services are identified, located, and evaluated; and a practical method is developed and implemented to determine which children are currently receiving needed special education and related services and which children are not currently receiving needed special education and related services" (Sec. 300.128). This proactive stance by districts and states further supports the zero reject principle of IDEA (Turnbull, 1993). The zero reject policy proposes that no students who have been identified as eligible to receive services under IDEA be denied a free, appropriate, publicly supported education (Turnbull, 1993; Underwood & Mead, 1995).

Evaluation, Classification, and Placement

Educational testing occurs for various reasons, including (1) assessing student progress; (2) determining the effectiveness of a particular teaching method or technique; (3) determining the eligibility for "supplemental" services; and (4) planning an educational program for the child. Similarly, on the federal level, evaluation occurs to (1) determine if a child is eligible under one or more of the federal categories of disability (e.g., receive federal funds); (2) determine placement within the range of least restrictive environment settings; (3) plan for the individual child's education; (4) determine if the child has met the goals and objectives of his or her educational program; and (5) determine if the child *no longer meets the definition* of his or her current disability label (e.g., reevaluation), or meets a different one.

Because of these reasons, evaluation plays a critical role in the education of a child with a disability. "Evaluation" is defined as "procedures used . . . to determine whether a child has a disability and the nature and extent of the special education and related services that the child needs. The term refers to procedures used selectively with any individual child and does not include basic tests administered to or procedures used with all children in a school, grade, or class" (Sec. 300.500). As a result of the multifaceted outcomes of evaluation, IDEA provides several safeguards to ensure that improper testing does not lead to misclassification, an inappropriate placement, an inappropriate educational program, or an inappropriate education (e.g., if the child has already met goals and objectives).

Parents should be involved in any planning of the child's evaluation and education. This is done through the prior notice and parental consent portion of IDEA. First, the content of the notice must include "an explanation of the procedural safeguards available to the parents; a description of the action proposed or refused by the agency (or an explanation of why the agency proposes or refuses to take the action) . . .; a description of each evaluation procedure, test, record, or report the agency uses as a basis for the proposal or refusal; and a description of any other factors that are relevant to the agency's proposal or refusal" (Sec. 300.505). Moreover, the notice must be written in an easily understandable language, written in the native language of the parent or other mode of communication used by the parent (unless it is clearly not feasible to do so) (Sec. 300.505) and provided within a reasonable time prior to the school district initiating or changing the identification, evaluation, or educational placement of the child, or refusing to initiate any change (Sec. 300.504).

Second, in terms of obtaining parental permission, consent must be obtained before conducting an evaluation and before initial placement of a child in a special education program (or before he or she receives any related services). *Parental consent* refers to the parent being fully informed of all information relevant to the evaluation and placement, and the parent understands and agrees in writing (Sec. 300.500).

Once parental consent is obtained for the initial evaluation, a team of individuals pursues the evaluation, classification, and placement of the eligible child. Because of the importance of such decisions by the multidisciplinary team (MDT), IDEA states that extensive and specific procedures be followed during the evaluation. First, all tests and other evaluation materials "are provided and administered in the child's native language or other mode of communication; have been validated for the specific purpose for which they are used; and are administered by trained personnel in conformance with the instructions provided by their producer" (Sec. 300.532). Second, tests and other evaluation materials include those tailored to assess specific areas of educational need and not merely those designed to provide a single general intelligence quotient. Tests are selected and administered so as to best ensure that when a test is administered to a child with impaired sensory, manual, or speaking skills, the test results accurately reflect the child's aptitude or achievement level or whatever other factors the test purports to measure, rather than reflecting the child's impaired sensory, manual, or speaking skills (except where those skills are the factors that the test purports to measure). No single procedure is used as the sole criterion for determining an appropriate educational program for a child. The evaluation is made by a multidisciplinary team or group of persons, including at least one teacher or other specialist with knowledge in the area of suspected disability. The child is assessed in all areas related to the suspected disability, including— if appropriate—health, vision, hearing, social, and emotional status; general intelligence; academic performance; communicative status; and motor abilities (Sec. 300.532).

Once the evaluation is completed, the MDT must determine if the child has a disability and is eligible for special education or related services. Following this decision, the individualized education program (IEP) is determined and, based on this information, setting or placement is determined. As when evaluating children suspected of having a disability, placement decisions must also incorporate a variety of evaluative data. As stated in Sec. 300.533, any decision making should

1. Draw upon information from a variety of sources, including aptitude and achievement tests, teacher recommendations, physical condition, social or cultural background, and adaptive behavior;
2. Ensure that information obtained from all of these sources is documented and carefully considered;

3. Ensure that the placement decision is made by a group of persons, including persons knowledgeable about the child, the meaning of the evaluation data, and the placement options; and

4. Ensure that the placement decision is made in conformity with the least restrictive environment (LRE) rules.

In addition to the use of evaluative data, the MDT should also consider educational placement of the child based on his or her IEP and proximity to the child's home. In other words, "unless the IEP of a child with a disability requires some other arrangement, the child should be educated in the school that he or she would attend if non-disabled" (Sec. 300.552). Last the educational placement of the child should be determined at least annually (Sec. 300.552), and any reevaluation that is completed should be "conducted every three years, or more frequently if conditions warrant or if the child's parent or teacher requests an evaluation" (Sec. 300.534).

Parents who do not agree with the evaluation conducted by the school district have the right to an independent evaluation; however, the school may initiate a due process hearing to demonstrate that its evaluation was appropriate. "If the final decision is that the evaluation is appropriate, the parent still has the right to an independent educational evaluation, but not at public expense" (Sec. 300.503). In addition, if the parents request information, the school will provide to parents information about where to obtain an independent evaluation.

Appropriate Education and the IEP

Free appropriate public education (FAPE) refers to providing special education and related services to students with disabilities (without charge) at public expense and under public supervision and direction (Sec. 300.8). FAPE covers students with disabilities in preschools, elementary schools, and secondary schools. Each state should ensure that FAPE is available to all children with disabilities ages 3 through 21 within its borders. Although this covers a wide range of ages, certain stipulations pertain to states providing FAPE to children with disabilities ages 3, 4, 5, 18, 19, 20, and 21. Under IDEA, Section 300.300 specifies that "if State law or a court order requires the State to provide education for children with disabilities in any disability category in any of these age groups, the State must make FAPE available to all children with disabilities of the same age who have that disability." In addition, IDEA states that "if a public agency provides education to non disabled children in any of these age groups, it must make FAPE available to at least a proportionate number of children with disabilities of the same age . . . and if a public agency provides education to 50 percent or more of its children with disabilities in any disability category in any of these age groups, it must make FAPE available to all its children with disabilities of the same age who have that disability."

Finally, under this provision, "a State is not required to make FAPE available to a child with a disability in one of these age groups if State law expressly prohibits, or does not authorize, the expenditure of public funds to provide education of non disabled children in that age group . . .; or the requirement is inconsistent with a court order that governs the provision of free public education to children with disabilities in that State" (Sec. 300.300).

As part of FAPE, special education is meant to be instruction that is different (specially designed instruction) from instruction offered in the regular education classroom and that addresses the unique needs of the child. Moreover, the term includes speech pathology or vocational education, or any other related services (if the service consists of specially designed instruction) at no cost to the parents, to meet the unique needs of a child with a disability (Sec. 300.17).

Related services cover a wide range of FAPE services that includes speech pathology and audiology, psychological services, physical and occupational therapy, recreation (including therapeutic recreation), early identification and assessment of disabilities in children, counseling services (including rehabilitation counseling and parent counseling and training), and medical services for diagnostic or evaluation purposes. The term also includes school health services, social work services in schools, and parent counseling and training (Sec. 300.16). Finally, included under Section 300.16 as part of related services is transportation. *Transportation* is defined as any travel to and from school and between schools; in and around school buildings; and that uses specialized equipment (such as special or adapted buses, lifts, and ramps), if required to provide special transportation for a child with a disability.

One of the most important documents pertaining to the rights of a child who receives special education services is the IEP. The IEP should be developed at a meeting "within 30 calendar days of a determination that the child needs special education and related services" (Sec. 300.343), and a copy of it is given to the parent on request (Sec. 300.345).

Under the revised IDEA 2004, the contents of the IEP should include the following:

1. A statement of the child's present level of academic achievement and functional performance;
2. A statement of measurable annual goals, including academic and functional goals designed to:
   • Meet the child's needs that result from the child's disability to enable the child to be involved in and make progress in the general education curriculum; and
   • Meet each of the child's other educational needs that result from the child's disability;
3. For children with disabilities who take alternate assessments aligned to alternate achievement standards, a description of benchmarks or short-term objectives;
4. A description of:
   • How the child's progress toward meeting the annual goals described in 34 CFR 300.320(a)(2) will be measured; and
   • When periodic reports on the progress the child is making toward meeting the annual goals (such as through the use of quarterly or other periodic reports, concurrent with the issuance of report cards) will be provided.
5. A statement of the special education and related services and supplementary aids and services, based on peer-reviewed research to the extent practicable, to be provided to the child, or on behalf of the child . . .
6. A statement of any individual appropriate accommodations that are necessary to measure the academic achievement and functional performance of the child on State and districtwide assessments consistent with section 612(a)(16) of the Act; and if the IEP Team determines that the child must take an alternate assessment instead of a particular regular State or districtwide assessment of student achievement, a statement of why the child cannot participate in the regular assessment and why the particular alternate assessment selected is appropriate for the child. . . .

Also required in an IEP is information about transition services that will be provided for the student, "taking into account the student's preferences and interests" (Sec. 300.342), often "beginning not later than the first IEP to be in effect when the child turns 16, or younger, if determined appropriate by the IEP team and updated annually."

The IEP must then include "appropriate measurable postsecondary goals based upon age-appropriate transition assessments related to training, education, employment, and, where appropriate, independent living skills" and "transition services (including courses of study) needed to assist the child in reaching those goals" (Sec. 300.320[b]). These transition statements are meant to include information about who will provide the services because *transition services* refers to "a coordinated set of activities for a student, designed within an outcome-oriented process, that promotes movement from school to post school activities, including post secondary education, vocational training, integrated employment (including supported employment), continuing and adult education, adult services, independent living, or community participation" (Sec. 300.18).

Finally, a number of participants should contribute information at the IEP meeting:

- The parents of the child;
- Not less than one regular education teacher of the child (if the child is, or may be, participating in the regular education environment);
- Not less than one special education teacher of the child, or where appropriate, not less than one special education provider of the child;
- A representative of the public agency (who has certain specific knowledge and qualifications);
- An individual who can interpret the instructional implications of evaluation results and who may also be one of the other listed members;
- At the discretion of the parent or the agency, other individuals who have knowledge or special expertise regarding the child, including related services personnel as appropriate; and
- Whenever appropriate, the child with a disability. (Sec. 300.321(a))

For a child with a disability who has been evaluated for the first time, the public agency shall ensure (1) that a member of the evaluation team participates in the meeting; or (2) that the representative of the public agency, the child's teacher, or some other person is present at the meeting, who is knowledgeable about the evaluation procedures used with the child and is familiar with the results of the evaluation (Sec. 300.344).

The Least Restrictive Environment

The least restrictive environment (LRE) principle serves to ensure that children with disabilities are educated, to the maximum extent appropriate, with children who are nondisabled (Sec. 300.550). In addition to this requirement, students with disabilities should be placed in special classes or separate schools (removed from the regular education environment) "only when the nature or severity of the disability is such that education in regular classes with the use of supplementary aids and services cannot be achieved satisfactorily" (Sec. 300.550). In other words, procedures should be in place to ensure that students with disabilities participate, to the maximum extent practicable, in regular education programs and that a continuum of alternative placements be available (Sec. 300.227 and Sec. 300.551).

In cases where parents place the child in "a private school or facility, the public agency is not required . . . to pay for the child's education at the private school or facility" (Sec. 300.403). This section also states that any disagreements between the parent and school regarding the availability of appropriate educational services or any questions pertaining to payment for the private school or facility are subject to due process procedures (Sec. 300.403).

Parent Participation

Because parents are a large part of their child's life, the requests of parents should always be respected and considered, particularly in reference to their child's educational needs. Prior to the passage of the Act, parental input was little more than lip service during the decision-making process of public agencies (Turnbull, 1993). With the passage of IDEA, parents are now much more involved in decisions pertaining to their child's education, resulting in a much more collaborative process. IDEA has stipulated that LEA will take the necessary steps to ensure that one or both of the parents or legal guardians (or in some cases surrogate parents) (Sec. 300.13) are present at meetings involving the educational needs of their child. Moreover, IDEA specifies procedures such as "notifying parents of the meeting early enough to ensure that they will have an opportunity to attend and scheduling the meeting at a mutually agreed on time and place" (Sec. 300.345). In addition, the notice sent to parents "must indicate the purpose, time, and location of the meeting and who will be in attendance" (Sec. 300.345). If, for whatever reason, neither parent can attend the meeting, the school should "use other methods to ensure parent participation, including individual or conference telephone calls" (Sec. 300.345).

Finally, for any meeting in which parents were not present, the school should "have a record of its attempts to arrange a mutually agreed on time and place . . . and copies of correspondence sent to the parents and any responses received" (Sec. 300.345). IDEA also encourages school personnel to take such unique steps as visiting the parents at work or home.

Due Process

Procedural due process procedures were included in IDEA to ensure that parents would have some recourse if schools failed to fulfill their educational obligation (e.g., zero reject, appropriate education, and LRE). *Procedural due process* refers to a set of procedures that allow parents "an opportunity to present complaints with respect to . . . the identification, evaluation, or educational placement . . . or the provision of a free appropriate education" for their child (Sec. 1415). These complaints are presented before an impartial hearing officer (Sec. 300.507) during an "impartial due process hearing" at which parents have "the right to present evidence and confront, cross-examine, and compel the attendance of witnesses" (Sec. 1415).

If the issue before the hearing officer involves an inappropriate evaluation, "the results of the evaluation . . . must be considered by the public agency in any decision made with respect to the provision of FAPE to the child and may be presented as evidence at a hearing . . . and if a hearing officer requests an independent educational evaluation as part of a hearing, the cost of the evaluation must be at public expense" (Sec. 300.503). Last, Section 300.503 states that "whenever an independent evaluation is at public expense, the criteria under which the evaluation is obtained, including the location of the evaluation and the qualifications of the examiner, must be the same as the criteria which the public agency uses when it initiates an evaluation."

In some cases, the issue before a hearing officer involves classification, placement, inappropriate education, or LRE issues. In such cases, the child remains in his or her current educational placement pending the outcome of the hearing, "unless the public agency and the parents of the child agree otherwise" (Sec. 300.513). In certain cases in which the child is being initially admitted to a school, with the consent of the parents, the child "must be placed in the public school program until the completion of all the proceedings" (Sec. 300.513).

Confidentiality and Privacy

Parents of children with identified disabilities have the right to keep confidential any personally identifiable information about the child. "Parental consent must be obtained before personally identifiable information is . . . disclosed to anyone other than officials of participating agencies collecting or using the information" (Sec. 300.571). In addition, the parents have "an opportunity to inspect and review all education records with respect to . . . the identification, evaluation, and educational placement of the child and . . . the provision of FAPE to the child" (Sec. 300.502).

If parents want to review information that also involves another child, the school must make certain that the parents "inspect and review only the information relating to their child or to be informed of that specific information" (Sec. 300.564). If a parent believes that information in the educational records is inaccurate, misleading, or violates the privacy of their child, the parents may request that the school amend the information. In turn the school will then decide whether to amend "within a reasonable period of time of receipt of the request" (Sec. 300.567).

In certain cases of disagreement between the school and parent concerning information in the child's records, either party may initiate a hearing. For example, if a school refuses to amend information that a parent has requested, it should inform the parent of the refusal, and advise the parent of the right to a hearing (Sec. 300.567). The purpose of the hearing is to provide either party with an opportunity to challenge information in educational records to ensure that it is not inaccurate, misleading, or otherwise in violation of the privacy or other rights of the child (Sec. 300.568). If, as a result of a hearing, the information is inaccurate, misleading, or in violation of the privacy of the child, "the school shall amend the information accordingly and so inform the parent in writing" (Sec. 300.589). If, as a result of the hearing, the information is not inaccurate, misleading, or otherwise in violation of the privacy or other rights of the child, the school "shall inform the parent of the right to place in the records it maintains on the child a statement commenting on the information or setting forth any reasons for disagreeing with the decision of the agency" (Sec. 300.589).

In developing and setting procedures for confidentiality and privacy, the state assumes the ultimate responsibility to "the protection of the confidentiality of any personally identifiable information collected, used, or maintained" (Sec. 300.129). On the local level, schools must "protect the confidentiality of personally identifiable information at collection, storage, disclosure, and destruction stages" (Sec. 300.572). At each school, one official "shall assume responsibility for ensuring the confidentiality of any personally identifiable information and each participating agency shall maintain, for public inspection, a current listing of the names and positions of those employees within the agency who may have access to personally identifiable information" (Sec. 300.572).

USING THE IEP IN THE INCLUSIVE CLASSROOM

Purpose of an IEP

The main purpose of an IEP is to ensure that the student with disabilities receives an appropriate education, one that has been agreed upon by all parties who are concerned for the student (e.g., parent, teachers, social worker, speech pathologist). However, simply writing out the various components of the IEP does not guarantee an appropriate education for the student. For some students, IEP goals and objectives are not written clearly or are too ambiguous to be of use. In other cases, parents may have unrealistic or high expectations for their child, and the IEP goals and objectives are unable to be met by the student.

The IEP, as developed during the IEP meeting, has other purposes as well. Pierangelo and Giuliani (2007) point to other purposes of the IEP that include serving as a communication tool between school personnel and parents, allowing parents to participate in their child's educational process; providing a forum for parents to discuss and resolve differences in the child's education; supplying parents with a written document that describes the obligations of all parties involved and can be used by government entities to ensure that schools are in compliance with certain parts of

IDEA; making available to parents the means by which progress will be monitored toward meeting the benchmarks or goals of the IEP; and although not a contract per se, the IEP serves as outline or management tool of the student's program.

Content of the IEP

As stated earlier, the IEP should contain the following elements: a statement of the child's present level of academic achievement and functional performance; a statement of measurable annual goals, including academic and functional goals (including elements that will allow the student to be involved in and make progress in the general education curriculum and meets the child's other needs that result from the disability); for students who take alternate assessments that are aligned to state standards, a description of benchmarks or short-term objectives; how progress will be monitored and when it will be reported; special education and related services and supplementary aids and services; and any individual-appropriate accommodations that are necessary to measure the achievement and functional performance of the child on state and districtwide assessments.

Writing Measurable Goals, Objectives, or Benchmarks for an IEP

Measurable goals must meet the students needs and allow the student to progress in the general education curriculum, as well as meet any other needs that result from the disability. When determining measurable annual goals, use the following information to assist you in writing goals, benchmarks, and short-term objectives:

1. *Determine which academic or functional skills the student needs to develop or build upon.* Goals, benchmarks, and short-term objectives listed in the student's IEP should relate to the student's needs pertaining to his or her disability and the needs as the disability interferes with the ability to participate in and make progress in the general education curriculum.

2. *Use the present levels of performance as starting points.* Present levels are determined by test results and observations completed during the evaluation for eligibility. If the student has a previous IEP, present levels can come from test results or observations that were completed during the school year.

3. *Determine how much progress the child can achieve in the upcoming year.* In other words, the IEP team has to determine what skills, knowledge, and behavior—based on the student's areas of need—the student can achieve by the end of the upcoming year or on an annual basis. The IEP team determines the number of goals necessary to meet the student's needs based on the student's disability. How many is too many and how many is not enough? In some cases, IEP team members can review the student's previous IEP to look at the number of annual goals that the student achieved in the past year, as a possible gauge in planning how many new goals, benchmarks, and short-term objectives the student might be able to achieve in the new IEP. According to the Federation for Children with Special Needs, ". . . it is best to choose only the goals that will make the biggest difference. If there are too many goals it will be difficult for your student to make effective progress in each goal area." (p. 3)

When writing measurable goals, Gibbs and Dyches (2007) suggest that the following four components be included:

1. *Condition*—Under what conditions will the student perform the task? Examples include statements that refer to materials or settings such as "Student given 20 double-digit addition problems without carrying over" or "Student given a 400-word, fifth-grade reading passage."

2. *Behavior*—What behavior or skill should the student perform while completing the task? Examples should include behaviors that are observable and measurable (countable) such as "Nina will verbally count objects," "Keisha will write the correct answer," or "Langford will read aloud."

3. *Criteria*—What is the criteria for achieving the goal? Examples might include statements that measure percentages ("80% accuracy"), number correct ("15 spelling words"), rate ("read 20 words correct per minute"), latency ("will sit down in seat within 2 minutes of the bell ringing"), or duration ("works quietly for 10 minutes").

4. *Trials*—How many times should the student perform the task at the set criteria? Once? Twice? Two of three days?

In addition, some goals might also include statements that refer to generalization or maintenance of the skill over time (Gibbs & Dyches, 2007). These statements might mention that the student will complete the objective—independent of teacher support, in different settings, or without teacher cues. In some cases the goals themselves will suffice for a student's IEP; in other cases benchmarks or short-term goals will have to be written for particular goals.

IDEA requires the use of benchmarks and short-term objectives only for students who take alternate assessments that are aligned to state standards; otherwise, measurable goals, as described above, will suffice. Benchmarks or short-term objectives represent interim steps that are needed to achieve the goal.

Benchmarks can be thought of as statements of *close approximations needed toward achieving the goal by the end of a designated timeframe or by a certain date* (e.g., in 5 weeks, in 10 weeks, by January, by May). These can be written using increasing levels of accuracy (e.g., 50%, 60%, 70%), increasing numbers of items (e.g., 5 problems, 10 problems, 20 problems), increasing levels of generalization (accurately counts change in class, accurately counts change at home, accurately counts change in public stores), or successive levels of reduced assistance (e.g., with written teacher cues, with partial teacher cues, without teacher cues) (Gibbs & Dyches, 2007). For example, the *annual goal* for counting change might be:

Given quarters, dimes, nickels, and pennies, Mikal will correctly count the amount of change needed for five items priced one dollar or less with 95% accuracy, in 3 of 5 days.

Benchmarks for the goal might extend over four marking periods (by the end of the fourth period it is hoped that Mikal will accomplish the goal) and look like the following:

1. By the end of the first marking period and given quarters, dimes, nickels, and pennies, Mikal will correctly count the amount of change needed for five items priced one dollar or less with *70% accuracy*, in 3 of 5 days.

2. By the end of the second marking period and given quarters, dimes, nickels, and pennies, Mikal will correctly count the amount of change needed for five items priced one dollar or less with *80% accuracy*, in 3 of 5 days.

3. By the end of the third marking period and given quarters, dimes, nickels, and pennies, Mikal will correctly count the amount of change needed for five items priced one dollar or less with *90% accuracy*, in 3 of 5 days.

These same benchmarks could also be written using statements about increasing numbers of items given, successive levels of reduced assistance, or increasing levels of generalization.

Although similar to benchmarks, short-term objectives can be thought of as statements that reflect *subskills of a task or goal.* As the student masters each subskill, he or she moves closer to achieving the goal. Using our previous example of counting change, three short-term objectives might look like this:

1. Given nickels and pennies, Mikal will correctly count the amount of change needed for five items priced 25 cents or less with 95% accuracy, in 3 of 5 days.
2. Given dimes, nickels, and pennies, Mikal will correctly count the amount of change needed for five items priced 50 cents or less with 95% accuracy, in 3 of 5 days.
3. Given quarters, dimes, nickels, and pennies, Mikal will correctly count the amount of change needed for five items priced 75 cents or less with 95% accuracy, in 3 of 5 days.

Changing or Modifying Goals, Objectives, or Benchmarks for an IEP

If changes are needed after the annual IEP meeting, do schools have to convene an IEP meeting? According to the U.S. Department of Education (2006), if there are "changes to a child's IEP after the annual IEP Team meeting for a school year, the parent of a child with a disability and the public agency may agree not to convene an IEP Team meeting for the purposes of making those changes, and instead may develop a written document to amend or modify the child's current IEP" (p. 4). However, the public agency (school) must ensure that the child's IEP Team is informed of those changes and, upon request, the parent must be provided with a copy of the revised IEP.

Using the IEP in the Inclusive Classroom

Teachers can take a number of steps to incorporate IEPs into the classroom. It all begins during the planning stage. During daily planning, teachers should always incorporate IEP goals, objectives, or benchmarks into their lesson plans whenever possible. For teachers who are co-teaching, incorporating the IEP into lesson plans can occur through co-planning, so that both teachers are aware of each special education student's goals, benchmarks, and objectives, as well as accommodations.

Once in inclusive classes, teachers need to make sure students with disabilities work on their goals and objectives during daily lessons. In addition, teachers should monitor progress in inclusive classrooms to make sure students are making progress with goals, particularly as they relate to students' accessing the general education curriculum. One method to monitor each student's progress on IEP goals is through the use of an IEP accountability form that can be used in a number of different settings (Cheney, 2000). This form uses these categories: objectives, data source, collection schedule, person responsible, and the date with performance.

Lindberg, Walker-Wied, and Forjan Beckwith (2006) recommend that teachers use a similar form called an IEP snapshot. The IEP snapshot lists goals and objectives, testing information, brief notes on behavior, present levels of performance, related services, and space to record progress of each goal and/or objective. The snapshot could be used for lesson planning and grouping of students with similar IEP goals. These authors also recommend developing easy-to-use methods of recording student progress, such as recording notes on index cards or in a notebook.

Finally, a number of state and federal government web sites are available that provide information on IEPs. We list several here and recommend that the reader be familiar with the specific format for the state where they will teach.

U.S. Department of Education's (DOE) sample IEP form can be found at the following link: http://idea.ed.gov/static/modelForms

More information about the IEP process and IEP form can be found by accessing the Major Topic "Individualized Education Program (IEP)" at the following U.S. DOE web site: http://idea.ed.gov/explore/home

National Dissemination Center for Children with Disabilities (NICHCY) web site provides an overview of the IEP process and form, and can be found at the following link: http://www.nichcy.org/Laws/IDEA/Pages/BuildingTheLegacy.aspx

Massachusetts Department of Education IEP form (model and annotated) can be found at the following link: http://www.doe.mass.edu/sped/iep/

New Jersey Department of Education IEP form (model and annotated) can be found at the following link: http://www.state.nj.us/education/specialed/form/

Virginia Department of Education IEP form (model and annotated) can be found at the following link: http://www.doe.virginia.gov/VDOE/sped/iep.shtml

California Department of Education IEP form (model and annotated) can be found at the following link: http://www.cde.ca.gov/sp/se/sr/ieptraining.asp

National Dissemination Center for Children with Disabilities (NICHCY) web site provides an overview of transition planning as it relates to the IEP at the following link: http://www.nichcy.org/EducateChildren/IEP/Pages/TransitionPlanning.aspx

U.S. Department of Education—Office for Civil Rights provides information about transition planning at the following link: http://www.ed.gov/about/offices/list/ocr/transition.html

U.S. Department of Education's (DOE) sample transition plan can be found at the following link: http://www.edu.gov.on.ca/eng/general/elemsec/speced/transiti/8.pdf

References

Cheney, C.O. (2000). Ensuring IEP accountability in inclusive settings. *Intervention in School and Clinic, 35*, 185–189.

Federation for Children with Special Needs. Available online at http://www.fcsn.org/pti/topics/iep/tools/annual_goals_faq.pdf

Gibbs, G. S. & Dyches, T. T. (2007). *Guide to writing quality individualized education programs* (2nd ed.) Boston, MA: Allyn and Bacon.

Individuals with Disabilities Education Improvement Act of 2004, P.L. 108-446, 20 U.S.C. $ 1400 et seq.

Lindberg, J., Walker-Wied, J., & Forjan Beckwith, K. (2006). *Common sense classroom management for special education teachers.* Thousand Oaks, CA: Corwin Press.

Pierangelo, R. & Giuliani, G. (2007). 100 Frequently Asked Questions About the Special Education Process. New York: Corwin Press.

Raymond, E. (2008). *Learners with Mild Disabilities.* Upper Saddle River, NJ: Pearson

Rothstein, L. (1995). *Special Education Law.* New York: Longman

Turnbull, H. R. (1993). *Free appropriate public education.* Denver, CO: Love Publishing Company.

Turnbull, H.R., & Turnbull, A.P. (2003). *Free appropriate public education*: Law and the education of children with disabilities. Denver, CO: Love. Turnbull.

Underwood, J. K., & Mead, J. F. (1995). *Legal aspects of special education and pupil services.* Boston, MA: Allyn & Bacon.

U.S. Department of Education. (2006). *Individualized Education Program Team Meetings and Changes to the IEP.* Retrieved August 30, 2009, from http://idea.ed.gov/explore/home

3

Cases About Special Education Law and Students with Disabilities in Inclusive Classrooms

CASE 1

Is This the Least Restrictive Environment?

Jill is a general education teacher in her third year of teaching at an inner-city school in a large urban school district in Florida. Since beginning her teaching career, she has taught second and third grades. This year she will teach third grade again with a new twist: Jill's classroom is designated as the inclusion classroom for students with disabilities. She expects to have a class of 26 students, with 8 of them receiving special education support services. Jill is nervous about this change, but hopes that her relationship with the special education teacher will help.

Amy is the special education teacher assigned to support students with disabilities in first, second, and third grades. Amy pulls 25 (first- through third-grade) students out of their general education classrooms for resource support (3.5 hours per day, 4 days per week), and she provides support to 13 students (0.5 hours per day, 2 days per week respectively) in the designated second and third grade general education inclusion classrooms.

The elementary school has 925 students, 150 of whom receive special education services. Another 100 students are either at risk for or are failing the general curriculum. The school employs four special education teachers, one full-time paraprofessional for special education services, one speech-language pathologist, and one part-time (one day per week) school psychologist. The service models used at the school include self-contained primary (grades K–2), self-contained intermediate (3–5), resource (1–3), resource (4–5), inclusion (2–3), inclusion (4–5), and consultation (K–5). The special education teachers are spread very thin at this elementary school and work hard to meet the needs of all of their students.

A few months into the school year, a new student joins Jill and Amy's third-grade inclusion classroom. Jordan transferred from a public school in the Midwest. His previous school implemented a schoolwide inclusion model that was supported by one special education teacher and one paraprofessional at each grade level. Jordan's individual education program (IEP) indicates that the least restrictive environment (LRE) that best meets his instructional needs is the general education classroom with special education support. Jordan's IEP indicates that his primary disability is mild intellectual and cognitive disability and that he has a secondary eligibility for speech (articulation) and language impairments. He receives 90 minutes of in-class direct services per week by the speech-language pathologist.

Jill and Amy's charge is to meet Jordan's educational needs through the inclusion model used at their school. They are worried: Jordan will receive significantly less direct support from special education faculty and staff in his new school with the current model. The "Big Question" is, Will inclusion continue to be the LRE for Jordan with the delivery systems provided at his new school?

Jill typically begins her day with an independent work assignment for the students, which includes copying the day's activities and homework assignments into their respective agenda books. While her students complete the independent assignment, she takes attendance and checks the students' homework. Jill then provides an overview of the day's activities and upcoming homework assignments. Next, she conducts a read-aloud that is related to one or more of the topics addressed in the core content. Following the read-aloud, Jill begins her language arts block. The block is organized into four sections: phonics and phonological awareness activities, working with words, fluency and oral reading, and vocabulary development and reading comprehension. While Jill conducts small-group reading and writing instruction, the students rotate through learning centers focused on these instructional areas. Each center is designed to provide individualized practice and learning opportunities for every student. After the 2-hour block, the students have 45 minutes of math instruction. During the ensuing independent practice phase, Jill provides small-group instruction for students needing additional assistance. At 11:00 a.m., the students have lunch for 25 minutes and then spend 20 minutes at recess. At 11:50 a.m., the students report to fine arts or physical education (P.E.) for 45 minutes. Finally, the students return to class at 12:40 p.m. to complete instruction for the day. Jill integrates science and social studies during the last time block. She implements a multimodal approach for teaching that includes hands-on learning experiences, cooperative learning group work, and performance-based assessment. At 1:45 p.m., the students prepare for dismissal and participate in teacher-supported independent reading.

Following Jordan's arrival, Jill and Amy meet daily to collaborate on how to best meet his instructional needs. They are concerned over Jordan's ability to make progress toward his IEP goals with the current level of support being provided. Jordan has difficulty learning the routine in Jill's classroom and working independently. He seems lost. He is frequently observed to be out of his area, off task, and/or napping. Jill tries to keep Jordan engaged, but is having trouble meeting his needs while simultaneously working with the other students with disabilities and her "regular" students. Amy attempts to support Jill and all of the students with disabilities, but is also having trouble. Her caseload and schedule make it very difficult to meet the needs of her inclusion students.

Discussion Questions

1. Jordan was successful in making progress toward meeting his IEP goals in an inclusion model of instruction at his previous school. He received daily support from a paraprofessional for a minimum of 4.5 hours per day, a special education teacher for a minimum of 4 hours per day, and the general education teacher. At the new school, Jordan receives support twice a week for 30 minutes from a special education teacher and daily from the general education teacher. Do these inclusion models provide the same level of LRE? Why or why not?

2. Jordan's new elementary school delivers an array of services for students with disabilities. Because many of these students require pull-out resource room support, teacher resources (time) have been focused in this area. Unfortunately, this leaves Jordan and the eight other students with disabilities access to Amy only two times per week for a total of 60 minutes. Should the IEP team convene a meeting to discuss a change in LRE? Why or why not?

3. Jill and Amy are working diligently to do the best they can in a very difficult situation. What steps could they take to improve the inclusion services in their classroom and their school?

4. The paraprofessional who works with students with disabilities splits her time between the self-contained classrooms. She also is assigned 30 minutes of lunch duty per day. She is entitled to a 30-minute lunch break and an additional 15-minute break during the day as well. With this information in mind, how would you use the paraprofessional to support inclusion in Jordan's class?

5. Based on your current knowledge of special education law, what recourse do you think Jordan's parents might take to force appropriate inclusion services?

CASE 2

"Oh, No: Another Due Process Hearing!"

Note: This case is based on information provided in Case 1.

Jill and Amy have decided to hold an interim IEP meeting to discuss Jordan's educational placement, or LRE. Amy completed the necessary paperwork to invite Jordan's mother to the meeting and hopes that she will agree with the team's recommendations. Amy doesn't want to change her schedule just to match the level of service that Jordan received at his last school. She knows that school districts are supposed to design programs based on the needs of students, but is aware of the reality. Her district isn't funding special education programs sufficiently so the "squeaky wheels" seem to get the services they need and others get the leftovers. Additionally, the school district has cut paraprofessionals in an effort to balance the budget. It takes almost an act of God to get a one-on-one aide in a classroom for a student with a disability.

During the time between Jordan's arrival and the pending IEP meeting, Jill works hard to try to meet Jordan's needs. Jordan is far behind both academically and socially. He requires almost constant attention and unfortunately annoys the other students. He acts like a 4-year-old child. He whines and cries when he doesn't get his way. He has trouble sitting at his desk for extended periods of time. Jordan also has great difficulty with any transition. Jill is about to pull her hair out, but is waiting patiently for the IEP meeting. Amy feels terrible that she can't support Jill more with Jordan, but her present schedule isn't set up for more inclusion time. They meet daily before and after school to plan instruction for him and to develop strategies to address his behavior, but things are not going smoothly.

Jill and Amy decide that they need to meet to make sure that they are in agreement for the upcoming IEP meeting. They want to let Jordan's mother know that they want the best for her son and that the general education classroom with inclusive support may not meet his needs at their school. Because Amy has such a large caseload and the other special education teachers are also overextended, they want to propose either a resource or a self-contained model of service for Jordan. They know that inclusion for Jordan, in the best of circumstances, will promote appropriate social skills and role models. Because Jordan's IQ is 57 and his adaptive skill deficits cover multiple areas, he will more than likely receive a certificate of completion at the end of his public school education. Jill and Amy realize that their efforts may not allow Jordan to achieve a regular high school diploma.

The day of the IEP meeting with Jordan's mother arrives. The IEP team convenes with the special education coordinator (Paula), the parent (Julie), the general education teacher (Jill), the special education teacher (Amy), and the speech-language pathologist (Susan). Introductions are made and the current IEP from the previous school district is reviewed. Jordan has goals in the areas of language arts (reading and letter identification [lowercase manuscript letters], recognizing and identifying sight words on a preprimer list, reading text with repetitive patterns); writing (letter formation, writing first and last name, writing simple sentences [agent-action-object]); math (one-to-one correspondence skills, adding to 18, greater than and less than, measuring with a ruler by the inch, telling time to the hour on an analog clock); communication (articulation of /s/, /r/, /p/ sounds; language (answering "wh" questions, following one-step directions, increasing average utterances from three to five words); and independent functioning (increasing time on-task from 3 to 7 minutes, increasing in-seat behavior from 5 to 15 minutes, raising hand to request assistance, using words rather than hitting to indicate "no"). The progress report from Jordan's previous school showed that he was making progress toward meeting his goals and short-term objectives. Presently, Jill and Amy note that Jordan seems to be regressing in most areas except for communication. Susan shares that there has been no major change in service in this area. Her caseload is such that she has been able to go into Jill's classroom to work with Jordan. Julie is noticeably upset by Jordan's reported regression. She doesn't understand why the school isn't following the IEP that was written at the previous school. Paula tells Julie that the school is implementing Jordan's IEP, but lacks the staff to provide the level of in-class direct support that he needs to be successful. Amy shares that Jill doesn't have a paraprofessional assigned to her classroom and that her schedule permits her to be in the classroom for only 60 minutes per week. The school recommends that Jordan's LRE is changed from inclusion to either resource or self-contained support. Julie is not happy about this recommendation. She wants the best education possible for her son and wants him in a general education classroom with support throughout the day. Jill and Amy recognize Julie's viewpoint, but argue that this level of support is not available at their school. Julie leaves the meeting in tears, refusing to sign the new IEP. She plans to implement due process proceedings in an attempt to get the level of service her son received at his previous school.

Discussion Questions

1. Based on your knowledge of LRE and FAPE, do you think that the school will be successful in changing Jordan's LRE from inclusion to resource or self-contained? Why or why not?

2. FAPE requires that appropriate educational services are provided, not the "best" educational services. As a special education teacher, how would you persuade Julie that a resource or self-contained setting is an appropriate placement for her son?

3. Julie understands her rights as a parent of a child with a disability. Once she calms down, what do you think she should focus on in her upcoming due process hearing (an inclusion placement, the need for a paraprofessional, compensatory services by a special education teacher) and why?

4. Generally speaking, school districts don't want to battle with parents over services needed by students with disabilities. Paula and Amy need to investigate all options that might be available to meet Jordan's needs at their school in preparation for the outcome of the due process hearing. The easiest option would be if Julie just gives in and lets them change Jordan's LRE, but they don't think that's going to happen. Paula phones the director of special education at the district to see what input she might provide. If you were Paula, what would you ask the director for (e.g., a special education teacher, a paraprofessional for Jordan's classroom, assistance with scheduling)?

5. Prior to getting to the final stage in due process, the school district agrees to meet Julie's demands for Jordan. Jordan will stay in the general education classroom. Jill will have the assistance of a full-time paraprofessional trained in meeting the needs of students with disabilities. Amy and/or another special education teacher will be required to provide 40 hours of compensatory educational service (after school) for Jordan in an effort to address the regression he exhibited since moving to the new school. Do you think that this agreement complies with FAPE? Why or why not?

CASE 3

Why Won't All Teachers Cooperate?

Jinny is a special education teacher who works at an inner-city middle school on the West Coast of the United States. Her certification is noncategorical, but she specializes in working with students with emotional and/or behavior disorders. Jinny has taught students at the middle-school level for 7 years in an inclusive model. She considers herself easy to get along with and a team player. This year Jinny will support 15 sixth-grade students with a variety of disabilities across the content areas. In doing this, she will work with four general education teachers.

Mike teaches sixth-grade English at Jinny's school. His class is designated as the inclusion class for students with a range of disabilities that include, but are not limited to, learning disabilities, emotional and/or behavior disorders, mild intellectual and/or cognitive disabilities, and Asperger syndrome. Mike is in his first year of teaching. He has limited experience working with students with disabilities and was actually hoping to teach honor's English this year.

Ann teaches sixth-grade math. Her class is designated as the inclusion class for students in grades 6 through 8. She is beginning her ninth year of teaching and is looking forward to the new year. Ann enjoys teaching in an inclusion model and loves co-teaching with Jinny. They share the same philosophy and compliment each other's strengths and weaknesses.

Valerie is beginning her second year as the sixth- and seventh-grade science teacher. Last year was her first year teaching in an inclusion model. At first she had some issues with having students with disabilities in her classroom, but after working with Jinny for a month she saw that these students were being successful in her class. She looks forward to another year of inclusion and is actually thinking of taking some graduate classes at the local university to enhance her knowledge and skills in pedagogical practices in special education.

Gertrude is the social studies and history teacher for sixth and eighth grades. This will be her 30th and last year of teaching. Gertrude is looking forward to her retirement. She just wants to get through this year. Unfortunately, she gets to do inclusion in sixth grade this year with Jinny's kids. This is going to make what should have been a walk in the park a walk through an obstacle course. Gertrude likes Jinny, but would have preferred to do what she's always done.

In an effort to get ready for implementing inclusion this year in sixth grade, Jinny, Mike, Ann, Valerie, and Gertrude set up a time for planning. Jinny gathers all of the information that she has received from the sending schools about their new group of students with disabilities. She makes copies of each student's IEP and provides a copy to each teacher. Three of the incoming students have behavior intervention plans (BIPs). Jinny makes copies of these as well. After reviewing the BIPs, Jinny feels that one of the plans may prove difficult to implement consistently in all classroom settings. She decides that the group will need to discuss this at length so that the student will be successful.

The group meets for 2 hours on the day before school begins. Jinny reviews all of the information with the teachers and answers questions. After everyone seems comfortable, the teachers review their lesson plans for the first day of school and plan instruction for the rest of the week. By the end of the meeting, all of the teachers seem ready for school to begin. All student schedules are finalized, and Jinny proceeds to phone each student to discuss expectations for the first day of school.

All of the students with emotional and/or behavioral disorders have the same schedule for the first 9 weeks of school. Jinny has grouped them this way so that she will be able to support their needs and provide daily assistance to their general education teachers. Some of Jinny's other students with disabilities will receive instruction in other general sixth-grade classrooms. She meets with these students and teachers at least three times per week. The students and teachers are asked to request assistance immediately if they need help. Jinny has found that this system works well at her school, and it makes inclusion work for her students. She doesn't like the idea of placing all of the students with disabilities in one classroom and calling it *inclusion* (it's not inclusion if the majority of students in a class have disabilities).

All in all, the first week of school goes well. Although there is confusion about the schedule for a couple of the sixth graders and some of the students aren't happy about their electives, there are no significant scheduling problems. None of the students exhibit any major behavior problems, and overall most of Jinny's inclusion team members have no complaints. Jinny realizes that it is only the end of the first week but is a little concerned about Gertrude's attitude about Sam's BIP.

Sam is an 11-year-old male diagnosed with bipolar disorder. He receives special education services due to his emotional/behavioral disorder (EBD). He takes medication daily and receives private therapy after school one time per week. Sam has difficulty handling frustration as evidenced by "shutting down"; he angers quickly—he may be physically and/or verbally aggressive and then has trouble regaining his composure. Sam has a comprehensive BIP that requires frequent reinforcement and documentation.

A summary of Sam's BIP provides the following information. *Brief profile:* Sam is an 11-year-old Asian American male entering the sixth grade. He was diagnosed with bipolar disorder when he was 9 years old. He began receiving special education services in kindergarten for a language disorder. In the third grade, he began exhibiting symptoms of depression and had trouble with anger management. At this time, his parents took him to see a psychiatrist for an evaluation. The school initiated a reevaluation to determine eligibility for EBD. He was found eligible for EBD at the beginning of fourth grade. He was dismissed from the language-impaired program at the end of fifth grade because he no longer demonstrated a need for services. Sam's behavior stabilized with the initiation of medication and his BIP. By the end of fifth grade, Sam rarely exhibited episodes of aggression, but continued to "shut down" when frustrated.

Brief list of strengths: Sam is verbal. He is able to follow basic directions and communicate the steps for problem solving. He can complete favored tasks independently. He is able to remove himself from an area when frustrated. Sam is also able to self-monitor his own behavior (data recording) with minimal prompting. *Brief list of challenges:* Sam has difficulty with transitions and changes in routine. When frustrated, he frequently shuts down and occasionally becomes aggressive to people (hits, kicks, throws objects, spits, threatens to kill others). *Support team members in middle school:* Sixth-grade inclusion team, guidance counselor, and assistant principal. *Intervention settings:* Involve the entire school campus. *Target behaviors: Maladaptive—* Shutting down (no eye contact, refusal to speak, refusal to work, refusal to move) and aggression (hitting, kicking, throwing objects, spitting, verbal threats). *Adaptive—*Removing self to an area to calm down, using words to express frustration, and self-monitoring points for adaptive/maladaptive behaviors. *Current status:* Sam's behavior was stable in elementary school and is unstable in middle school. *Desired outcome:* Sam will develop necessary coping skills in order to be successful in the middle school environment. *Middle school observations:* In the first week of middle school, Sam has had no episodes of aggression. In most of his classes, he has handled any frustration with academic or social tasks appropriately. Sam is having trouble in social studies. In 4 out of 5 days, he has shut down. He refused to self-monitor his own behavior (self-charting of adaptive/maladaptive behaviors). He has also refused to complete tasks assigned by Gertrude, but will attempt tasks assigned by Jinny. *Environmental adjustments and preventative strategies:* Sam will be provided with verbal and visual cues prior to transitions. He will be praised for transitioning appropriately. Transitions will be limited as much as possible. Sam will be taught what classroom expectations are and reinforced for compliance. *Alternative skills to be taught:* Sam will learn impulse control. He shall perform and participate in transitions without incident. Sam will keep his hands, feet, and objects to himself. He will use words (appropriate) to express frustration and conference with his teacher and/or peers when in a calm state. *Consequences and reinforcers:* When Sam exhibits one of his targeted maladaptive behaviors, he will not earn corresponding points on his point sheet. If his behavior warrants, he will be removed from the classroom and given an opportunity to calm down (with work). Sam's mother will be notified of behavioral incidents. When Sam exhibits one of his targeted adaptive behaviors, he will earn points on his point sheet. Points may be exchanged daily and weekly for selected reinforcers that are developed between him and his teachers. If Sam has 15 days without exhibiting a targeted maladaptive behavior, he will receive a special reinforcer (menu of reinforcers developed by teachers and Sam). *Crisis management procedures:* If Sam's behavior escalates to an extent that he is a danger to himself or others, Crisis Response Team management strategies will be used. *Generalization and maintenance strategies:* Once Sam's behavior is stable in his inclusion classrooms, the frequency of reinforcement will be faded in all-academic settings.

During the first week of school, Sam is successful in transitioning to middle school in all of his classes except for social studies. In this class, he has issues with shutting down, following directions, and completing his work. If Jinny approaches him and asks him to comply, Sam usually does. Gertrude has yet to develop a rapport with Sam. She hasn't bought into his BIP and doesn't think that he should have a plan that is so different from the rest of the other students. Jinny plans to speak to Gertrude after school on Friday to discuss how they should proceed to ensure that Sam is successful in social studies.

Discussion Questions

1. Gertrude seems resistant to implement Sam's BIP as written by the elementary school. If you were Jinny, how would you proceed?

2. Jinny has the choice between Gertrude and another sixth-grade teacher who delivers social studies instruction for students in sixth grade. If you were Jinny, would you work with Gertrude to get her to implement Sam's BIP or move Sam to the other class? Provide a rationale for your response.

3. Gertrude is from the "old school" with regard to educating students with disabilities. She feels that these students should be served in another setting—not her classroom. As a teacher for students with special needs, how would you go about arguing for inclusionary practices?

4. In reading this case history, it was necessary for you to review the summary of Sam's BIP. Do you think that the plan should be modified for Gertrude's class? Why or why not?

5. IDEA 2004 requires individualized BIPs for students with emotional and/or behavioral disorders. These plans must include a program to address both maladaptive and adaptive behaviors. Do you think that the plan for Sam meets the standard set forth in the law? Why or why not?

CASE 4

Medical Procedures: A Liability Issue

Donna Carter is a second-grade teacher at Babbling Brook Elementary School. She is in her fifth year of teaching and first year of supporting students with disabilities in an inclusion model. Babbling Brook is a small school with an enrollment of 340 students in a mid-size school district. The school is so small that there is no school nurse on staff. The office staff and/or secretaries dispense any medication that students require. The secretaries are not thrilled about this responsibility but have no choice. The classrooms lack locking medicine cabinets, and they have a clinic connected to the office.

Lauren Johnson is a special education teacher assigned to support students receiving inclusive services in first and second grade. She also works with a group of third-grade students in a resource room for 2 hours per day. Lauren is in her third year of teaching at Babbling Brook Elementary School. She is certified to teach students with learning disabilities in grades K–12 and is thinking about going back to school to get her master's degree in severe disabilities.

Lauren provides support to Donna's classroom for 90 minutes per day. During this time, Donna completes 1 hour of the 2-hour language arts block and begins math instruction. While in the classroom, Lauren works in a small group with the students eligible for special education services and a few other students who are struggling with the general curriculum. Occasionally Donna and Lauren co-teach a math lesson, but typically Donna acts as the primary teacher and Lauren supports her instruction. The situation is not ideal, but works for them.

One of the female students with a learning disability, Tonisha Brown, requires a lot of support in the regular classroom. She is a very active child who frequently requires direction to stay in her area, work cooperatively with others, and be quiet during instruction. Tonisha is into everything. She enjoys being the center of attention and seems to generate quite a bit of it. Tonisha rarely misses a day of school.

One day during language arts instruction, Lauren notices that Tonisha is unusually quiet. In reading group, Tonisha doesn't blurt out words when others are reading or swing her legs, kicking Lauren repeatedly under the kidney-shaped table where they sit. Lauren asks Tonisha, "Are you okay? Are you feeling alright, honey?" Tonisha doesn't respond. In between reading and math, Lauren approaches Donna and tells her that she thinks Tonisha is ill. She is going to take her to the school's front office so that one of the secretaries may take her temperature.

Lauren tells Tonisha that she wants her to go to the office with her. She is not in trouble; Lauren is worried about her. Tonisha goes quietly to the office with Lauren. One of the school secretaries escorts both of them into the clinic and proceeds to take Tonisha's temperature. Her temperature is normal. Lauren tells the secretary that Tonisha is not acting like herself. She is worried that there is something wrong with her. They decide to phone Tonisha's mother. Mrs. Brown is contacted and shares that she noticed that Tonisha didn't seem to be herself that morning. She says that she will call the doctor to see if she can get an appointment and will be there within the hour to pick her up from school.

Tonisha misses the next 2 days of school. On Friday afternoon, Mrs. Brown calls the school. She speaks to one of the secretaries, Janice Marchant. She tells her that the doctor determined that Tonisha has diabetes. When Mrs. Brown took her to the doctor on Wednesday, Tonisha's blood sugar was extremely high. The doctor has started Tonisha on injectable insulin. She must have her blood sugar checked before and after each meal and any time she begins to act sluggish. Tonisha will need to monitor her blood sugar at school and receive insulin there. Mrs. Brown shares that Tonisha still needs assistance with this routine, and she isn't always very co-operative about it. Tonisha will be ready to return to school on Monday. She will drive Tonisha to school and bring all of her medical supplies and doctor's orders.

After the phone call, Janice tells the school principal about her conversation with Mrs. Brown. She leaves notes in Lauren and Donna's mailboxes to see her after school. Janice telephones the director of nursing for the school district and relays the situation to her. The director of nursing says that she will arrange for a nurse to be at the school on Monday morning to meet with the school principal, the secretaries, the classroom teachers, and the parent.

On Monday morning before Tonisha and Mrs. Brown arrive, a meeting is held to discuss the situation. Cora Geoffrey, the nurse, provides information to the group concerning diabetes and diabetic care. Cora tells the group that she will work at the school this week to get them up to speed on Tonisha's care, but after that they will be on their own. The principal and secretaries are not happy about this situation. The secretaries do not have medical training and don't want to be responsible for Tonisha's medical care. Donna and Lauren don't have the resources in their classroom (e.g., locked refrigerator, private area for medical treatment) to provide the care there. The school personnel feel that this is a huge liability issue and wonder what their legal recourse might be.

Discussion Questions

1. Prior to the situation arising with Tonisha, the school secretaries routinely dispensed oral medication to students. Do you believe that this was appropriate? What liability issues did this create?

2. The law mandates that students with disabilities must receive appropriate medical care and treatment at school so that they can access education in the LRE. Do you feel that diabetic care falls under the scope of this law? Why or why not?

3. Do you believe that the school district has the authority to mandate that school secretaries be responsible for testing blood sugar and administering injectable insulin to students? Why or why not?

4. In this situation, who do you think has the most power to initiate change, and why?

5. If you were the school principal, what steps would you take to rectify this situation?

CASE 5

Does Mom Have a Case?

Chuck Venning is a 10-year-old boy in fourth grade. He receives special education services through the language-impaired program (expressive and receptive language skills) at his school. Chuck repeated third grade due to significant issues with reading (decoding) and reading comprehension. Unfortunately, Chuck is still struggling in the area of reading, and he is not progressing well in fourth grade.

Vicky Santiago is Chuck's fourth-grade teacher. She has been teaching fourth grade for 12 years. She has also served as the fourth-grade inclusion teacher on and off for 5 years. Vicky enjoys teaching in an inclusion model and doesn't mind having students with disabilities in her classroom.

Evelyn Petty is the speech-language pathologist who provides language therapy to Chuck. Evelyn prefers to conduct language therapy in a resource model because it is easier to work with students in a quiet environment without distractions. She pulls Chuck out of class twice weekly for 45 minutes of language therapy. Evelyn meets with Vicky quarterly to discuss what she is working on in therapy and to receive input as to Chuck's progress in the general education classroom.

Monica Rainey is the special education teacher who provides inclusive support services to Vicky's students. She is not a stickler for the rules and works with any student who needs extra assistance. Occasionally, she even pulls students out of the general education classroom for additional support during their special-area class time.

During the first teacher workday of the school year, Vicky, Evelyn, and Monica meet informally to discuss the progress of Vicky's students during the first grading period of the year. Vicky and Monica share with Evelyn that they have concerns about Chuck's progress in fourth grade. He is failing most of his subjects and appears to need more academic support than Vicky and Monica can give him in an inclusion model. Evelyn tells the group that Chuck is continuing to make steady progress in his expressive and receptive language skills, but she is beginning to wonder if he might have a learning disability that is hindering his academic performance. The ladies agree that it might be time to request permission to reevaluate Chuck. Vicky and Monica will document the interventions they have implemented so far this year with accompanying data to share at the meeting. Evelyn will prepare the parent participation notice and invite the school psychologist to attend the meeting as well.

The next day, Evelyn gives Chuck a copy of the parent participation form for his meeting (scheduled to occur in 2 weeks). She tells Chuck that she wants to speak to his mother about how he is doing in school and to see if she will give her permission to do some testing to see if Chuck qualifies for more assistance at school. Evelyn assures Chuck that he is not in trouble and offers him a reward if he brings back the form signed by his mother. The next time Evelyn meets with Chuck for language therapy, she asks him if he has the signed form. Chuck says, "I gave the form to my mom, but she never gave it back to me." Evelyn says, "That's okay. I will give you another form. Please make sure to get your mom to look at it, sign it, and then I want you to bring it to me. Okay?" Chuck agrees. The next day Evelyn drops by Chuck's classroom to see if he has the signed parent participation notice. He doesn't. Evelyn decides she should phone the house and leave a message for his mother.

On the day of the scheduled meeting, Chuck's mother doesn't show up. Because there were three documented attempts to contact the parent, the IEP team meets without her. The team agrees that a reevaluation is warranted. They send home notes of the meeting and a consent-for-reevaluation form. When after a few days the form is not returned, they mail a second copy home for signature. Chuck's mother then signs and returns the form to the school via Chuck. After consent is received, Evelyn and the school psychologist test Chuck. Reports are written and a meeting to review the results of the reevaluation is scheduled. Multiple notices are again sent home to the parent concerning the meeting and are never returned.

The reevaluation meeting is conducted without Chuck's mother. It is determined that Chuck is eligible for a learning-disabilities program and continued eligibility for the language-impaired program, with learning disabilities designated as his primary disability. A new IEP is developed, a change of placement form completed, and notes of the meeting documented and sent home to the parent. Chuck's mother has 10 working days to respond to the change of placement. If the school receives no response, the placement is automatic. Chuck's mother never responds to the change of placement.

In the spring, Vicky receives a phone call from Chuck's mother. She is upset to discover that Chuck is being pulled out of his general education classroom for support in reading, which no one told her about. She demands to know what is going on. Vicky relays to her what had happened earlier in the school year and how the team made repeated attempts to contact her. She tells the mother that Chuck is doing much better now in his subjects with the additional support services. Chuck's mother is still very upset that a change was made without her permission. She threatens to phone the school superintendent and the governor.

Discussion Questions

1. Based on what you know about special education law, is it appropriate for Monica to pull students out of their special-area classes to provide additional academic support? Why or why not?

2. Evelyn made three attempts to contact and invite Chuck's mother to the consent-for-reevaluation meeting. Should the meeting have been rescheduled when the mother did not attend?

3. After the reevaluation meeting, signed consent for reevaluation was received from the parent. Was the team authorized to conduct the reevaluations at this point? Why or why not?

4. When the IEP team met to discuss the results of the reevaluations, Chuck's mother was not present. The information was sent home and 10 days notice provided prior to the change of placement. Should the team have changed the placement without direct permission from the parent? Why or why not?

5. Chuck's mother is very angry about her son's change of placement. Do you believe that she has any legal recourse? Why or why not?

4

Teaching in the Inclusive Classroom

INCLUSION AND COLLABORATION

Teaching within an inclusion classroom can be a challenge not only for students with disabilities, but also for the teachers. Before we discuss collaboration, co-teaching, and the teaching models used in an inclusion classroom, we first define, or try to define, what is meant by inclusion.

The word *inclusion* means many things to many people as evidenced by the varied definitions of the word (see Smith, 2007, for a discussion of the problems involved with defining inclusion). A common definition of inclusion is *the education of students with disabilities within the general education setting and under the direction of both the general education teacher and special education teacher* (Friend & Bursuck, 2006; Mastropieri & Scruggs, 2007). Others (Giangreco, 1997; Giangreco, Baumgart, & Doyle, 1995) have elaborated on the term *inclusion*, and its definition comprises the following parts:

1. All students are welcome in general education classes in their local schools. *Inclusion for some* is a contradiction in terms.
2. Students are educated in classes where the number of those with and without disabilities is proportional to the local population.
3. Students are educated with peers in the same age groupings available to those without disability labels.
4. Students with varying characteristics and abilities participate in shared educational experiences while pursuing individually appropriate learning outcomes with necessary supports and accommodations.
5. Shared educational experiences occur in settings predominantly frequented by people without disabilities (e.g., general education classroom, community work sites).
6. Educational experiences are designed to enhance individually determined valued life outcomes for students and therefore seek an individualized balance between the academic/functional and social/personal aspects of schooling.
7. Inclusive education exists when each of these characteristics occurs on an ongoing daily basis (Giangreco, 1997, p. 194).

33

Using various components of this definition, in this book *inclusion* refers to a student with disabilities who is being taught with nondisabled peers and are *active participants* in the learning process. Additionally, the inclusion classroom includes at least one general education teacher and one special education teacher, whereby both work with and teach all of the students in the classroom.

The main components of teaching in an inclusion classroom discussed in this chapter include professional collaboration, co-planning and co-teaching, co-teaching models, and monitoring student progress (Friend & Bursuck, 2009; Giangreco, 1997; Giangreco, Baumgart, & Doyle, 1995).

PROFESSIONAL COLLABORATION

One component of teaching in an inclusive classroom is professional *collaboration*. Collaboration involves two people working together to achieve a *shared goal.* It can include a variety of educators, professionals, and parents. In the case of co-teaching, collaboration usually involves teachers working together to instruct students with disabilities in a regular education setting. Teacher–teacher collaboration is the most common type of collaboration that occurs in schools. In special education, the most common pairing is a special education teacher collaborating with a regular education teacher. These teachers commonly collaborate or co-teach in content-area classes (e.g., science, social studies, history, English) to teach students with and without disabilities; however, in primary grades collaboration can occur throughout the entire day in every subject area.

Collaboration really involves more than just two teachers working together. It involves learning about collaboration, as well as learning specific skills about how to collaborate, co-teach, and co-plan effectively. As teachers become more comfortable working together and learning how to teach more diverse learners, they become more effective teachers. Furthermore, through ongoing training and development, they can continue to meet the challenges of teaching diverse students who have varied levels of knowledge and skills.

Morsink, Thomas, and Correa (1991) define collaboration as "a mutual effort to plan, implement, and evaluate the educational program for a given student" (p. 6). A slightly different version of this definition is presented by Friend and Cook (1992), who refer to collaboration as a "*style* of interaction" (p. 5) used by professionals as they work together. Viewed in this manner, collaboration is a "*style* [that] professionals choose—to accomplish a goal they share" (Friend & Bursuck, 2009, p. 79). These authors further point out that just because two people are working on the same activity does not ensure that collaboration is occurring; hence, their reference to collaboration as a "style of interaction" can occur during different activities. In this textbook, we view collaboration as *two teachers working together to plan and teach students with and without disabilities in an inclusive or collaborative setting.*

Collaboration is a critical component in co-taught classrooms. What makes an inclusive program successful are teachers who develop collaborative partnerships (i.e., effective styles of interactions) with each other, and their efforts are reflected by the fact that *all* students in the classroom benefit from this collaborative relationship. A study by the National Center on Educational Restructuring and Inclusion (NCERI) found that teachers who used collaborative teaching or the co-teaching model reported several positive outcomes for students with and without disabilities (NCERI, 1995). Their data found positive student outcomes on academic, social, and behavior measures for students with disabilities who participated in inclusive programs. Moreover, the report indicated positive "behavioral and social outcomes" for nondisabled students as well and no negative effects on academic skills.

Effective collaborative relationships do not happen instantly—it takes two or more partners working together over a long period of time to make for a successful collaborative partnership. In fact, Gately and Gately (2001) believe that collaboration and co-teaching develop through three distinct stages. First, teachers work politely with one another in a *beginning stage* of collaboration. This stage is characterized by teachers communicating in a guarded manner as they seek to interpret both verbal and nonverbal messages. At first, they may clash in their level of openness or honesty so as not to offend their teaching partner. Some general education teachers may feel as if their class is being intruded upon by the special education teacher. On the other hand, special education teachers may feel awkward and excluded working in the general education classroom. If both teachers don't have mutual goals of sharing and collaborating, they could become entrenched in this stage and never move on to the next stage. In the second stage, the *compromising stage,* both teachers use more open and effective communication with each other. As Gately and Gately put it, there is a sense of *give and take* that develops as they move to a more real collaborative partnership. As the special education teacher begins to take a more dynamic role in classroom teaching and responsibilities, special educators must be willing to give up something in return. In the third and final stage, *collaborative stage*, "teachers openly communicate and interact" with one another (Gately & Gately, p. 42). Teachers have the comfort zone in this professional relationship as they work as one to teach all students. Like most experienced collaborative teachers during this stage, observers often have a difficult time discerning who is the special education teacher and who is the general education teacher.

Friend and her colleagues (Friend & Bursuck, 2009; Friend & Cook, 1992) identified several key characteristics of effective collaboration that include:

- Collaboration is a voluntary process.
- Collaboration is based on respect, trust, and support for one another.
- Collaboration uses mutual goals and shared accountability of outcomes.
- Collaboration engages in a shared participation and decision-making.
- Collaboration encourages equal contributions and shared resources.

First, collaboration is based on a voluntary process, whereby both teachers are willing participants. In the early stages of collaborative relationships, teachers often volunteer to work with each other on a regular basis, and in some cases, have already worked with each other. Voluntary collaboration represents a willingness on the part of both individuals to work with each other. Second, true collaboration is based on individuals with a mutual respect and trust for one another. Their relationship is very much based on parity or each equally valuing the other person's decisions and contributions. These relationships are not based on power, but on treating each other with mutual respect and valuing everyone's opinion equally. Teachers in these collaborative relationships support one another, yet understand that there will be times when both may not see eye to eye on certain issues. Despite disagreements, these teachers respect each other's opinions. Third, related to mutual respect, effective collaborators develop shared goals for what they hope to accomplish while collaborating and working together toward accomplishing these goals. Likewise, they also have shared accountability for their students and themselves. Very often these teachers are proud of their knowledge and working relationships and will put forth the extra effort to accomplish their teaching goals or help students accomplish their learning goals. Fourth, collaboration involves shared participation and decision making. Because both teachers view themselves as equal, both respect each other's opinions during the decision-making process and value each other's views on issues or topics. Like good collaborators, they are in sync in terms of mutual decisions about class rules, students' assignments, discipline, and other aspects of an inclusive classroom. Fifth, collaboration involves equal contributions and shared resources. Similar to shared participation and decision making, collaborators encourage and expect equal contributions from each other. Each individual is heard in an effective collaborative relationship, and each opinion is respected by the other. Along with respecting each other's contributions, collaborative teachers also are willing to share resources with each other. We often see what we affectionately call "nomad teachers" in schools. When classes change, these teachers are often seen pushing their cart up and down the hallway as they head off to their next class. Usually their cart is full of materials and supplies that will be used on that particular day to teach in different classrooms throughout the school. Like a man without a country, this collaborator is a teacher without a homeroom. Despite the lack of a homeroom, we have seen their collaborative partners provide them with a desk or space in their room for their materials, often to such an extent that their partner's classroom becomes a second home for them.

CO-TEACHING AND CO-PLANNING SKILLS

For teachers to work together effectively, they must possess or acquire skills that allow them to clearly communicate to their partner and to support each other in the classroom. Typically, teachers attend professional development workshops prior to or while working as co-teachers. This training helps them prepare to work with other professionals.

The four key areas for effective collaboration are *interaction skills*, *support skills*, *solution-building skills*, and *problem-solving skills*.

1. *Interaction Skills.* Friend and Bursuck (2009) break interaction skills into two components: "communication skills and steps to productive interactions" (p. 83). The first component—communication skills—uses effective *listening skills* (i.e., *active listening*) and an awareness of both *nonverbal communication* and *verbal communication* skills. Effective collaboration involves active listening and effective communication skills (Friend & Cook, 2000). In fact, Clark (1996) developed a collaborative model whereby communication and language are two components that both people perform together rather than separately. As such, active listening involves being engaged in the conversation; the listener tries to understand what is being said and shapes what is being said by the speaker. Whether the teacher is listening to their partner describe a student's problem or how their day went, active listening is a crucial skill. People who are active listeners often use both nonverbal cues (e.g., body language, facial expressions, spatial relations) and verbal communication skills to shape interactions when communicating with others. The listener provides nonverbal feedback to the speaker and, in turn, this feedback is used by the speaker to modify the conversation (i.e., interaction) Manusov & Trees 2002. Working in tandem with the speaker, the listener often becomes a co-narrator in conversations through nonverbal facial expressions (e.g., winces, frowns) or verbal utterances (e.g., supplying words or using fillers such as, "uh huh") (Bavelas, Coates, & Johnson, 2002).

Others have reported similar relationships between verbal and nonverbal communication, with as much as 93% of our communication coming from facial expressions and vocal intonations, much of it nonverbal in nature (e.g., frowning, smiling, or nodding your head) (Miller, 2005). Moreover, there may be times when the speaker may be too distressed or embarrassed to verbalize what they are really thinking or feeling; therefore, the listener has to rely on nonverbal cues to understand the individual's true intent.

Another component of interaction skills is the effective use of *verbal communication skills*. When listening to others speak or when communicating with others, it is important to be precise in your understanding of their message and likewise, try to be precise when communicating messages. As a listener, hearing someone describe an issue, you have to be able to understand both the verbal measure and their feelings associated with the message. Teachers who work together must have a mutual understanding of a problem or issue in order to effectively resolve it.

2. *Support Skills.* Along with interaction skills, support skills also play a crucial role in collaboration. People use support skills to show caring and support for one another during their interactions. They typically include both verbal and nonverbal forms of communication that help develop bonds between teachers. These skills are the cement that holds the co-teaching team together. Knackendoffel (2005) breaks these skills into two broad categories: *equality builder* and *solution builder* skills. Collaborative teachers use equality building skills to show that they view their partner as an equal and value their partner's knowledge and skills. Typical statements are, "I really enjoy working with you because you have such a caring attitude toward teaching all the students," or "Rather than try to design the lesson by myself, I would appreciate your expertise in terms of the content that we'll both teach." These statements show that the collaborative teacher enjoys working with his or her partner and values the partner's teaching expertise. Along with these statements, partners can also include compliments and *statements of appreciation* to show appreciation for the hard work and efforts and *empathic statements* to show empathy with difficult situations and recognition of problems or issues.

3. *Solution-Building Skills.* Collaborators use these skills and statements to help focus back to the task at hand or to help direct the conversation toward mutually acceptable solutions. These solutions help solve a problem and provide a solution that meets the needs of all of the parties. Solution-building statements might include, "I am glad that we decided that Steve should show his homework to me so I can reinforce his behavior, and to you so you can give him feedback about his performance," or "I like your idea of using proximity control to help reduce talking in the back of the class. It will also help the students to remain on task." Again, these statements reflect a benefit for all parties involved and are solutions that both teachers can agree on.

4. *Problem-Solving Skills.* Problem solving represents another crucial area for collaborators. These skills can be used with students' academic or behavior problems or to solve other nonstudent issues (e.g., problems with colleagues or administrators, managing schedules, or personal problems). A number of problem-solving models have been suggested in the literature (Knackendoffel, 2005; Morsink, Thomas, & Correa, 1991; Rubinson, 2002; Santangelo, 2009). The model described next borrows components taken from several sources to form a generic problem-solving model and includes the following steps:

1. Identify the problem.
2. Generate and analyze solutions.
3. Develop an intervention plan and implementation steps.
4. Monitor intervention and evaluate.

IDENTIFY THE PROBLEM.   Any problem or issue that is identified must be clearly defined. This involves describing it in specific, observable, and measurable terms (Barnhill, 2005). During this process, background information about the behavior or issue should also be gathered to see if there are any related factors that may be pertinent. For example, if a student doesn't record notes during class, does this affect the student's grade? What techniques have been used in the past to help this student with note taking? Is this a skill or behavior that should be addressed, or should other, more important skills and behaviors be addressed? How is the student's lack of notes affecting his or her grades? Is this a skill-based deficit (i.e., student lacks the skills to complete the task) or is it a performance-based deficit due to a motivational or discrimination problem (e.g., student has skills, but does not use them)? These questions help determine if note taking is an important skill to be addressed for this student.

GENERATE AND ANALYZE SOLUTIONS.   When generating possible solutions, all possible solutions should be considered. This part of the problem-solving process is typically analogous to brainstorming, whereby no solutions are rejected—each is recorded. Once these solutions are generated, collaborators should develop a criterion for accepting or rejecting possible solutions. For example, co-teachers who are working with a student with poor note-taking skills might reject ideas that could be easily implemented by either teacher or ideas that could not be implemented during regular school hours. Once the solutions are analyzed, collaborators should consider the best solution (or solutions) that they want to implement.

DEVELOP AN INTERVENTION PLAN AND IMPLEMENTATION STEPS.   Once the best solution(s) is selected, teachers need to develop an action plan. This action plan should include the task (i.e., solution), the person responsible for each task, when each task will begin, and when each task will be completed.

MONITOR INTERVENTION AND EVALUATE.   Along with this action plan, teachers should discuss how each task will be monitored and the specific criteria for success for each task. By establishing a criterion for success for each task, teachers can discuss their expectations (i.e., pseudo-criteria), which then helps to determine if the goal has been met based upon meeting the criteria. At some point, teachers should meet again to discuss student progress on each task and whether the criteria have been met or need to be adjusted.

CO-PLANNING SKILLS.   Co-planning is just as important as co-teaching. A well-planned lesson may not always guarantee that a well-taught lesson will succeed, but it certainly increases the chances that the lesson will go well. Conversely, having no plan is an invitation for disaster. Therefore, it is important to have a plan that is developed by all who will teach the lesson and that has been well thought out ahead of time. During co-planning, it is important to establish a routine and, initially, use a written plan (see Table 4.1) to structure co-planning time. The written guide should cover the previous lesson and break down the new lesson into sections that can be discussed, as well as include an area for assigning who will be responsible for carrying out that portion of the lesson. Each portion should be assigned based on each teacher's skills or expertise, as well as students' needs. A guide or lesson plan is needed so that both teachers are clear about their roles and responsibility during teaching.

In middle or high school math classes, the special education teacher might be responsible for the warm-up portion of the class. The warm-up reviews problems that were previously taught and ensures that the students understand previous material before moving on to new material. The regular education teacher might then take over for teaching of new content while the special education teacher walks around and monitors students, checking for correctness of work and understanding of new information. Each of these areas should be worked out ahead of time and assigned so someone is responsible for each.

Establishing a routine ahead of time prevents teachers from downtime during their co-planning periods. Routines are especially important for novice teachers or new co-teachers.

TABLE 4.1	Co-Planning Guide and Lesson Plan

Evaluation of Previous Lesson:

Which portion of the lesson went well?

Which portion of the lesson went poorly?

Which content should be reviewed or retaught?

Which activity could be used to review content that is being retaught?

Are there parts of co-teaching that could be improved (e.g., introduction, preview, transitions, review, preparation/distribution of materials, monitoring of students, feedback to students)?

Lesson Considerations:

What cognitive supports could be used in the lesson to ensure that all students learn the content?

What accommodations do students with disabilities need?

What effective teaching methods or supports are used in the lesson to enhance learning?

What classroom management components are needed for the lesson?

New Lesson Format:

Advanced organizer or review of previous content or skills

What will you say/do? Who does this? How long?

Partner teacher does what?

Introduction to new content or skills

What? Who? How long?

Partner teacher does what?

Guided Practice of Content or Skills Through Activities

Activity 1

What? Who? How long?

Partner teacher does what?

Activity 2

What? Who? How long?

Partner teacher does what?

Activity 3

What? Who? How long?

Partner teacher does what?

Assessment of learning

What? Who? How long?

Partner teacher does what?

Summary or review

What? Who? How long?

Partner teacher does what?

Filler, enrichment, or follow-up activity

What? Who? How long?

Partner teacher does what?

Source: J. R. Boyle & D. Scanlon. *Methods and strategies for teaching students with mild disabilities.* Belmont, CA: Wadsworth Cengage Learning.

Routines require that each person knows what they are responsible for during planning and what materials are needed. For example, an effective co-planning routine might involve meeting in the same room every time to plan out the next day's lesson, having all of the necessary materials that will be used during planning (e.g., the textbook, the teacher's guide, paper, pencils, ancillary materials related to the lesson, the teacher's gradebook, student work, master copies of handouts), having the school secretary hold all calls during your meeting time, having a method for recording the lesson plan (e.g., a scribe is selected for each meeting to record notes), following a set procedure (see Table 4.1), and ending within a reasonable amount of time. Again, the purpose of a routine is to minimize downtime and make the meeting flow smoothly. Planning time is such an important part of co-teaching for teams that protecting it is often a number one concern for teachers (Dieker, 2001).

The actual co-planning guide and lesson plan can serve as a record of agreed-upon components and roles. The first section, the *Evaluation of Previous Lesson*, reviews the previous lesson. If planning takes place in the afternoon, an evaluation of the lesson taught that day would be recorded here. The purpose of this section is to learn from what worked and what did not work, and then make the appropriate changes. Be sure that you base your decisions on data from the previous lesson. If students did not adequately learn a new concept or skill, to what extent did they not learn it? Is it based on test or quiz results, or on oral questions? Similarly, if students mastered content or skills, how do you know they reached mastery? Did all students reach mastery, or a just small minority? High-achieving students can frequently master content and skills despite the teacher's lack of skills at teaching it. Many of these students are self-motivated learners capable of learning on their own. Because you are teaching a diverse group of learners, consider if other students (e.g., average, low-achieving, and students with disabilities) reached mastery on specific skills or content (e.g., commonly referred to as HALO—High achiever, Average achiever, Low achiever, and Other achievers, such as students with disabilities). For some students, reviewing or even re-teaching of content or skills may be needed for them to progress on to the next skill level.

The *Lesson Considerations* portion serves to remind teachers about cognitive supports (e.g., guided notes, cognitive maps and organizers, outlines, mnemonics, study guides) that could be used to help students record better notes and remember the content of lectures. This section also prompts teachers to identify and include effective teaching methods (e.g., differentiated instruction, direct instruction, discovery learning, mnemonics techniques, pause procedure) or supports that could be used to deliver content to students. The accommodations question serves to remind teachers to consider appropriate accommodations for students with disabilities.

The classroom management component reminds teachers that different management components might be needed when using different co-teaching models. For example, if using station teaching, teachers might provide additional reinforcers (e.g., stickers, tokens, points) to students who are quiet, transition quietly, cooperate while working in groups, or follow directions.

The last portion of the co-planning guide and lesson plan, *New Lesson Format*, is the actual lesson plan. These could be modified depending on the lesson, but be sure to use the following components: advanced organizer, introduction, guided practice activities, assessment of learning (e.g., independent practice) Filler, enrichment, or follow-up activity, and summary of lesson.

Finally, as co-teachers become more comfortable working together in an inclusive classroom, they can begin to examine ways to improve their interactions, planning, and teaching with one another. Gately and Gately (2001) developed a useful informal instrument whereby teachers can assess their working relationship in the inclusive classroom (see the Gately & Gately, 2001, article for their co-teaching rating scale). Their *Coteaching Rating Scale* comes in two formats: Special Education Teacher format and General Education Teacher format. This scale can be used to gauge where the co-teaching pair feel they are currently at in terms of their collaborative relationship and can provide them with aspects of their co-teaching that could be useful for collaborative discussions for further growth.

MODELS OF CO-TEACHING

According to a 1994 study by the NCERI, several models are used to support inclusive education; however, the most frequently cited model used by schools with inclusive programs is the co-teaching model. Although a number of co-teaching models are presented in the literature (Cook & Friend, 1995; Friend & Bursuck, 2006; Thousand, Villa, & Nevin, 2006; Walther-Thomas, Korinek, McLaughlin, & Williams, 2000), this text presents the following four models of co-teaching: *station teaching*, *interactive teaching*, *alternative teaching*, and *parallel teaching* (Figure 4.1). Each model can be used with different content and each model has its advantages.

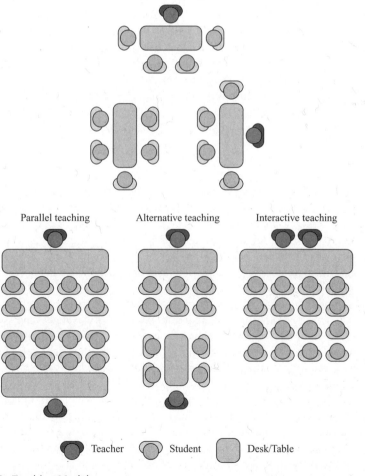

FIGURE 4.1 Co-Teaching Models

Depending on the purpose of a lesson, one model might work better than others. For example, *parallel teaching* might be used when teachers want to review content before a test. On the other hand, *alternative teaching* might be used if a portion of the class has missed content and the purpose is to catch those students up with the rest of the class.

STATION TEACHING. When using station teaching, depending on the size of the class, teachers set up three to five stations around the room, and students move in groups from one station to another after a designated period of time (10 to 15 minutes). Station teaching requires quite a bit of preparation on the part of the teachers. Prior to the lesson, the teachers have to prepare each station with the appropriate materials and make sure that the directions are clear. If directions are not clear or if expectations for student behavior are not explicit, students may become sidetracked trying to figure out what to do or may end up using materials in an inappropriate manner. In station teaching, teachers have to monitor the noise level and monitor behaviors.

When used in a collaborative classroom, each teacher will work at a station that requires teaching or direct supervision; at the remaining stations the students are expected to work independently. For example, if students were studying the characteristics of rocks, there would be five stations. One station might have a computer where students can view video clips from the web site "Rock Hounds" (http://www.fi.edu/fellows/fellow1/oct98/create/index.html) that shows them how different types of rock form (e.g., igneous, sedimentary, and metamorphic); one station might contain a word search or activity that students have to complete to practice using vocabulary words commonly associated with rocks (e.g., granite, marble, metamorphic, quarts, sandstone, volcano); at another station students can make the three different types of rocks using common materials (see the following web site for these activities: http://www.rogersgroupinc.com/ourcommunities/rockology/types.htm); one station might have a teacher explaining and discussing the rock cycle, and another station might have a teacher discussing the hardness of rocks and gives students some rocks to test.

INTERACTIVE TEACHING. With interactive teaching, one teacher assumes the lead, teaching in front of the class, while the other teacher supports by monitoring student learning. After a short period of time, the teachers switch roles. Remember, in effective co-taught classes, teachers work efficiently so that it becomes a symbiotic relationship. Each teacher has multiple opportunities to serve in both the *teach* and *support* modes. In the support role, the teacher is engaged in the lesson and asks questions or rephrases details when she or he sees a student having difficulty understanding a concept. The support teacher also supervises practice and monitors behaviors.

As an example of interactive teaching, while one teacher discusses how light refracts through a convex lens, the other teacher monitors students' notes, checking for understanding. Occasionally, when the support teacher sees a student having difficulty, she or he stops and asks questions to the lead teacher such as, "Did you say the light refracts as it passes through the lens? You also mentioned that 'refracts' means to bend, is that correct?" The support teacher uses questions in this fashion, rather than drawing attention to a student who is having difficulty understanding the concept. Shortly after convex and concave lenses are explained, the support teacher becomes the lead teacher and walks the class through a lab in which the students project images onto different types of lenses to see the effects of each. The same teacher then continues to explain how light changes when it comes from air and enters water. She or he explains to students how light refracts in water at a different angle than when it was in the air. In the meantime, the support teacher now monitors students' notes to ensure their accuracy. Although interactive teaching can be an enjoyable way to teach, both teachers have to know the content well and must plan ahead of time to ensure smooth transitions between their teaching. Teachers should be careful not to get stuck performing the same limited tasks, because they might be viewed as less than equals in students' eyes. For example, if one teacher is the one who handles disruptive behavior, one day when that teacher is absent, students may be more likely to behave inappropriately. If one teacher typically teaches the content, then students are more likely to turn to that one for their questions. The point is that both teachers should share the different roles—roles that are burdensome, as well as roles that are rewarding.

ALTERNATIVE TEACHING.   Alternative teaching involves creating a small group of students and then teaching them in one section of the room, usually in a corner or at a table in the back of the class. While one teacher works with the small group, the other teacher instructs the rest of the class. The purpose of the grouping is for re-teaching concepts, providing enrichment activities, catching students up who were absent, or addressing special problems that students may have (e.g., students who are talkative or disruptive, students who need prerequisite content, or students who need extra assistance taking notes). Using this model, teachers will alternate roles on a regular basis so that they do not become cast as the person who always works with small groups (the implication being that the particular teacher cannot handle large groups or that she or he works only with a certain type of student). Likewise, the group should be heterogeneous and not include the same students every time, lest the small group take on the appearance of students who have behavior and academic problems. All students should be given opportunities to participate in both large and small groups. For example, if a student with a mild disability is having difficulty understanding the concept of a recessive gene, that student might be paired up with a high achiever who understands the concept well, and then both could be given practice activities in a small group. In this way, both the teacher and high achiever could explain the concept to help the student with mild disabilities understand it. The purpose of the alternative teaching configuration is still met: because the students with the highest needs have been distributed between the two teachers, they will be able to receive the levels of attention they need.

PARALLEL TEACHING.   Parallel teaching involves dividing the class in half and having each instructor teach students the same content. Each group of students is heterogeneous (i.e., high, average, and low achievers). This configuration provides a good format for students who are reluctant to respond in larger groups or during those times when teachers want more interactions with students. As such, it would be an appropriate format to use when teaching difficult-to-understand concepts, when students need a lot of practice with skills, or when teachers want to make sure that all students have mastered a set of content or skills. Parallel teaching does require careful planning so that both teachers cover the same content and maintain an adequate pace to ensure that all of the designated content will be covered by the end of class. Of course, two instructors teaching in the same classroom may be more distracting, and there will be higher levels of noise. For some teachers, it will take some time to get acclimated to this format, particularly teachers who are unsure of their teaching and classroom management skills.

The problem with some of the co-teaching models is that the regular education teacher does the actual "teaching" and the special education teacher ends up assisting the teacher or is delegated to nonteaching tasks (e.g., grading papers, monitoring student behavior, or preparing materials for the lesson). The biggest complaint that special education teachers in ineffective co-taught classes have is that they are often "stuck" doing nonteaching tasks and thus feel like a teaching assistant. Of course, with better communication between teachers and the willingness of both teachers to share the teaching role, they can usually resolve many of these problems.

MONITORING STUDENT PROGRESS

The last major topic pertains to monitoring instruction in inclusive classrooms. Monitoring student progress is critical for helping students with disabilities succeed in inclusive classrooms. When used with differentiated instruction, monitoring progress becomes a valuable tool for teachers to see how students are responding to instruction. Of course it all begins with using an instructional model, such as direct instruction, whereby the teacher models a new skill to the students, uses guided practice with feedback to guide the students as they practice the new skill, and then uses independent practice to assess whether the students can use the new skill on their own. To support student learning, teachers also need to use an ongoing form of assessment to measure student progress over time.

Curriculum-based measurement (CBM) represents perhaps one of the best methods of monitoring student progress. CBM involves taking "brief assessments that serve as indicators of overall proficiency in an academic area" (Stecker, Lembke, & Foegen, 2008, p. 49). Because CBM is sensitive to small changes in student learning, particularly when data is recorded multiple times within a short period of time, it is ideal for teaching students with disabilities in inclusive classrooms. Unlike traditional progress measures, which are administered only once or twice per semester, CBM can be used frequently (e.g., weekly, twice a week, every other day) to detect minor changes in learning as students respond to various teaching methods. In fact, research has shown that when teachers use CBM to make changes in instruction, students obtain higher achievement levels than with traditional assessment practices (Stecker, Fuchs, & Fuchs, 2005). More important in inclusive classrooms, CBM has been shown to be successful not just for students with disabilities, but also among general education students. For example, when used with whole classes in math, CBM has been shown to be more effective than traditional assessment in terms of increasing overall student achievement (Fuchs, Fuchs, Hamlett, Phillips, & Bentz, 1994).

How do teachers use CBM? Typically, a teacher begins by choosing one skill area (e.g., reading the number of words correctly per minute is a common CBM skill—see Figure 4.2).

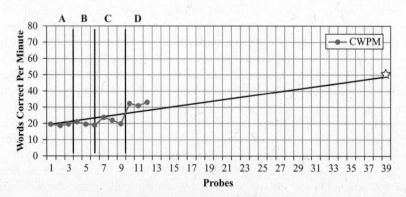

FIGURE 4.2 Curriculum-Based Measurement—Oral Reading Rate

Once a baseline or starting point is established, the teacher needs to decide on a goal. A goal can be determined using a variety of methods such as tables that use established scores per grade level (Hasbrouck & Tindal, 1992; Hudson, Lane, & Pullen, 2005; Rasinski & Padak, 2004), the performance of grade level peers (Howell & Kaplan, 1980; Salvia & Hughes, 1990), or academic growth standards which are then multiplied by the number of weeks remaining in the school year (Deno, Fuchs, Marston, & Shin, 2001; Hosp & Hosp, 2003; Scott & Weishaar, 2003). Other useful methods for determining goals and materials can be found at a number of web sites, including the Curriculum-Based Measurement Warehouse from Intervention Central (http://www.interventioncentral.org/htmdocs/interventions/cbmwarehouse.php) or Research Institute on Progress Monitoring (http://www.progressmonitoring.org).

Once the goal is plotted on a chart or graph (e.g., represented on our chart by a star), the teacher then draws a line to connect the goal (data point) to the baseline point (e.g., on our chart this is 20 words correct per minute). This line is known as the *aimline*. The aimline serves as a guide for teachers as they plot data points on the chart and informs them how students have performed in relation toward meeting the goal. Data points plotted above the aimline generally represent student performances that will eventually achieve the goal. In other words, the technique or method that the teacher is using is working in terms of student performance. As a general rule, three or more data points above the aimline indicate that the student is on the way toward achieving the goal (Scott & Weishaar, 2003). Conversely, if three or more data points are below the aimline, the teaching technique or method is not working and, therefore, needs to be changed or modified until the student performance is above the aimline.

CBM is a useful tool for teachers to use as they work in inclusive classrooms. If used judiciously, it can be a meaningful assessment tool that does not monopolize much teaching time and can be used in coordination with IEP goals and objectives (Scott & Weishaar, 2003; Stecker, Lembke, & Foegen, 2008). Used frequently, this tool can inform teachers about the effectiveness of their teaching practices and alert teachers to how student performance is changing over time.

Conclusion

Effective collaborative teaching, or co-teaching, does not happen overnight. As with any change in teaching, it takes time to develop a collaborative partnership with others. As those partnerships develop, attitudes begin to change among teachers as they co-plan and co-teach lessons. They begin to develop better communication and support skills and become more adept at problem solving and co-planning.

The use of different co-teaching models such as station teaching, interactive teaching, alternative teaching, and parallel teaching can be beneficial to student learning. Using these different models of teaching, along with supports and modifications in the classroom, teachers can manage and effectively instruct a large heterogeneous group of students. Over time, co-teachers also begin to modify their instruction to find better ways to help all students learn. They begin to modify their roles and responsibilities with each other and through co-planning begin to better understand their roles and responsibilities during co-taught lessons. As teachers become more proficient at co-planning and teaching, they begin to work not as two teachers, but as one team.

References

Barnhill, G. (2005). Functional behavioral assessment in schools. *Intervention in School & Clinic, 40*(3), 131–143.

Bavelas, J. B., Coates, L., & Johnson, T. (2002). Listener responses as a collaborative process: The role of gaze. *Journal of Communication, 52,* 566–580.

Clark, H. H. (1996). *Using language.* Cambridge: Cambridge University Press.

Cook, L., & Friend, M. (1995). Co-teaching: Guidelines for creating effective practices. *Focus on Exceptional Children, 28(3),* 1–16.

Deno, S., Fuchs, L., Marston, D., & Shin, J. (2001). Using curriculum-based measurement to establish growth standards for students with learning disabilities. *School Psychology Review, 30,* 507–524.

Dieker, L. A. (2001). What are the characteristics of "effective" middle and high school co-taught teams for students with disabilities? *Preventing School Failure, 46*(1), 14–23.

Friend, M., & Bursuck, W. (2006). *Including students with special needs: A practical guide for classroom teachers.* Boston: Allyn & Bacon.

Friend, M., & Bursuck, W. D. (2009). *Including students with special needs: A practical guide for classroom teachers* (5th ed.). Upper Saddle River, NJ: Merrill.

Friend, M., & Cook, L. (1992). The new mainstreaming. *Instructor, 101*(7), 30–32.

Friend, M., & Cook, L. (2000). *Interactions.* New York: Longman.

Fuchs, L., Fuchs, D., Hamlett, C., Phillips, N., & Bentz, J. (1994). Classwide curriculum-based measurement— helping general educators meet the challenge of student diversity. *Exceptional Children, 60*(6), 518–537.

Gately, S. E., & Gately, F. J. (2001). Understanding coteaching components. *TEACHING Exceptional Children, 33*(4), 40–47.

Giangreco, M. F. (1997). Key lessons learned about inclusive education. *International Journal of Disability, Development, and Education, 44,* 193–206.

Giangreco, M. F., Baumgart, D. M., & Doyle, M. B. (1995). How inclusion can facilitate teaching and learning. *Intervention in School and Clinic, 30*(5), 273–278.

Hasbrouck, J. E., & Tindal, G. (1992). Curriculum-based oral reading fluency forms for students in grades 2 through 5. *Teaching Exceptional Children, 24,* 41–44.

Hosp, M., & Hosp, J. (2003). Curriculum-based measurement for reading, spelling, and math: How to do it and why. *Preventing School Failure, 48*(1), 10–17.

Howell, K., & Kaplan, J. (1980). *Diagnosing basic skills: A handbook for deciding what to teach.* Columbus, OH: Merrill.

Hudson, R. F., Lane, H. B., & Pullen, P. C. (2005). Reading fluency assessment and instruction: What, why, and how? *The Reading Teacher, 58,* 702–714.

Knackendoffel, E. A. (2005). Collaborative teaming in the secondary school. *Focus on Exceptional Children, 37*(5), 1–16.

Magiera, K., Smith, C., Zigmond, N., & Gebauer, K. (2005). Benefits of co-teaching in secondary mathematics classes. *TEACHING Exceptional Children, 37*(3), 20–24.

Manusov, V., & Trees, A. R. (2002). "Are you kidding me?" The role of nonverbal cues in the verbal accounting process. Journal of Communication, 52, 640–656.

Mastropieri, M. A., & Scruggs, T. E. (2007). *The inclusive classroom: Strategies for effective instruction.* Upper Saddle River, NJ: Merrill/Pearson Education.

Miller, P. W. (2005). Body language in the classroom. *Techniques: Connecting Education and Careers, 80*(8), 28–30.

Morsink, C. M., Thomas, C. C., & Correa, V. I. (1991). *Interactive teaming: Consultation and collaboration in special programs.* New York: MacMillan

Morsink, C.V., Thomas, C.C., & Correa, V.I. (1991). *Interactive teaming: Consultation and collaboration in special programs.* New York: Macmillan.

National Center on Educational Restructuring and Inclusion. (1995). *National study of inclusive education.* New York: Author.

Rasinski, T., & Padak, N. (2004). *Effective reading strategies.* Upper Saddle River, NJ: Pearson.

Rubinson, F. (2002). Lessons learned from implementing problem-solving teams in urban high schools. *Journal of Educational and Psychological Consultation, 13,* 185–217.

Salvia, J., & Hughes. C. A. (1990). *Curriculum-based assessment: Test what is taught.* New York: McMillan.

Santangelo, T. (2009). Collaborative problem solving effectively implemented, but not sustained: A case for aligning the sun, the moon, and the stars. *Exceptional Children, 75,* 185–209.

Scott, V., & Weishaar, M. (2003). Curriculum-based measurement for reading progress. *Intervention in School and Clinic, 38*(3), 153–159.

Scruggs, T. E., Mastropieri, M. A., & McDuffie, K. A. (2007). Co-teaching in inclusive classrooms: A metasynthesis of qualitative research. *Exceptional Children, 73*(4), 392–416.

Smith, P. (2007). Have we made any progress? Including students with intellectual disabilities in the regular education classroom. *Intellectual and Developmental Disabilities, 45*(5), 297–309.

Steckler, P., Fuchs, L., & Fuchs, D. (2005). Using curriculum-based measurement to improve student achievement: A review of the literature. *Psychology in the Schools, 42,* 795–819.

Stecker, P., Lembke, E., & Foegen, A. (2008). Using progress-monitoring data to improve instructional decision making. *Preventing School Failure, 52*(2), 48–58.

Thousand, J., Villa, R., & Nevin, A. (2006). The many faces of collaborative planning and teaching. *Theory Into Practice, 45,* 239–249.

Walther-Thomas, C., Korinek, L., McLaughlin, V. L., & Williams, B. T. (2000). *Collaboration for inclusive education.* Boston: Allyn & Bacon.

5

Cases About Collaboration and Co-Teaching in Inclusive Classrooms

CASE 1

To Build a Better Mousetrap

As Janice Jenkins sat in the corner of the classroom and graded papers, she thought to herself how different this so-called "inclusion class" is from the wonderful inclusion models discussed in her college classes. As her mind drifted back to her college days, Janice remembered Professor Hanson's descriptions of inclusion schools and how he spoke of the harmony of two teachers working together to teach all kids in the class. It sounded so nice when he described it. "Why is it so different now? If only this guy would let me do some teaching, this could be such a great class," she thought to herself.

The "guy" that she was referring to was Ramone Sanchez, a veteran at Jefferson High School, with 20 years' teaching experience. He taught a number of science classes, including 10th-grade chemistry. He taught the same way for years and was not about to change just because the school was going "inclusion." He was, in his opinion, the content guy responsible for making sure that his students learned the content well enough to pass the state's standards test. Of those who took his end-of-the-year science tests, he had an 88% pass rate, one of the best passing rates in the school.

Janice, on the other hand, was fairly new to special education, having graduated from her Learning Disabilities (LD) master's program just 2 years earlier. When she was first hired, the principal, Vernon Savior, spoke of big changes occurring throughout his school. He told Janice about how he was looking for someone with her kind of fresh ideas, energy, and expertise in collaborative teaching. He also revealed his vision of his school as one in which all kids (those with LD and nondisabled students) would learn together, and all teachers would care about every student. He had wanted to be an inclusion leader within his school division and thought he had all of the proper staff on board at Jefferson to make it happen. Bringing Janice on board was, in his opinion, the final piece of the puzzle necessary for an "inclusive" year. The same year that Janice joined the staff, all students with LD were placed in inclusion classes. Each LD teacher traveled from class to class collaborating and supporting inclusion within the school. All resource and self-contained LD classes were eliminated.

Janice, excited at the start of her career, had slowly become more cynical about her ideals of inclusion, particularly at her school. Yes, it's true that in her two other collaborative classes, she does co-teach most of the time, but she thought everyone should be willing to allow her to co-teach. She felt that the only way to alleviate the effects of special education labels was to place students in inclusion or regular education classes full-time.

Now, relegated to the role of the "worksheet and test grader" in Ramone's class, Janice felt dejected because she was only permitted to complete menial tasks such as checking homework and going around the room to redirect students back on task. Occasionally, she also breaks up fights between students and even arguments between Ramone and students, including the special education students. She definitely felt that Ramone treated students with LD differently than the nondisabled students and that the gifted students earned a special status. Whether this was true or not depended on who you asked.

Today, she thought, is the day that things change in chemistry. As soon as class ended, Janice decided to approach Ramone with her ideas of co-teaching.

As students piled out the classroom door, Janice approached Ramone's desk. "Mr. Sanchez, another excellent lesson," remarked Janice, thinking she could prod him forward using compliments. "Thanks," said Ramone in a slow cautious manner. "I think the students really liked your analogy that you used of how chemical reactions are like factories," Janice said further. "I was thinking that, maybe, if you let me teach a quick review first or teach *some* content, that maybe, it might help students better understand the material," Janice elaborated, often stumbling over her words.

Ramone, seeing what was coming next, turned toward the blackboard and began erasing his notes. With his back toward her, he began, "You know Janice, we have been down this road before. You are well aware of how I feel about anyone, even someone as talented as you, teaching chemistry." He then continued in a very diplomatic fashion by stating, "Even though you are a great LD teacher, one of the best that I have seen here at Jefferson, I feel that I alone am responsible for getting the content across to these kids so that they can pass the standards test."

"I couldn't agree with you more," retorted Janice, "but why don't we team up to teach content and, thereby, help students to better understand it?" Without allowing Ramone a chance to speak, Janice continued, "Look, there are some students who still have a difficult time with the content. For example, Hillary (a student with LD) and Natasha (a nondisabled student who was failing chemistry) really had a difficult time understanding what was going on today." "Yes," Ramone fired back, "but she (Hillary) is one of *your* students, and Natasha spent the entire class time talking and passing notes. It's not my fault they didn't get it because they weren't paying attention." He went further to exclaim, "I have one of the highest pass rates in the school; why in the world would you want to mess with something that works? Why, it's like trying to build a better mousetrap." Rebutting his argument, Janice continued, "Yes, your pass rate is great, but what about the ones who don't get it? The ones who don't learn it? For example, what about Petrie and Gertrude?" "What *about* them?" replied Ramone. "Those kids are doing fine here."

Janice fired back, "Ramone, you know as well as I do that they also have trouble understanding what you are teaching them, and their notes are terrible. They often miss half the lecture points that you make. If it weren't for (me) pulling them aside (along with a few others) in study hall, they wouldn't make it."

Sensing the conversation was getting too intense, Janice backed down and extended an olive branch by saying, "Look, you are a great teacher yourself, but I feel that if we team up, we can really get *all* of these students to understand the content in class, and I feel that we can get *all* of the kids to pass the end-of-the-year standards test."

Temporarily silenced, Ramone retreated from his argument and replied in a more concilia-
tory tone, "Well, I'll . . . I'll think about it. In the meantime, could you please review their notebooks for tomorrow? I . . . I really need to get going." As Ramone hurried past her, Janice could
only feel as if he, once again, ducked the subject and brushed aside her concerns. "Well, back to
the same old grind," Janice thought as she grabbed the pile of ungraded student notebooks and
headed for the door. "Well, with any luck, he'll go home tonight, think about what I said, and
either take me up on my offer or take early retirement tomorrow," Janice joked to herself as she
lugged the box of notebooks down the hall.

Discussion Questions

1. What ideas could you suggest to Ramone to increase the amount of co-teaching that occurs
   in chemistry?
2. If you were Ramone what could you do to compromise?
3. Using different models of co-teaching, describe how you would use one of those models in
   his class. Develop a chemistry lesson and describe each teacher's role. Also, specifically
   describe the other teacher's support role if one teacher is doing the actual instruction with
   the class. Plan out one lesson and list the details of the co-taught lesson.
4. What role should the principal, Vernon Savior, play at increasing collaboration among the
   teachers in his school? What are some specific suggestions that might increase collaboration or co-teaching between the special education and regular education staff?
5. With increased pressure to pass state standards tests, should regular education teachers be
   solely responsible for teaching all of the content? Why or why not?
6. What are some other issues from the case that might hinder an effective collaborative
   partnership?

CASE 2

Her Reputation Precedes Her

Karen Bellum is an LD teacher at Boise Middle School. Boise is located in a predominantly
urban area in southeastern Pennsylvania. Karen has taught for 21 years and is now just 2
years from retirement. She has taught in many different collaborative settings, and this year is
no different.

Because Karen is a collaborative teacher, she does not have a classroom but instead, pushes
a cart from class to class. She currently teaches with three other general education seventh-grade
teachers. In science, she teaches with Larry Shaw; in civics, she teaches with Heather; and in
literature, she teaches with Sam Watson. All are veteran teachers and each is quite proud of their
achievement in the Collaborative Teaching Program at Boise.

For each of her collaborative classes, Karen co-plans and occasionally co-teaches with her
colleagues. Despite Karen's years of experience, other teachers find it difficult to team-teach
with her. Karen is often disorganized and has poor classroom management skills. A number of
her colleagues have complained about her teaching but Mr. Kearns, the principal, does little to
address the problems. Typically, he shuffles her from one teacher to another year after year.
Karen has a great personality and wants to improve, but she rarely makes substantial changes in
her teaching.

For example, yesterday in Heather class her students were so disruptive that Mr. Kearns had to interrupt her lesson to quiet them down. As Mr. Kearns was walking toward her class, he could hear the students well before he reached the door. "Ms. Bellum," asked Mr. Kearns as he opened the door abruptly, "what in the world is going on?" Her startled students quickly quieted down. "I, I, I was just going over a civics lesson," came a nervous reply from Karen. "Civics . . . civics . . . How could anyone learn civics in such a noisy environment?" an irritated Mr. Kearns replied. "I'll do my best to try to keep the noise level down," answered Karen. "Where in the world is Ms. Heather?" Mr. Kearns asked. Peter, sitting closest to the door, interrupted and pointed out that Ms. Heather went to run off some worksheets. "Yes, yes, she went to run off some copies," Karen followed up. With that, Mr. Kearns shut the door and walked back down the hall.

For Karen, this was just a typical lesson. She has learned to talk over the students and when too rowdy she has learned to yell at them. Mostly though, students are off task the majority of the time they are in her class. Later that day in science, Vernon had to stop the class five times because of the noise level. During her lesson on the ecosystem, one group of students was in the back of the room talking, another group was passing notes, and still another group was being entertained by the class clown, Eric Johnson. Throughout the lesson, Karen used many nonverbal signals in an attempt to quiet them down, yet it was only after Vernon yelled at them that they began to quiet down. After class, Vernon made it a point to express his anger at how noisy the class was, but Karen blamed it on being a "Friday" before the long weekend.

Karen seems to be oblivious of students' misbehavior and often ignores blatant violations of class rules. Yesterday in Sam's class, two students bickered throughout her lesson, disrupting those around them. At one point, Sam had to address the argument by yelling at the students and threatening to throw them out of class. Naturally, Karen apologized for their outburst and blamed the problem on two students who never get along. Karen's teaching is one of denial and excuses.

At a recent faculty meeting, all three teachers—Sandra, Vernon, and Sam—happened to be at the same table. As Sandra began to complain about Karen, the others jumped in with their own stories. All were amazed at the similarity of the problems, yet they weren't quite certain how to address the problem. They weren't quite sure whether the problems were student misbehavior or poor teaching. Together, they devised a plan to broach the topic with Karen.

Discussion Questions

1. What ideas could you suggest to the three regular education teachers to help address Karen's teaching problems?
2. If you were Mr. Kearns, what could you do?
3. Using different models of co-teaching, describe how you would use one of those models in one of the co-taught classes. Develop a lesson, and describe each teacher's role during co-teaching. Also, specifically describe the support role that the other teacher will do while one teacher does the actual instruction with the class. Plan out one lesson, and list details of the co-taught lesson.
4. With increased pressure to pass state standards tests, should regular education teachers be solely responsible for teaching all of the content? Why or why not? How could you assure that the special education co-teacher would cover the content sufficiently well?
5. What other issues from the case might hinder an effective collaborative partnership?

CASE 3

Letting Go!

Jim Johnson was not new to special education. He had been a special education teacher for the past 3 years and was now finishing his master's degree at Sican University. Concurrently, he was also completing his provisional certification and will become fully certified as soon as he completes his last college course. Jimmy currently teaches students with moderate mental retardation at Gator Middle School. Though some of the students are new, most have been in his class since last year. Most are working out of an academic curriculum, but many have more functional goals and objectives. Jim co-teaches only one class, due to the nature of his students' disabilities. Jim's kids are mainstreamed into art, physical education, and music and involved in an inclusion science class.

Jim is realistic of the demands of the regular education curriculum, but is baffled as to why the seventh-grade teacher, Judy Warner, won't let him teach the entire class and won't let him alone with students in the class. Now in their second year of working together, Jim feels as if Judy does not trust him to teach or lead the class in science instruction. For Judy, her main concerns are having her students pass the Southern States Standards. Using these test scores, schools have been accredited when they pass and criticized when they fail. Their school, Gator Middle School, has passed and received accreditation over the past 3 years. Despite their passing scores and above-average performance, there is always pressure to pass the tests and receive accreditation. In some rare cases, teachers have been demoted because of their students' poor performance.

Jim has studied the standards, prepared lessons, and motivated students to learn science. Over the past 2 years, he feels that he has made great strides at helping students understand and enjoy learning science. He has transformed the class from one in which weary students took notes from Judy's traditional lectures, to one of excitement as students actually complete "hands on" experiments. During these activities, Jim allows for interactions and movement in class, behaviors which tended to frustrate Judy. Judy feels comfortable with quiet and attentive students who occasionally ask questions. When Jim first observed her class, he thought about how exciting it would be to see students interact with science, rather than sit back passively as they learn science facts.

Jim's lessons were indeed exciting and enjoyable for students. However, during many of Jim's lessons, Judy would interject comments or attempt to correct him. Jim knows that there is nothing he can do but capitulate to her and listen attentively as she re-teaches his lesson. In fact, her unscheduled "mini-lessons" frequently cause Jim to run out of time with his own lessons. Jim feels that Judy just can't "let go of the class" so that he can teach an entire lesson.

Just as their teaching styles differ, so too do their classroom management styles. Judy seems to be a stickler for rules and regulations. She is a strict disciplinarian who often draws attention to inappropriate behaviors by calling out the name of the offender and writing it on the board. If a student receives a second warning, a checkmark is placed next to his or her name, and with a third warning, they are sent to the principal's office to receive detention. She does not agree that students should be given any leeway when they exhibit inappropriate behaviors, even those with disabilities. She believes that all students should be treated in the same fair manner. Keep in mind that Jim has two students who have been diagnosed with attention deficit hyperactivity disorder, and they often have particular trouble controlling their hyperactive behaviors. Judy also feels that students should not be bribed to behave appropriately. Even though Jim has explained that these students are on a behavior management plan, Judy refuses to allow reinforcers to be given to his students during her class time. Her philosophy is that everyone should be treated the same.

Discussion Questions

1. What ideas could you suggest to Jim to help him address the differences in teaching style?
2. What ideas could you suggest to Jim to help him address the differences in behavior management style?
3. Using different models of co-teaching, describe how you would use one of those models in one of the co-taught classes. Develop a lesson, and describe each teacher's role during co-teaching. Also, specifically describe the support role that the other teacher will do while one teacher does the actual instruction with the class. Plan out one lesson and list details of the co-taught lesson.
4. With increased pressure to pass state standards tests, should regular education teachers be solely responsible for teaching all of the content? Why or why not? How could you ensure that the special education co-teacher would cover the content sufficiently well?
5. What other issues from the case might hinder an effective collaborative partnership?
6. What role or influence should the principal play when teachers have different teaching or management styles?

CASE 4

Inclusion Gone Wrong

Tara Moore always got her way. When she was young, she excelled in all that she did and made sure that nothing stood in the way of her success. When charm and flattery did not work to her advantage, she would find other methods to manipulate people so that she would always get her way. While some were impressed by her hard work and ambition, others saw her as merely a sycophant: one who would manipulate the system to get her way. Despite excelling quickly through high school and college, Tara often alienated those around her. In college, she received many awards and accolades and later became one of the youngest teachers ever to be hired in her school district, Markley County Schools.

While completing her student teaching in special education at Teaberry Elementary School, she caught the eye of the principal, Dr. Peter Bradford. Dr. Bradford knew talent when he saw it and recruited young Tara to lead his new Inclusion Initiative. Dr. Bradford had big plans. He was going to have an inclusion class at every grade level of Teaberry during its first year and, during the second year, he planned to have every class become an inclusion classroom. He felt that the only way to incorporate inclusion properly was to begin it on a grand scale. When he announced his plans in May at the end of the school year, many teachers were dismayed and disappointed. Over the summer, he saw many of his best teachers transfer to other schools because they did not want to be part of his mandated inclusion. He was surprised to see some of his top teachers leave, but happy that others, the "dead wood" as he called them, would soon leave Teaberry as well. He knew that many of the older teachers and those who could not deal with change would leave and expected some to request transfers, but was surprised by the high number of teachers who chose to leave.

As the new school year began, Tara began to conduct a series of workshops to teach her colleagues about inclusion. She paired three regular education teachers with one special education teacher. Tara's workshops focused on describing the concept of inclusion, co-teaching, and effective communication. As the new year began, Tara felt like teachers had some skills to at least begin inclusion, and planned for a series of workshops later in the year that would focus on behavior management and effective teaching. Despite these initial workshops, many teachers expressed apprehension with inclusion. As the school year began, many teachers complained about the lack of support within the inclusion classroom.

Because of the limited number of special education teachers, most were not able to attend every inclusion class in which they had a special education student. Slowly, this too created problems as teachers complained that they were never trained to teach students with disabilities. Tara also greatly reduced the number of pull-out (resource room) sessions and informed the special education teachers that the individualized education plan goals and objectives should be covered in the inclusion (general education) classroom. Although regular education teachers were grateful to have the special education teachers in their classes, the shortage of special education teachers meant that many classes went without a special education teacher (or teaching assistant).

Soon, problems began to occur. Regular education teachers complained that they could not keep up with all of the modifications being made to the curriculum, they did not have time to make supplemental and support materials (e.g., study guides, guided notes) to meet the needs of special education students, and they had an increased number of behavior problems associated with students becoming frustrated or classes being staffed without a special education teacher. Special education teachers similarly complained that they were overwhelmed with requests to make support materials and modify tests, quizzes, and worksheets, and also lacked sufficient time in each class to address the academic and behavior problems of special education students. As the number of referrals to the office rose, tensions in many classrooms also rose. Soon, staff meetings were turning into complaint sessions, and Dr. Bradford faced pressure from parents who also wanted changes.

Before long, many teachers began to dislike Tara and their work in the inclusion classroom. Tara tried to respond to these problems by directing teachers to an inclusion web site and asking teachers to send her e-mail. For Tara, her lack of preparation and understanding about inclusion hampered her efforts to effectively respond to teachers' and parents' complaints. It was only a matter of time before Tara herself requested to be transferred to another school.

Discussion Questions

1. When planning for inclusion, should it be mandated that everyone be involved in inclusion, or is there a better way to incorporate inclusion models into schools?
2. From the workshop topics listed above, describe other topics that might be helpful to teachers as they begin teaching in inclusion classes.
3. How should parents be informed and educated about inclusion?
4. What skills or attributes should the lead specialist have to deal with inclusion problems that arise?
5. What role or influence should the principal play when initiating inclusion in schools?

CASE 5

A Clash with the Titan

Sonny Thompson recently won the Teacher of the Year Award from the *Association for Persons with Intellectual Challenges*. Sonny had been a teacher for 22 years in special education, with most of these years at Milford High School. He works hard to make sure that his students are prepared to live independent, self-sufficient lives. Sonny was credited as being one of the first teachers in the county to get his students clerk jobs within the State Department of Environmental Protection Services. These clerk jobs meant good pay and full health care coverage. Students in these jobs run errands, file and copy paperwork, and deliver interoffice mail. Sonny recently made connections with the State Department of Wildlife Welfare and was able to develop a cooperative program with them.

In this cooperative program, Young Adults for Wildlife Welfare (YAWW), Sonny was able to get two of his recent graduates to work for them and earn decent pay and health benefits. Because Sonny works with students with moderate intellectual challenges, his students often have him for their teacher for a few years. Sonny is a firm believer that students need functional skills first, and then academic skills. He also weaves prevocational and vocational skills into his student's daily educational program. One day a week Sonny also accompanies his students on the job, as a job coach, particularly when they begin a new job. He feels he helps them to make a smoother transition, rather than send them off by themselves.

Although Sonny believes in teaching both academic skills (e.g., state standards testing) and functional skills (e.g., life skills), not all of his students are capable of the intense workload. During part of the day, Sonny's students attend Silvia Tarta's special education inclusion classes. In her class, students learn mostly academic skills; however, most students graduate with only a certificate of attendance, as opposed to a diploma or GED.

Sonny teaches in two inclusion classes: U.S. history and advanced biology (Bio II). In each, Sonny switches roles from one of teaching to that of support. Sonny especially looked forward to working with Tendra Domes, an experienced Bio II teacher. Tendra was new to the high school, having just transferred from Parson's High School, which had closed because of funding issues. Despite Tendra being new, she was a giant in the eyes of the district's administration because her students had such a high pass rate on state science tests, and her 20 years of experience meant she was a shining star in the district. In addition, her work in the teacher's union meant she had to occasionally clash with the school's superintendent, earning her the name "Tendra the Titan."

Bio II was one subject that students would need if they expected to be part of the YAWW program and get a job with the state. Sonny loved to work in this class because he could provide lots of support for his students. Sonny would provide the same content, yet provide lots of visuals, organizers, guided notes, modified readings, textbooks on tape, and re-teachings, as well as modified assignments. Of course, for Sonny this meant many late nights to prepare for the next day's lessons. Last year, Sonny had trouble with a different teacher whom he had previously worked with because that teacher did not think Sonny's students could keep up with the pace of the class. Sonny resented this teacher and others who felt the same way.

With the school year now in full gear, Sonny did his best to keep up with Tendra's pace, but many students were struggling, even some of the nondisabled students. The students who took Bio II had cognitive disabilities and IQ scores between 75 and 87. Over time, Sonny found that his students were performing poorly in quizzes and had earned C grades in the first unit test. In the meantime, Sonny was doing double time trying to assist his students. When Sonny requested that Tendra slow down the pace, she replied that she was simply following the state guide on science standards. When Tendra reviewed grades from the class with Sonny, she pointed out that all of the students were able to maintain at least a C average or better. She had posted all of the grades in an electronic gradebook on her laptop. As she went over the grades, the screens showed improved quiz scores over time, and when she clicked the "distribution" button, instantly the grades were transformed into a graph that looked like a bell-shaped curve, except it was slightly skewed (because there were no D or F grades). Further, she pointed out that students must be learning effectively from her teaching because of the grade distribution. Next, in a burst of frustration, Tendra told Sonny that he was essentially "spoon feeding" his students and she did not feel that it was fair, or realistic, for him to continue doing this. She also mentioned that Sonny's constant interruptions, to re-teach small portions or to re-explain certain concepts, often interrupted her pace in teaching. This slower pace prevented her from doing her weekly reviews and instead, she had to teach content that resulted from the slower pace—because of Sonny's re-teachings.

Before long, Sonny's students were earning worse grades because Sonny could not help them keep up with the class. Soon Tendra had to tell Sonny that she did not think that his students could pass the state biology test. Despite her concerns, Sonny believed his students could make it and would work overtime to get them to pass her class and the state test.

Discussion Questions

1. What ideas could you suggest to help these teachers address their concerns or differences?
2. Is it realistic to expect these students to learn and understand the content in Bio II?
3. Using different models of co-teaching, describe how you would use one of those models in one of the co-taught classes. Develop a lesson and describe each teacher's role during co-teaching. Also, specifically describe the support role that the other teacher will do while one teacher does the actual instruction. Plan out one lesson, and list the details of the co-taught lesson.
4. With increased pressure to pass state standards tests, should regular education teachers be solely responsible for teaching all of the content? Why or why not? How could you ensure that the special education co-teacher would cover the content sufficiently well?
5. What are the pros and cons of focusing on a more academic curriculum versus a more functional curriculum?

6

Effective Use of Behavior Management in Inclusive Classrooms

Behavior management is frequently a challenge for educators working in K–12 classrooms, as well as inclusive classrooms. Teachers and school administrators are all responsible for, and concerned with, student behavior as it affects the instructional environment and subsequent academic achievement (Simonsen, Sugai, & Negron, 2008). Numerous research studies have been conducted over the years investigating the relationship of classroom and behavior management routines to student learning (Gable, Hester, Rock, & Hughes, 2009; Maag, 2001; Simonsen, Sugai, & Negron, 2008). This body of research shows a direct correlation between effectively managed classrooms, student learning, and student/teacher satisfaction. Thus, the effective use of behavior management strategies and routines cannot be understated.

Teachers working in inclusion classrooms benefit from the opportunity to collaborate and actively problem solve how to manage student behaviors in their classrooms (Friend & Bursuck, 2006). Collaborative or co-teachers, by the nature of the instructional model, work with one or more certified teachers to meet the academic and behavioral needs of their students. In optimal situations, co-teachers develop and implement classroom rules and routines, monitor student behavior, identify and deliver reinforcement consistently, establish systems for providing consequences (positive and negative), and work collaboratively to gather functional behavior assessment data and create individualized behavior intervention plans as necessary for students. This chapter provides an overview of effective classroom and behavior management techniques for inclusion classrooms and a description of each of these tasks.

CLASSROOM AND BEHAVIOR MANAGEMENT

What exactly is classroom management? Are *classroom management* and *behavior management* interchangeable terms? For the purpose of this discussion, classroom management is defined to encompass all of the procedures and routines that teachers manage systematically in order to create environments conducive to teaching/instruction and student learning (Smith, Polloway, Patton, & Dowdy, 2008). Therefore, classroom management includes creating systems for handling instructional and noninstructional routines. For example, teachers develop rules and procedures for students to follow while participating in cooperative learning activities, transitions,

TABLE 6.1 Planning for Managing the Inclusion Classroom
Suggestions for Consideration
• Agree on System of Classroom Management • Adopt 4–5 Classroom Rules • Identify Rewards • Determine Consequences for Inappropriate Behavior

small group instruction, and whole group instruction (Gable, Hester, Rock, & Hughes, 2009). Additionally, teachers create rules and procedures for students to follow concerning when it is appropriate to sharpen pencils, use the restroom, get a drink of water, and so forth. These examples involve group behaviors and relate to effective classroom management. Behavior management, on the other hand, tends to be more individualized in nature while simultaneously incorporating classroom management procedures. Before we more fully examine behavior management procedures for the inclusion classroom, let's look at some effective techniques and teacher behaviors to avoid in managing the classroom.

Classroom Management in Inclusive Classrooms

When teachers are given the opportunity to work in inclusive classrooms, it is extremely important for them to collaborate and to come to a consensus on how they will manage their classroom and student behavior (Friend & Bursuck, 2006; Meadan & Monda-Amaya, 2008). Several issues should be considered before the partnership begins and possibly revisited throughout the school year (see Table 6.1 for a brief list). We suggest that the first issue to be considered and agreed upon is the system of classroom management. This system includes instructional and noninstructional procedures. While determining which procedures to use, teachers should engage in honest discussions of what behaviors they can and cannot tolerate. For example, are students allowed to talk quietly to each other when small-group instruction is in process? Do students need to sit at their desks while completing cooperative learning activities or may they stand at their seats as long as they are working? If students leave personal belongings in another location of the school, may they retrieve them? Are there any exceptions to the instructional and noninstructional procedures? Answering these questions before teaching students the procedures will reduce the likelihood of issues arising in the classroom later. Furthermore, discussing what teachers can and cannot tolerate in the classroom bridges the conversation to developing and agreeing upon classroom rules. After developing four to five classroom rules (Gable, Hester, Rock, & Hughes, 2009), inclusion teachers should determine how and by whom the rules will be taught to students. Finally, an agreed-upon process for delivering rewards and/or consequences for following instructional and noninstructional procedures should be established. We cannot overemphasize the importance of each teacher consistently managing the classroom and delivering rewards and/or consequences to students. Inclusion teachers who are inconsistent in classroom management run the risk of students playing Mom against Dad or teacher against teacher.

Behavior Management in Inclusive Classrooms

As noted previously, systems used to manage inclusion classrooms should be built on communication between, and collaboration of, the teachers and adults delivering instruction (Meadan &

TABLE 6.2	Examples of Positive Reinforcement
Target Behavior	**Reward/Reinforcer (desired by student)**
Complete work	Sticker, grade, point
Follow directions	Teacher praise, pat on back
Read aloud	Chart/graph personal progress
Walk in line	Extra computer time
Share material	Token, ticket, or edible treat

Monda-Amaya, 2008). Students who follow classroom rules and procedures should be rewarded. One frequently used reward system is positive reinforcement. Simply defined, positive reinforcement is the delivery of a consequence that increases the likelihood of a behavior occurring again in the future (Maag, 2001; Smith, Polloway, Patton, & Dowdy, 2008). For example, Steve raises his hand and waits to be called on by the teacher. The teacher calls on Steve and praises hand-raising. Steve is rewarded (reinforced) for raising his hand, and this behavior increases. Table 6.2 provides a brief list of other examples of possible positive reinforcement incentives for a variety of student behaviors.

Another reward system that may be applied to increase individual student behavior is negative reinforcement. Negative reinforcement involves the removal of an aversive that increases the likelihood of the behavior occurring in the future (Friend & Bursuck, 2006; Maag, 2001; Vaughn, Bos, & Schumm, 2007). For example, Sidney frequently leaves her backpack and belongings on the floor by her desk. Each time she does this, her teacher nags her about the behavior. Sidney finds her teacher's nagging behavior aversive, so she starts to put away her backpack and belongings. A note of caution about the use of negative reinforcement: Unfortunately, teachers may use negative reinforcement routines unknowingly. For example, Joseph does not like to read aloud. When prompted to read aloud, he throws his book and is removed from the classroom. The next time the teacher asks Joseph to read aloud, the behaviors are repeated. The teacher is negatively reinforcing book throwing by removing Joseph's requirement to read aloud. Table 6.3 provides other examples of negative reinforcement.

Extinction is an additional method that may be used to alter behavior. Extinction is exercised when a behavior that was previously reinforced is no longer reinforced (Smith, Polloway, Patton, & Dowdy, 2008). For example, Victor is a middle-school student with autism who whines and cries frequently. This behavior has been inadvertently reinforced by the adults working

TABLE 6.3	Examples of Negative Reinforcement
Target Behavior	**Aversive Removed**
Complete work	Numerous math problems—reduce amount of work
Complete work	Group work—complete work individually
Follow rules	Teacher reprimands
Walk in line	Rope (students forced to hold rope to ensure line behavior)
Wear seatbelt	Car buzzer, warning light, ticket

with him in the classroom by providing attention each time the behavior occurs. After realizing what has occurred, the adults decide to use extinction to reduce the behavior (withhold attention each time Victor whines and/or cries). Initially, the behavior escalates and then finally subsides. Teachers wishing to use extinction to eliminate and/or alter student behavior need to make sure that they are in control of delivering reinforcement for the behavior. For example, Elizabeth calls out during whole-group instruction. Her teachers decide to reinforce hand-raising in an attempt to eliminate call-outs. They use planned ignoring for call-outs, but the behavior is reinforced by student attention. Elizabeth continues to call out in class and, subsequently, the behavior is not extinguished.

These descriptions of positive and negative reinforcement as well as extinction show that there are numerous things that students may find reinforcing. Reinforcers can be classified into two distinct areas: primary and secondary. Primary reinforcers include items typically considered as edible or specifically associated with individual needs (Friend & Bursuck, 2006). Examples include, but are not limited to, juice, sodas, candy, and crackers. Secondary reinforcers tend to involve items and/or activities that are more socially based or abstract in nature. These may consist of stickers, tickets, points, homework passes, notes home, grades, social praise, self-affirmation, phone calls home, and/or recognition from peers or teachers. Although the research is mixed on the importance of contingent reinforcement and its effectiveness for students (Gable, Hester, Rock, & Hughes, 2009), it is strongly suggested that inclusion teachers consistently provide contingent reinforcement to their students while shaping behavior (Beattie, Jordan, & Algozzine, 2006). Each time students exhibit a behavior targeted for change, teachers must consistently and immediately reinforce the behavior. Table 6.4 depicts a variety of reinforcement

TABLE 6.4   Schedules of Reinforcement

Type	Description of Procedure
Continuous schedule of reinforcement (CRF)	Reinforcement is delivered for every occurrence of the target behavior.
Fixed-ratio (FR)	Reinforcement is delivered for exhibiting a predetermined number of target behaviors. For example, on an FR3 schedule, every third target behavior would be reinforced.
Variable-ratio (VR)	Reinforcement is delivered for exhibiting an average number of target behaviors. For example, on a VR3 schedule, on average every third target behavior would be reinforced.
Fixed-interval (FI)	Reinforcement is delivered for exhibiting the target behavior after a set amount of time has lapsed. For example, on an FI3 schedule, reinforcement of the target behavior would be reinforced on its first occurrence after each 3-minute period.
Variable-interval (VI)	Reinforcement is delivered for exhibiting the target behavior after a variable amount of time has lapsed. For example, on a VI3 schedule, reinforcement of the target behavior would be reinforced on its first occurrence after each time period averaging 3 minutes in duration.

schedules that inclusion teachers may wish to implement in their classrooms, from initiation to the maintenance of a behavior management plan (Alberto & Troutman, 2008; Beattie, Jordan, & Algozzine, 2006).

Whichever type of reinforcement system inclusion teachers choose to embrace, it is important for teachers to consider naturally occurring consequences and reinforcement for behavior in order to establish and maintain behavior (Malott, Whaley, & Malott, 1997). Behavior systems that are contrived, and reinforcement systems that are difficult to consistently deliver, may not be supported in natural environments and will most likely be unsuccessful over the long term. Furthermore, consequences for behavior may be viewed as positive, negative, neutral, or punishment (Alberto & Troutman, 2008). Neutral consequences tend not to influence behavior as far as increasing or reducing the likelihood of future occurrences.

Before moving into planning individualized behavior management techniques for students in inclusion classrooms, we need to explore two more methods traditionally used in K–12 settings: time-out and punishment. Time-out is a procedure that many teachers and schools use as a method for addressing student misbehavior (Albrecht, 2008). For example, students who act out in class are sent to the corner, another classroom, the office, or get an in-school suspension for violating classroom rules and/or routines. The duration of the time-out may be from a few minutes to several hours. The largest issue with time-out is whether or not time-in is reinforcing. For this example, look back at the text describing Joseph. He throws his book when asked to read aloud in class and is removed. He does not have to read and his book-throwing behavior is reinforced. Is time-out effective in managing his behavior? We would say no. Punishment is the second technique that many teachers working in K–12 environments use in an attempt to modify student behavior (Maag, 2001; Moore, 2005). Smith, Polloway, Patton, and Dowdy (2008) define punishment as "the presentation of something unpleasant or the removal of something pleasant as a consequence of the performance of an undesirable behavior" (p. 476). Teachers who use punishment procedures may see an immediate reduction in target behaviors (Maag, 2001), but may find that punishment is not effective for all students. Teachers are limited in the number and magnitude of punishers they may use with students and as such may lack the means to deliver a punishment that is strong enough to reduce an unwanted behavior. For example, Vinnie is frequently noncompliant (does not follow teacher directions the first, second, or third time given). Each time Vinnie exhibits noncompliant behavior, he loses a point (response cost) on his point sheet. Vinnie typically has no points by midmorning, becomes aggressive (throws materials, hits others, and/or uses profanity), and is removed from the classroom. This pattern of behavior is consistent across time and demonstrates that punishment (loss of points and removal from the classroom) is not effective in reducing Vinnie's noncompliance.

Another form of punishment is the use of teacher reprimands. Reprimands may be verbal or nonverbal and generally communicate displeasure with a behavior (Smith, Polloway, Patton, & Dowdy, 2008). Although reprimands may be simple to provide, they may not be effective and may even serve to positively reinforce the behavior that the individual aims to reduce. A classroom-wide form of punishment often used in inclusion classrooms is assertive discipline. Assertive discipline is typically composed of multiple levels of consequences (Bender & Mathes, 1995; Canter & Canter, 2001; Malmgren, Trezek, & Paul, 2005). In early elementary classrooms, it may be represented by students having an apple with their name placed on a paper tree that is displayed on a bulletin board. When students break a rule, their apple is moved to a lower branch on the tree. Each rule infraction or inappropriate behavior results in movement of the apple with the impending result of loss of reinforcement, a note or phone call home, and a possible trip to the principal's office. As with many punishment routines, assertive discipline may reduce inappropriate behavior for some, but not all, students. For students with significant behavioral issues, the movement of the apple may exacerbate inappropriate behavior. We suggest that teachers who use this form of punishment make sure to include systems or procedures for students to earn back position on the tree. This allows students the opportunity for reinforcement rather than losing the opportunity in the early morning and having no recourse for recovery for the remaining school day. In late elementary, middle, and high school, assertive discipline procedures may take the form of the teacher writing students' names on the board (Bender & Mathes, 1995). The first infraction results in the name being written on the board as a warning; each subsequent infraction results in a checkmark being placed next to the name with a corresponding consequence. Here again this method of discipline may prove effective for some, but not all, students. In sum, we concur with Smith, Polloway, Patton, and Dowdy's (2008) recommendation that punishment is employed only as a last resort.

Now that we have built a foundation for classroom management, reinforcement, and punishment procedures, let's explore functional behavior analysis procedures and individually designed behavior intervention plans and management techniques.

Functional Behavior Analysis and Behavior Intervention Plans

Unfortunately, not all students with and without disabilities respond to methods and procedures designed to increase positive behaviors and to decrease unwanted behaviors in the classroom. On occasion, teachers working in inclusion classrooms may find the need to formally determine the function of student behavior and to develop individualized behavior intervention plans (BIPs). When this is the case, completion of a functional behavior analysis (FBA) may be warranted. What is an FBA? According to Friend and Bursuck (2006):

> FBA is a problem-solving process implemented for any student with a disability with chronic, serious behavior problems. Its basis is the ongoing conflict between protecting the rights of students with disabilities and respecting teachers' and school administrators' concerns about preventing school violence, maintaining safe schools, and disciplining students with disabilities (Conroy, Clark, Gable, & Fox, 1999). An FBA is a detailed and documented set of procedures designed to improve educators' understanding of exactly what a problem behavior looks like, where it occurs, when it occurs, and what function it serves for the student. It leads to ideas about how to change the behavior and a specific plan for doing so (Asmus, Vollmer, & Borrero, 2002; Sugai, Lewis-Palmer, & Hagan, 1998). (p. 442)

As can be seen from Friend and Bursuck's (2006) definition, FBA entails a comprehensive set of procedures designed to address and understand student behavior. Furthermore, it requires input from multiple members of an interdisciplinary team as well as parental written consent for completion (Individuals with Disabilities Education Improvement Act of 2004 [P.L. 108–446]; Sugai, Lewis-Palmer, & Hagan-Burke, 2000). Therefore, the decision to complete an FBA for a student is not be taken lightly. The decision should be based on the nature and severity of the behavior targeted for change as well as data collected on the effectiveness of previous interventions.

TABLE 6.5 Differential Reinforcement Procedures	
Type	**Description of Procedure**
Differential reinforcement of higher rates of behavior (DRH)	Reinforcement is given when rates of the target behavior are above specified levels
Differential reinforcement of lower rates of behavior (DRL)	Reinforcement is given when rates of the target behavior are below specified levels
Differential reinforcement of incompatible behavior(s) (DRI)	Reinforcement is given when a behavior(s) that is incompatible with the target behavior is/are exhibited
Differential reinforcement of alternate behavior(s) (DRA)	Reinforcement is given when an alternate behavior(s) is/are exhibited
Differential reinforcement for omission of behavior (DRO)	Reinforcement is given when a behavior(s) is/are not exhibited

FBAs and BIPs should be developed based on observations of specifically defined and measureable student behavior and data (Friend & Bursuck, 2006; Sugai, Lewis-Palmer, & Hagan-Burke, 2000). Therefore, the first step in completing an FBA and developing a BIP would be to identify the behavior(s) targeted for change. After coming to consensus over the specific behavior, data as to antecedent events (what happens immediately before the behavior is exhibited), consequences (what happens immediately after the behavior is exhibited), frequency, latency (time between antecedent and emission of behavior), and/or duration (how long does the behavior last) should be collected. The next step in carrying out the FBA and developing the BIP would be developing one or more possible hypotheses concerning the function of the behavior for the individual. Following this, teachers should test the hypotheses to determine the function(s) of the behavior. Once this step is completed, the individualized BIP can be developed.

One point that teachers should consider while developing BIPs is what behavior they wish to replace the target behavior with through intervention. Because behavior does not occur in a vacuum (Sugai, Lewis-Palmer, & Hagan-Burke, 2000), it is important for teachers to differentially reinforce the replacement behavior at the same time as targeting the behavior for change (Alberto & Troutman, 2008). If teachers fail to do this, students may replace the target behavior with another behavior in their repertoire that teachers may not want exhibited (Sugai, Lewis-Palmer, & Hagan-Burke, 2000). Table 6.5 describes differential reinforcement procedures that inclusion teachers may wish to use for students with BIPs.

After the BIP is developed, implementation issues addressed (including crisis management procedures), and consensus gained from all involved, the BIP should be put into action. During this phase, data should be gathered as to the efficacy for implementation across individuals and settings and the effectiveness of the BIP (Smith, Polloway, Patton, & Dowdy, 2008). These data may be used to modify the BIP and to determine whether or not the plan is working. If the data show that the plan is not being implemented consistently across individuals and/or settings or the behavior is not changing in the desired manner, the BIP and FBA should be revisited. Table 6.6 briefly illustrates a BIP that might be used for a student receiving services in an inclusion classroom.

For further ideas and descriptions of BIPs, we recommend: Bryant, Smith, & Bryant, 2008; Friend & Bursuck, 2006; and Sands, Kozleski, & French, 2000.

TABLE 6.6 Sample BIP

Component	Description
Brief profile	Frank is in the fourth grade. He is eligible for special education services through programs for students with Other Health Impairments (Attention Deficit with Hyperactivity Disorder). He does not take medication. Frank has difficulty with impulse control, consistently following directions, staying in his area, and conflict management.
Strengths	Responds to verbal praise
	Enjoys independently working at the computer
	Is liked by most peers and teachers
Weaknesses	Following multistep directions
	Working on undesired tasks for extended periods of time, problem solving
	Reading, writing, and performing math at grade level
Support team members	Fourth-grade general and special education teachers, school counselor, and assistant principal
Intervention settings	Entire school campus
Target behaviors	Keeping hands, feet, and objects to self (no hitting, kicking, or throwing objects)
	Using school-appropriate language (no profanity)
	Count to 10 before responding to conflict
	Remove self from situation with peer and seek support
	Request help and/or a break from frustrating academic task
	Use alternate anger statements
Hypothesis statement	When in a conflict situation with a peer or feeling frustrated by an academic task, Frank uses aggression and/or inappropriate language to escape the situation/task.
Plan	Frank will be taught alternative methods to deal with conflict situations with peers and frustration with academic tasks. Embedded social skills techniques will be used as an intervention for the entire class. Individualized problem-solving techniques, including role play, will also be taught for addressing conflicts with peers. Frank will use an agreed-upon system for requesting assistance with and/or breaks from frustrating academic tasks. Alternate behaviors will be reinforced: Counting to 10 before responding to a conflict, removing self from peer and seeking support, asking for assistance or a break, and using alternate anger statements.
Crisis intervention	If Frank's behavior escalates to the point of being a significant danger to himself or others, he will be removed from the classroom or the classroom will be evacuated until he is calm.
Method of data collection	Event/frequency recording; discipline referrals
Reinforcement	DRL—reduced aggressive outbursts
	DRH—increased use of adaptive behaviors (as defined above)

SUPPORTING BEHAVIOR

This section briefly describes systems and procedures that may be used at the school, in the classroom, and/or on an individual level to promote appropriate student behavior and social skills.

Schoolwide Positive Behavior Supports (SWPBS)

Schoolwide positive behavior supports (SWPBS) and positive behavior supports (PBS) have become more widely used and recognized in schools since the late 1990s and early 2000s (Bryant, Smith, & Bryant, 2008; Vaughn, Bos, & Schumm, 2007). With the increased emphasis on academic achievement and inclusion of students with disabilities, PBS is now included as a component of IDEA 2004 (Vaughn, Bos, & Schumm, 2007). Simonsen, Sugai, and Negron (2008) define SWPBS as ". . . a proactive, systems-level approach that enables schools to effectively and efficiently support student (and staff) behavior" (p. 33). Furthermore, SWPBS solicits schools to identify outcomes, data sources, methods, and procedures that will be environmentally appropriate and significant for them. Schools that are successful in implementing SWPBS tend to see decreases in student misbehavior and increases in academic achievement. For more information on SWPBS primary, secondary, and tertiary practices, we refer the reader to Fairbanks, Simonsen, and Sugai, 2008; Simonsen, Sugai, and Negron, 2008.

CHAMPs

CHAMPs is a program developed by Randy Sprick's *Safe and Civil School* (http://safeandcivilschools.com/)series. The acronym CHAMPs stands for Conversation, Help, Activity, Movement, and Participation (Sprick, Garrison, & Howard, 1998). The authors share that, "*CHAMPs: A Proactive and Positive Approach to Classroom Management [for Grades K–9]* is a systematic guide for classroom teachers who want to improve their current classroom management plans" (p. 3 overview). This program is another example of an approach that teachers may choose to use in order to positively influence student behavior. Furthermore, it may also be used in conjunction with SWPBS. Although a recent database search of the existing research concerning the effectiveness of CHAMPs resulted in limited evidence, this program appears to still be used widely in the United States. For example, some schools in the Charleston County School District, South Carolina, are implementing CHAMPs (http://hursey.ccsdschools.com/home.aspx); a teacher working in Lexington County Schools, Kentucky, notes that this program is implemented in her classroom (http://staff.fcps.net/ngreen/behavior_management.htm); the state of Florida lists training for teachers on the Northeast Florida Educational Consortium web site (http://www.nefec.org/news/view.asp?id=62); and a book review for the National Association of School Psychologists lists it as a possible resource for teachers (http://www.nasponline.org/publications/cq/cq326safecivilschools.aspx).

Focusing Together

Focusing together: Promoting Self-Management Skills in the Classroom (Rademacher, Pemberton, & Cheever, 2006) is part of the Community-Building Series published by Edge Enterprises Inc. "The Focusing Together" program is an instructional program that promotes self-management behavior in association with a set of classroom expectations that defines responsible work habits, respect, and emotional and physical safety" (p. 1). Students learn the strategy in three steps: (a) learning about community expectations, (b) learning about making choices, and (c) learning the FOCUS self-management strategy. Table 6.7 lists the steps of the FOCUS strategy.

TABLE 6.7   FOCUS Strategy
Steps/Description
Free your mind of distractions Organize yourself Check the expectations and get started Use help wisely Supervise yourself (p. 63)

Research supporting the efficacy of Focusing Together revealed that the program was effective in (a) reducing off-task behaviors of students, (b) increasing student satisfaction with classroom management procedures, (c) increasing teacher satisfaction concerning the program and student behavior, (d) and increasing teacher perceptions of reducing students' off-task behavior (Rademacher, Pemberton, & Cheever, 2006).

Other Systems and Procedures

Over the years, numerous systems and procedures have been created to support teachers' instruction in, and students' development of, social skills in inclusive classrooms (Fenty, Miller, & Lampi, 2008; Iaquinta & Hipsky, 2006; Williams & Reisberg, 2003). In 2008, Fenty, Miller, and Lampi described 20 ways to embed social skills instruction in inclusive settings. In their article, they addressed issues from assessment to instruction to maintenance and generalization for embedding social skills instruction for students served in general education and inclusion classrooms. Iaquinta and Hipsky (2006) explored and reported on the possible use of practical bibliotherapy strategies for the inclusive elementary classrooms. They noted that teachers who use children's literature as a mechanism for teaching students to solve problems and produce alternative reactions to these situations will enhance their students' ability to become effective and independent problem solvers. Iaquinta and Hipsky briefly describe the methods teachers should follow in order to implement bibliotherapy strategies in the classroom. Williams and Reisberg (2003) illustrated how to teach social skills to students with disabilities in the "regular" classroom through an integrated curriculum approach. They offered brief descriptions of a number of procedures and/or curricula that are available to address social skills, including *Skillstreaming the Adolescent*, integrated unit planning, and the Violence is Preventable (VIP) Project.

These systems and procedures do not encompass the vast array of social skill resources available to teachers working in inclusive classrooms today. These descriptions were provided as a glimpse of just a few of these sources.

Conclusion

Classroom and behavior management continue to be among the most challenging aspects of a teacher's job. This chapter gives a brief overview of some of the issues and ways in which teachers may work to improve their skills. By actively collaborating on problem-solving methods and procedures designed to manage classroom routines and individual student behaviors, teachers should be more successful in meeting the diverse needs of the students they instruct.

References

Alberto, P. A., & Troutman, A. C. (2008). *Applied behavior analysis for teachers* (8th ed.). Upper Saddle River, NJ: Merrill/Pearson.

Albrecht, S. F. (2008, Fall). Time away: A skill-building alternative to discipline. *Preventing School Failure, 53*(1), 49–55. Retrieved March 15, 2009, from Academic Search Premier database.

Beattie, J., Jordan, L., & Algozzine, B. (2006). *Making inclusion work: Effective practices for all teachers*. Thousand Oaks: Corwin Press.

Bender W. M., & Mathes, M. Y. (1995). Students with ADHD in the inclusive classroom: A hierarchical approach to strategy selection. *Intervention in School and Clinic, 30*(4), 226–233. Retrieved March 15, 2009, from Academic Search Premier database.

Bryant, D. P., Smith, D. D., & Bryant, B. R. (2008). *Teaching students with special needs in inclusive classrooms*. Boston: Pearson/Allyn & Bacon.

Canter, L., & Canter, M. (2001). *Assertive discipline: Positive behavior management for today's classroom* (3rd ed.). Seal Beach, CA: Canter.

Fairbanks, S., Simonsen, B., & Sugai, G. (2008). Classwide secondary and tertiary tier practices and systems. *Teaching Exceptional Children, 40*(6), 44–52.

Fenty, N. S., Miller, M. A., & Lampi, A. (2008). Embedded social skills instruction in inclusive settings. *Intervention in School and Clinic, 43*(3), 186–192.

Friend, M., & Bursuck, W. D. (2006). *Including students with special needs: A practical guide for classroom teachers* (4th ed.). Boston: Pearson/Allyn & Bacon.

Gable, R. A., Hester, P. H., Rock, M. L., & Hughes, K. G. (2009). Back to basics: Rules, praise, ignoring, and reprimands revisited. *Intervention in School and Clinic, 44*(4), 195–205.

Iaquinta, A., & Hipsky, S. (2006). Practical bibliotherapy strategies for the inclusive elementary classroom. *Early Childhood Education Journal, 34*(3), 209–213. *Individuals with Disabilities Education Improvement Act of 2004*. P.L. No. 108-446.

Maag, J. W. (2001). Rewarded by punishment: Reflections on the disuse of positive reinforcement in schools. *Exceptional Children, 67*(2), 173–186.

Malmgren, K. W., Trezek, B. J., & Paul, P. V. (2005, September/October). Models of classroom management as applied to the secondary classroom. *The Clearing House, 79*(1), 36–39. Retrieved March 15, 2009, from Academic Search Premier database.

Malott, R. W., Whaley, D. L., & Malott, M. E. (1997). *Elementary principles of behavior* (3rded.). Upper Saddle River, NJ: Prentice Hall.

Meadan, H., & Monda-Amaya, L. (2008). Collaboration to promote social competence for students with mild disabilities in the general classroom: A structure for providing social support. *Intervention in School and Clinic, 43*(3), 158–167.

Moore, K. D. (2005). *Effective instructional strategies: From theory to practice*. Thousand Oaks, CA: Sage.

Rademacher, J. A., Pemberton, J. B., & Cheever, G. L. (2006). *Focusing together: Promoting self-management skills in the classroom*. Lawrence, KS: Edge Enterprises, Inc.

Sands, D. J., Kozleski, E. B., & French, N. K. (2000). *Inclusive education for the 21st century*. United States: Wadsworth.

Simonsen, B., Sugai, G., & Negron, M. (2008). Schoolwide positive behavior supports: Primary systems and practices. *Teaching Exceptional Children, 40*(6), 32–40.

Smith, T. E. C., Polloway, E. A., Patton, J. R., & Dowdy, C. A. (2008). *Teaching students with special needs in inclusive settings* (5th ed.). Boston: Pearson/Allyn & Bacon.

Sprick, R., Garrison, M., & Howard, L. M. (1998). *CHAMPs: A proactive and positive approach to classroom management for grades K–9*. Longmont, CO: Sopris West.

Sugai, G., Lewis-Palmer, T., & Hagan-Burke, S. (2000). Overview of the functional behavioral assessment process. *Exceptionality, 8,* 149–160. Retrieved February 21, 2009, from Academic Search Premier database.

Vaughn, S., Bos, C. S., & Schumm, J. S. (2007). *Teaching students who are exceptional, diverse, and at risk in the general education classroom* (4th ed.). Boston: Pearson/Allyn & Bacon.

Williams, G. J., & Reisberg, L. (2003). Successful inclusion: Teaching social skills through curriculum integration. *Intervention in School and Clinic, 38*(4), 205–210. Retrieved February 21, 2009, from Academic Search Premier database.

http://hursey.ccsdschools.com/home.aspx
http://staff.fcps.net/ngreen/behavior_management.htm
http://www.nefec.org/news/view.asp?id=62
http://www.nasponline.org/publications/cq/cq326safecivilschools.aspx

7

Cases About Behavior Management in Inclusive Classrooms

CASE 1

Dumb as a Doornail!

"What sounds like a tank and walks like a penguin?" asked Samuel as he waddled back and forth like a penguin in front of the class. "I know . . .," replied Cleo, as tears practically streamed down his face from laughter. "Ms. Flock," blurted Samuel as he broke into uncontrollable laughter. With that, the rest of the students in his seventh-grade class broke out in laughter. Suddenly the door opened and the class became quiet. Samuel raced to his seat and ducked his head down behind the student in front of him. Ms. Flock had just returned from running off copies of an English worksheet. As she searched on her desk for the answer key, most of the students were still giggling about Samuel's joke. Looking up over her glasses, Kay Flock began to question students about their silliness. "What's so funny? Did I miss a joke?" she asked the class. Upon getting no response, she began to get back to the task at hand of teaching students about analogies, similes, and metaphors. On the board was the standard that they were working on this week*: 7.4. The student will use analogies, idioms, similes, and metaphors to extend understanding of word meanings.*

"Turn to number one on the worksheet coming around," Ms. Flock explained. "Okay. What does it mean to be 'red as a beet'" she asked. Jonathan replied, "It means that your face turns red from embarrassment." "Right. Excellent," said Ms. Flock, beaming from ear to ear because the brightest student in the class knew the answer. Ms. Flock routinely called on Jonathan when she was not sure about how she taught a lesson. His correct responses gave her a false sense of success because little did she know that most of the other students often had no idea what she was talking about.

Pointing at the worksheet she continued, "You try number two on your own and then we'll compare answers." From out of the back of the room came the remark, "trash." Looking up, Ms. Flock asked, "What about trash?" Everyone in the class was quiet. "Why do you make us do this trash?" demanded Samuel. "Well for one. . . ." Ms. Flock stumbling for an answer was thrown off balance by Samuel's straightforward question. "We do these so that you can enhance your creative writing skills," Ms. Flock retorted. With that, Samuel shook his head and put it down. Ms. Flock ignored Samuel and moved on with her teaching, but it did not take long until Samuel was making noises and inappropriate remarks. He started with the comment "fat as an elephant," asking whether it was a simile, metaphor, or analogy. The class laughed because they knew exactly for whom the remark was directed—Ms. Flock. This continued throughout the entire class. Even other students begged Ms. Flock to quiet him down.

Ms. Flock was used to Erin Purser, the special education teacher, handling such outbursts. Erin taught these students in pull-out classes when they were not in the inclusion class and Erin also co-taught in inclusive classes. Erin had a certain matter-of-fact way about her that would often quiet even the toughest crowd. On this particular morning, Erin was called away to an individualized education plan meeting and Ms. Flock was left alone with her unruly bunch of special education boys. The boys were usually okay when separated, but when they were together, trouble was not far behind. The "ring leader," as Ms. Flock calls him, is Samuel.

Samuel is currently identified as having two labels: Emotionally Disturbed and Learning Disabilities (LD). It seems that depending on the time of year that he is evaluated, he could qualify for either label. In the past, Samuel has given other teachers "fits." He has caused much mischief in his classes and is known as the troublemaker in the school. Some of Samuel's behaviors include talking back to and disobeying teacher requests, making jokes and inappropriate remarks during class, and playing practical jokes on teachers (e.g., Last year he let all of the research mice out of their cages in the psychology lab). Mrs. Purser currently has him on a behavioral contract, but its effectiveness is questionable. For some teachers, Samuel is a problem; yet, for others they have learned to give him a warning and then kick him out of their class. His numerous in-school suspensions (ISS) are an indicator of his problems and serve as bragging material for him. For Ms. Flock, her good-hearted nature often prevents her from taking immediate and decisive action. Ms. Flock claims that her best days of teaching are those days when Samuel is absent.

At home Samuel has similar problems. He is disrespectful to his parents and other authority figures and frequently does not come home at night until well beyond his curfew. On a number of occasions, his parents have locked him out of the house. When this happens, Samuel sleeps in the bed in the pool house. His parents run a successful computer consulting business and work odd hours, leaving Samuel to care for himself. It's not that his parents don't care about Samuel, but their business takes up the majority of their time, and their social parties take up the rest. Samuel does have the housekeepers and gardeners to talk to about his problems, but they too are often the target of his vengeful remarks and pranks. One way that his parents keep tabs on Samuel is via his cell phone or beeper. They check in at least once a day, yet Samuel considers these intrusions rude and cursory. In response to his inappropriate behaviors, his parents have threatened to send him to boarding school and have sent him to a number of "tough love" camps. Even at these camps, Samuel causes many problems for the counselors. One recent camp in the mountains of North Carolina threatened to kick him out.

Discussion Questions

1. From the case, what behavior(s) would you target for remediation? Or what behavior(s) would you target for further assessment or observation?
2. In the class, choose a maladaptive behavior that you would like to target, and write an objective for either the maladaptive behavior or an appropriate target behavior.

3. Design a behavior plan for Samuel. Decide how you will measure the behavior and how you will change the maladaptive behavior.
4. How would you monitor his progress? Describe how and when you would monitor progress.
5. Choose a social skill area, and describe how to teach him the social skill.

CASE 2

It Doesn't Add Up

Antonio sat at his desk muttering to himself, "I just can't do this." Antonio's paper was full of holes indicating how he had tried to answer and change answers numerous times. When Mr. Larkson looked up from his desk to see what he was doing, Antonio let out a loud yell and banged his head on the desk. Antonio was supposed to be completing a worksheet of 10 multiplication problems, but instead was carrying on at his desk. Mr. Larkson went to his desk and tried to redirect him back to his worksheet. "Now, come on Antonio. You can answer these problems," he said as he handed him a clean worksheet. Again, Antonio let out a yell and shouted "I just can't do this crap." With that, the other students let out simultaneous "ooohhhs" and "ahhhs." Mr. Larkson, who was now becoming angry, gave Antonio one final command: "Get back to work or take a trip to the hall." Antonio did nothing but sat in his seat motionless, overcome with stubbornness. As Antonio sat contemplating his demise, Mr. Larkson snapped at the other students, "Get back to work." Again, he looked at Antonio and growled at him, "Get to work." Within seconds of Antonio's refusal, Mr. Larkson let out, "That's it! You go to the hall, and you can finish this paper for recess!" Again, Antonio sat still refusing to move. Mr. Larkson then went to the board and in large letters wrote "ANTONIO—NO RECESS." With chalk cracking as he wrote it, the other students again chimed in with "ooohhhs" and "ahhhs." Antonio, unfazed by his teacher's action, defiantly held up the clean worksheet and ripped it in half.

During the entire incident, Ms. Ziglar watches as she tries to redirect the attention of the other students in her inclusion math class. Ms. Ziglar knows to stay out of Mr. Larkson's way when he disciplines students. Although she occasionally has to deal with them, for the most part she takes a hands-off approach to behavior problems of the special education students. Ms. Ziglar had approached Mr. Larkson in the past about the way he handles behavioral problems, but he does not want to be told how to deal with behavior problems.

Antonio is a 13-year-old with Cognitive Impairments (CI) who currently attends Toolesville Elementary School in downtown Northumberland, Pennsylvania. Antonio has been in Mr. Larkson's class for 2 years and has caused problems for Mr. Larkson on a number of other occasions. Antonio is considered borderline CI because of his earned IQ score of 69 on the Wechsler Intelligence Scale for Children, but was placed in two inclusion classes this year because he had shown improvements in behavior and academic skills over the past year. In addition to his lower-than-average IQ, he also has academic deficits in all of the basic skill areas: reading, math, and written language. To complicate matters, Antonio has also been identified as having attention deficit hyperactivity disorder (ADHD) and currently takes Ritalin to help control his attention and hyperactivity.

Antonio lives at home with his mother, Silvia, in a nearby townhouse. Silvia is always concerned with Antonio's progress in school. Mr. Larkson has often told her that he wishes his other students' parents were as involved in their child's education as she. Silvia is familiar with

Antonio's stubbornness. At home, Antonio frequently refuses to complete work for her and is defiant of her requests. Silvia has related to Mr. Larkson that morning is the worst time of day for her. During the morning hours, Silvia spends long periods of time getting Antonio ready for school. Even though he goes to bed early enough, he does not like to go to school; instead he would rather sleep all day. She knows her son well, so it came as no surprise when she received a note that night from Mr. Larkson describing the incident during math. When she spoke to Antonio about the incident, he refused to discuss it.

That same evening, Mr. Larkson also pondered Antonio's unusual behavior. He asked himself a series of questions: "Did I handle it properly?" "Could I have not gotten so angry?" "Should I have immediately put him in the hall?" Because this was his second year of teaching, Mr. Larkson still isn't quite certain how to handle some of his students' problems. He remembers back to his class in behavior management, but draws a blank as to what he could have done differently. A "control freak" at heart, Mr. Larkson likes a quiet, business-like classroom. In the past, he has been able to manage many of the inappropriate behaviors that his students have exhibited, but Antonio's behavior is often worse the closer it gets to the weekend.

Being the only special education teacher in the school, Mr. Larkson is well aware that he has to walk on eggshells around the other teachers and principal. Two years ago, he pleaded with the principal, Mrs. Gunnison, to allow him to co-teach in math and English, and after much negotiating he was permitted to do so. Mrs. Gunnison herself has a no-nonsense type of management style. "Gunnie," as she is known to other teachers, is the type of administrator who would suspend a student rather than discuss their inappropriate behavior. Mr. Larkson was chosen as the first special education teacher at Tannerville because of his diplomatic style while conferring with other teachers. He was told by his supervisor, Ginny Frew, that he needs to establish a good working relationship with the other faculty so that next year they can try to place other special education classes in the school and so that the county's special education program can expand its inclusion movement into city schools.

The next day, Mr. Larkson decides to discuss Antonio's behavior with his aide, Trudy Stellar. "It just doesn't add up," said Mr. Larkson as he began to explain the incident in math class. As the two discussed the incident, Trudy told him that Antonio got into a heated discussion with another student on the playground prior to coming to math class. As she described the incident, Trudy said that it was a student from another class—Nerby—who sparked the quarrel. Trudy added that Antonio was playing nicely at recess when Nerby walked by and hit him. "Antonio seemed to calm down when I asked him to line up to come inside," Trudy remarked, "but once inside, as we were walking down the hall, I could tell that he was upset about something." At that point, Mr. Larkson began to wonder if this incident had anything to do with Antonio's behavior during math.

Discussion Questions

1. From the case, what behavior(s) would you target for remediation? Or what behavior(s) would you target for further assessment or observation?
2. In the class, choose a maladaptive behavior that you would like to target, and write an objective for either the maladaptive behavior or an appropriate target behavior.
3. Design a behavior plan for Antonio. Decide how you will measure the behavior and how you will change the maladaptive behavior.
4. How would you monitor his progress? Describe how and when you would monitor progress.
5. Choose a social skill area, and describe how to teach Antonio the social skill.

CASE 3

The Girl Who Couldn't Stop Talking

Trisha was an overly active student in Judy Hall's third-grade inclusion class. Judy was a general education teacher who worked with the special education collaborative teacher, Toby Tevesco. On a daily basis, Judy and Toby witness how Trisha's talkative behavior can be disruptive to the class. Whether she's calling out an answer without raising her hand or telling on another student; her teachers have to constantly reprimand her for disrupting the class. This makes it extremely difficult to get through daily lessons.

Trisha was identified earlier this year as having ADHD. She was assessed by the eligibility team at the request of her parents, and her teachers supported this request. The test results showed that Trisha has minor problems in academic areas, such as reading and math, and scored within the average range on the Wecshler Intelligence Scale for Children III. She performed poorly on measures of attention and impulsivity as measured on a continuous performance computer game and an impulsivity scale. In addition, her teachers and parents rated her poorly on measures of attention and hyperactivity on the *Attention Deficit Hyperactivity Disorder Diagnostic Scale*. As a result of these measures and other tests, Trisha qualified under IDEA 2004 category Other Health Impaired as having ADHD. Soon after the school's testing, Trisha's parents, Nevell and Georgia Centrinas, went to the local children's hospital, Peterson-Ashburn Children's Medical Center, to have Trisha retested. Just as the school found, the clinical psychiatric unit determined that indeed Trisha had ADHD, as well as obsessive compulsive disorder, OCD. Trisha's psychiatrist immediately suggested that Trisha be placed on the ADHD medication Adderall.

Despite Trisha being on Adderall for the past several months, she still exhibited many of the traditional ADHD and OCD behaviors such as inattention, impulsivity, and perseveration on tasks and excessive explanations. In particular, her excessive talking seemed to be the behavior for which she is constantly being reprimanded and is the most disruptive. The other day, Judy mentioned to Toby that, "Even when she does raise her hand, Trisha's responses are usually drawn out and tend to be off topic," to which Toby quickly agreed. Toby added, "I thought having her on medication would have helped with her talkativeness, but it seems to be the same as before or worse." "Yea," Judy remarked, "even when we call on her, we have to tell her to get straight to the point and save the stories for later, after her work is done." Toby agreed and said, "Just the other day I was helping Trisha with a math word problem that asked her to identify the number of widgets in a basket, and she misread the word 'widgets' and called them 'witches.' Well, before you know it, she was telling me a story about the Halloween that she dressed up as a witch."

Still, on another occasion, Trisha would talk to the classmates as if she were the teacher. Trisha likes to boss around her classmates, particularly during group work. On one recent day, Judy and Toby arranged students in the class to work in cooperative learning groups. Trisha was working with Kristi, Jacob, and Austin. Soon after the group received their assignment (students have to first estimate the length of various items—spoon, pencil, erasure, water bottle, umbrella—and then are given a ruler to measure each), Trisha began her dominating behavior. It started with her asking everyone in the group to pass each item to her so that she had all of the items. "Okay," began Trisha, "I'm gonna estimate each one, and Austin, you write down on the worksheet what I say." "Hey, you're not the boss," Kristi yelled out. Jacob seconded Kristi's comment by adding "You don't even know what you're doin'." To this Trisha began calling out her own estimated length of each item: "8 inches for the pencil, 15 for the umbrella, 10 for the bottle, 5 for the spoon, and 5 for the erasure." Despite Jacob's attempt to get Trisha to accept other answers, Trisha stuck to her answers, grabbed the worksheet from Austin, and furiously began writing down her answers in pen. As she was recording her answers for the group, Jacob yelled out, "Mr. Tevesco and Mrs. Hall! Trisha's not letting us work on this game." When Mrs. Hall arrived at the group's table, she immediately wanted to know what was going on. "Okay, okay, wait, quiet. One person at a time explain to me what happened," Mrs. Hall demanded. As they described Trisha's behavior, Mrs. Hall told Trisha to go out in the hall so that she could speak to her.

Still another problem that teachers have with Trisha is that she constantly calls out answers or requests help without raising her hand to be called on. Unfortunately, this occurs repeatedly no matter how many times her teachers try to address it. One solution that is already used is that her teachers *reinforce* her for raising her hand. They are pretty consistent in praising her for raising her hand and have seen Trisha about to call out an answer, but she raises her hand instead. Because she likes to be the teacher, She could be given time at the end of the day to read a short story to the class, or just sit in the rocking chair during independent reading time if she remembers to raise her hand all day. This solution might work because being able to read to the class would be her ultimate reward (she has been asking to do this since the second week of school), and therefore would probably work. Despite both teachers' best attempts, Trisha still calls out and her teachers often yell at her when this happens. If this occurs too frequently throughout the day, Toby calls Trisha's parents at home. In a few instances, Toby has written an e-mail to Trisha's parents about her impulsivity. Interestingly, the following day, Trisha behaves better, but only for that day. Another solution that her teachers have tried is writing Trisha's name on the board. Using this technique, if Trisha misbehaves she gets one letter of her name written. If her teachers have to write her entire name (one letter for each instance of inappropriate behavior), Trisha loses recess. The only problem is that one of her teachers must remain in the room to watch her. Although this technique has been rarely used, Trisha becomes frustrated when they begin to write one letter of her name on the board. Usually, Trisha becomes so upset that she is unable to control her behavior, resulting in her entire name being written on the board and losing recess.

On a recent day after school, Toby and Judy get some free time to reflect on Trisha's behavior and what to do next. "Well, Judy, I have had about as much of Trisha's talking as I can stand," remarked Toby as he shuffled papers around looking for Trisha's math worksheet. "Look at this," handing the incomplete math worksheet to Judy. "Trisha hardly did any work on it because she was too busy talking to Jacob." Judy looked it over and shook her head in acknowledgement. "I know how you feel. It seems like everything we do has no effect on her talking," Judy responded. "What should we do next?" asked exhausted Toby. "We need to do something, but I'm not quite sure what. Let me go home and look through my college textbooks to see what might help," Judy replied.

Discussion Questions

1. From the case, what behavior(s) would you target for remediation? Or what behavior(s) would you target for further assessment or observation?
2. In the class, choose a maladaptive behavior that you would like to target, and write an objective for either the maladaptive behavior or an appropriate target behavior.
3. Design a behavior plan for Trisha. Decide how you will measure the behavior and how you will change the maladaptive behavior.
4. How would you monitor her progress? Describe how and when you would monitor progress.
5. Should you have Trisha not speak at all in class? Is this a reasonable behavior to modify? Why or why not?

CASE 4

Math Is No Joke!

In his high school algebra class, Willie Mascue frequently passes time by making jokes to the teacher, Peter James (or Mr. J, as most kids call him), or other students. Willie's latest joke went like this: "Hey Mr. J, what's a polygon?" Mr. J shrugs his shoulders and Willie says, "a dead parrot." Although funny, it is difficult to get Willie to work because he always has a joke or humorous remark for the teacher or other students. He recently made fun of a classmate, George, by saying that, "George smells so bad that he is the only kid he knows who can get an 'A' for not raising his hand." His off-task antics continue most of the day. Mr. J counters this by telling Willie to get back to work. Over and over again, Mr. J is always redirecting Willie back to task. Willie's jokes aren't so bad, except they disrupt other students and prevent Willie from completing his tasks. His jokes place him in danger of flunking algebra. Only after a last-minute reprieve (extra credit) from Mr. J is Willie able to pass. To make matters worse, Willie dislikes math and frequently complains to Mr. J that he will never use it.

Typically, Mr. J's lessons center around using examples from the book and explaining them on the board to students. Between Mr. J's explanations and Mr. Naylor's (the Behavioral Disordered [BD] teacher) reiterations, most students can master the content. Mr. J takes the time to explain the content to all students in the class and offers tutoring classes after school for those who need additional help. His stoic lessons are interspersed with real life examples and games. Mr. J also believes that practice makes perfect, so he frequently gives his students a number of homework problems to work on. When Willie does get homework, he often does not complete it. Or, if he does bring it back, it is done incorrectly.

Willie is not only inattentive (he has been identified as BD), but impulsive. Diagnosed by his pediatrician at an early age with ADHD, Willie has bounced on and off many different types of medications, yet few are effective at controlling his inattention or impulsiveness. A more serious matter could be Willie's impulsiveness. Several times Willie has placed himself or others in danger because of his impulsiveness. For example, he was showing off for friends by hanging out of a car and nearly got hit by a passing car. Another time, Willie jumped out from the curb in front of a bus, just as a "joke" to amuse his friends. His stunts have earned him the nickname "Wild-Ass Willie." Of course, his stunts have also landed him in ISS.

Peter has spoken to Grant Naylor, his co-teacher from the BD program. Grant and Peter collaborate for math and science for both general education and LD and BD students. Willie represents one of their milder problems. Grant and Peter have collaborated for several years and comprised one of the first collaborative teams in their school and county. They love teaching together and provide a light, fun atmosphere for students to learn. They meet weekly to discuss student problems and problem solve. Peter really knows his stuff in math and science, and Grant is proficient in terms of instructional techniques and behavior management. Although some progress has been made with Willie, both teachers feel that he could perform and behave much better.

Willie provides a challenge to not only his teachers, but also his parents. Willie's parents, separated for the past 3 years, have dealt with the wild side of Willie on several occasions. Willie has been dropped off by the local police a number of times over the past 3 years. Willie's father, now in Alcohol Anonymous, caused much pain in the family, yet his mother is marginally friendly with his dad. His father's years of drinking and anger took their toll on both Willie and his mother. After attending several juvenile court hearings, Willie's mother is now close to kicking him out of the house. Willie's younger brother, Sykes, still lives at home, but he too is having problems with his mother. Similar to Willie, Sykes likes to stay out past curfew and skip school.

In school, Peter and Grant try to focus on the things that they can control and affect in Willie's life, like grades and behaviors. Both have tried ignoring the jokes and inappropriate behaviors, but it doesn't seem to work. Grant recently took data to get a baseline on Willie's on-task behavior. He found that over a 3-day period, Willie was off task 60% of the time. Of his off-task time, 70% was spent talking, 20% was spent looking around the room, and 10% was spent on other activities (tapping pencil, looking in his desk, etc.). For Willie, math was really just a joke. After Grant and Peter examined the data, they decided that it was time to get serious about Willie and for Willie to get serious about algebra.

Discussion Questions

1. From the case, what behavior(s) would you target for remediation? Or what behavior(s) would you target for further assessment or observation?
2. In the class, choose a maladaptive behavior that you would like to target, and write an objective for either the maladaptive behavior or an appropriate target behavior.
3. Design a behavior plan for Willie. Decide how you will measure the behavior and how you will change the maladaptive behavior.
4. How would you monitor his progress? Describe how and when you would monitor progress.
5. Choose a social skill area, and describe how to teach Willie the social skill.

CASE 5

Lui Learns History the Hard Way

Lui Ti is a 10th-grade student who has an LD. Lui is currently in Young Manson's history (co-taught) class. In class, Lui is often off task, talking to other students, out of his seat, or not paying attention. Lui often spends time either in the office or in the hall. Although the special education teacher, Gabbie Soo, often defends him, Lui's continued inappropriate behaviors offend Mr. Manson and break many unwritten class rules. Mr. Manson is patient up to a point, and Lui's rudeness and brashness grate on Mr. Manson's nerves to the point where he has to kick Liu out of the class. If not for Ms. Soo, Lui would have been suspended on a number of occasions. Ms. Soo frequently steps in and takes Lui in the hall for a talk or to calm him down.

In this particular history class, Mr. Manson usually takes the lead role while Ms. Soo records notes on the board for students to copy. She also helps with grading papers and circulates throughout the class to monitor learning and behavior. Mr. Manson is an expert on U.S. history, particularly World War II history. Some students say that he actually fought in the "big one," as Mr. Manson calls it, but he is actually younger than he looks. He has worked at the local museum giving tours of their World War II exhibit. Ms. Soo, on the other hand, is a fairly new teacher and is often intimidated by the older Mr. Manson. Despite occasional friction between the two teachers, both have agreed to work together for the good of the kids.

Having taught for 15 years, Mr. Manson's auditory style of presentation is a "less-than-perfect" lecturing style. He often reads notes to his class and rarely provides any support materials for students to use to take notes or learn materials. Talking can be a problem with students in the class, and lack of interest in the subject runs rampant during many lectures. Despite these problems, Mr. Manson's students score well on the state standards tests and earn strong grades. What seems to help students keep up with the content is the large number of pop quizzes that Mr. Manson gives. As students will tell you, shear memorization of facts is the Manson way.

When problems do occur in class, Mr. Manson first tries using verbal reprimands and planned ignoring with students, especially with Lui, but usually nothing seems to work. Eventually, Lui's outlandish behavior earns him a trip to the office. The other day, for example, it all began when Lui started making airplane noises as Mr. Manson spoke about the German blitzkrieg Funny at first, the students began to laugh, and even Ms. Soo chuckled. But, as Lui continued after being told to stop, Mr. Manson's face began to turn beet red. With anger seething through, he eventually raced toward the back, grabbed Lui by the arm, and rushed him out. With Ms. Soo in tow, the students began laughing, clapping, and betting each other that Lui would be suspended once again.

"Mr. Manson," Ms. Soo timidly yelled. "Could you slow down. I think I can help," she continued. "Not this time, Gabbie," Mr. Manson replied. The expression on Mr. Manson's face let Ms. Soo know that she could only sit and watch. As Mr. Manson spun Lui around and pushed his back up against the hallway wall, Lui's body made a loud thud. For the first time ever, Lui had a sickening expression on his face. Perhaps he realized he had gone too far. As Mr. Manson put his face in front of Lui's, he began to rant about how "punk kids" like him did not belong in his class. When Lui heard a pause in the conversation, he began to speak. With his lower lip quivering, he spoke, "I . . . I . . . I really didn't mean to make you soooo angry." "Too bad," shot back Mr. Manson. "This time you're out of here!" Ms. Soo could only watch and wait. She knew that both needed to blow off some steam. When she saw the action slowing down, she jumped in and said to Lui, "Look, let's just take a few minutes to calm down and consider the consequences of your actions." Realizing that no one was left in the room, Mr. Manson remarked to Ms. Soo, "From the sounds of it, I had better get back in there to calm things down."

As Mr. Manson left, Lui confessed at how he hated being in Mr. Manson's room and how he thought Mr. Manson was an evil person out to get him. Lui explained that he thought Mr. Manson was the irrational one and thought "the old man" should be fired or brought up on charges.

Later that day, Ms. Soo met Mr. Manson in the teacher's lounge and approached him about the incident. "Young" she began, "I'm really sorry about the incident this morning. Lui has quite a few disabilities besides his LD. He has been identified as ADHD." "Well," Mr. Manson countered, "there's no excuse for acting as weird as he does." After a few minutes of uncomfortable quiet, Mr. Manson finally spoke, "What do you suppose we could do?"

Discussion Questions

1. From the case, what behavior(s) would you target for remediation? Or, what behavior(s) would you target for further assessment or observation?
2. In the class, choose a maladaptive behavior that you would like to target, and write an objective for either the maladaptive behavior or an appropriate target behavior.
3. Design a behavior plan for Lui. Decide how you will measure the behavior and how you will change the maladaptive behavior.
4. How would you monitor progress? Describe how and when you would monitor progress.
5. Choose a social skill area, and describe how to teach Lui the social skill.

8

Effective Techniques for Teaching Basic Skills: Reading and Written Language

Teaching students with and without disabilities to read can be a challenging task for teachers working in K–12 classrooms. Additionally, teaching in inclusive classrooms may compound this task for some. Teachers need to be aware of the major components of reading and knowledgeable of instructional practices and research-based strategies designed to increase competency in phonemic awareness, phonics, fluency, vocabulary, and text comprehension (National Reading Panel, 2000).

In 2000, the National Reading Panel (NRP) produced a report that identified and defined the five major components of reading. The first component is phonemic awareness. NRP posited that "Phonemic awareness refers to the ability to focus on and manipulate phonemes in spoken words" (p. 2-1). The NRP report went on to describe the common tasks involved in the assessment and instruction of phonemic awareness:

1. Phoneme isolation, which requires recognizing individual sounds in words; for example, "Tell me the first sound in *paste*." /p/
2. Phoneme identity, which requires recognizing the common sound in different words. For example, "Tell me the sound that is the same in *bike*, *boy*, and *bell*." /b/
3. Phoneme categorization, which requires recognizing the word with the odd sound in a sequence of three or four words; for example, "Which word does not belong? *bus*, *bun*, *rug*." (*rug*)
4. Phonemic blending, which requires listening to a sequence of separately spoken sounds and combining them to form a recognizable word. For example, "What word is /s/ /k/ /u/ /l/?" (*school*)
5. Phoneme segmentation, which requires breaking a word into its sounds by tapping out or counting the sounds, or by pronouncing and positioning a marker for each sound. For example, "How many phonemes are there in *ship*?" (three: /š/ /I/ /p/)
6. Phoneme deletion, which requires recognizing what word remains after a specified phoneme is removed. For example, "What is *smile* without the /s/?" (*mile*) (p. 2-2)

The second major component of reading is phonics. The report noted that, "An essential part of the process for beginners involves learning the alphabetic system, that is, letter-sound correspondences and spelling patterns, and learning how to apply this knowledge in their reading" (p. 2-89).

The third major component is fluency. According to NRP, "Fluent readers can read text with speed, accuracy, and proper expression" (p. 3-1). The report goes on to note that fluency is based on word recognition and/or decoding skills, but that skills in these areas may not lead directly to fluency.

The fourth major component is vocabulary.

> *Researchers distinguish between many different "vocabularies." Receptive vocabulary is the vocabulary that we can understand when presented to us in text or as we listen to others speak, whereas productive vocabulary is the vocabulary we use in writing or when speaking to others. It is generally believed that one's receptive vocabulary is much larger than one's productive vocabulary because we often recognize words that we would rarely use. Vocabulary is also subcategorized as oral versus reading—oral vocabulary refers to words that are recognized in speaking or listening; reading vocabulary are words used in print. Sight vocabulary is a subset of reading vocabulary that does not require explicit word recognition processing. Conclusions about some of these different types of vocabularies often do not apply to all; what may be true for one may or may not be true for another (pp. 4-15–4-16).*

And finally, the fifth major component is text comprehension. Text comprehension is the ultimate purpose for reading and involves constructing meaning from text through an interactive process.

READING INSTRUCTION IN "TYPICAL" INCLUSION CLASSROOMS

Teachers working in early elementary-, elementary-, and middle-school inclusive classrooms may observe and/or participate in multiple models of instruction for teaching and supporting student reading. These models may include one or more, or a combination, of the following forms: one teach–one support, station teaching, parallel teaching, alternative teaching, and team teaching (Friend & Cook, 2007; Tomlinson, 1999, 2001; Tomlinson & McTighe, 2006). The instructional model used by teachers and schools may be influenced by state mandates, school district initiatives, school-based decisions, enrollment issues, staffing patterns, scheduling problems, or teacher preferences. Additionally, the instructional method or reading program (e.g., phonics versus whole language, basal versus literature-based, Reading First, *Read 180*, SRA Direct Instruction guided reading) used may be influenced by these factors.

READING INSTRUCTION IN HIGH SCHOOL

Students with mild disabilities at the high school level do not typically take reading. High school students normally complete 4 years of English or English language arts. General education teachers providing this instruction frequently have little to no course work in how to teach reading because students are expected to know how to read fluently by the time they enter high school (Beers, 2003). As a result, special education teachers supporting students with mild disabilities in inclusive high school English classes play a pivotal role in reading instruction. Furthermore, special education teachers may be called on to support reading instruction across the content areas. Fortunately for teachers and students, researchers have begun to address effective techniques for teaching reading across the content areas at the secondary level (Beers, 2003; Deshler, Palincsar, Biancarosa, & Nair, 2007; Lenz, Deshler, & Kissam, 2004).

RESEARCH-BASED TECHNIQUES FOR TEACHING READING

This section describes instructional strategies designed to increase reading competency. Each strategy is introduced to the reader, defined, and explained. A brief description of the research supporting the use of these strategies is then provided.

Phonological Awareness and Word Identification Strategies

A number of phonological awareness and word identification strategies are available in the literature. All are backed by research that demonstrates their effectiveness. This section describes three of these strategies.

STOP—Phonological Awareness Strategy

The first strategy is the phonological awareness strategy (Boyle, 2008; Boyle & Seibert, 1998). This strategy aims not to teach initial letter sounds (i.e., students should know most of their letter sounds), but to teach the next logical step—segmenting and blending. Therefore, as a prerequisite step, students must know at least 80% of the initial letter sounds (phonemes) from a list of phonemes (consonant and short-vowel sounds).

Because of the young age of students learning this strategy, it incorporates familiar keywords (e.g., stare, tell, open, put) that they can easily understand. The phonological awareness strategy incorporates both segmenting and blending skills through the mnemonic STOP (Stare, Tell, Open, Put; see Table 8.1). The specific steps of the strategy were developed because: (a) previous studies demonstrated that segmenting and blending were two skills essential for pronouncing words (Rack, Snowling, & Olson, 1992); (b) training students in one subskill (e.g., segmenting) does not result in increases in other subskills (e.g., blending) (O'Conner, Jenkins, Leicester, & Slocum, 1992); (c) segmenting and blending must be taught together to help students pronounce words (Torgesen, Morgan, & Davis, 1992); and (d) phonological awareness training that explicitly links phonological awareness skills with reading, and teaching specific strategies to implement those phonological awareness skills was proven to be more effective than a "skill and drill" approach (i.e., teaching skills in isolation and out of context) (Cunningham, 1990).

The first step, stare, cues the student to look at each letter of the unknown word (i.e., the first step of segmenting). In the second step, tell, the student is asked to tell him/herself each letter sound (the second step of segmenting). The third step, open, cues the child to verbalize aloud the segmented sounds. The fourth step, put, cues the student to blend the letter sounds together to say the word.

Strategy instruction consists of introductory and mnemonic practice training, during which students are instructed on the components of the phonological awareness strategy. Initially, the teacher describes and models the strategy to students and then they begin using the mnemonic STOP while the teacher provides feedback. Once students are proficient at using the strategy steps, they

TABLE 8.1 Phonological Awareness Strategy

STOP Strategy Steps

S—Stare at the unknown word.

T—Tell yourself each letter sound.

O—Open your mouth and say each letter.

P—Put the letters together to say the word.

begin using the strategy with actual words. The initial phase involves using the strategy with 10 monosyllabic words (three- to four-letter words that contain short-vowel sounds) per training session. Each monosyllabic word is placed on individual index cards. Each subsequent session uses 10 new words. During each session, two or three of the words are nonsense words that students pronounce using phonetic rules. Nonsense words should be used to ensure that students are applying the strategy steps and not just remembering the words as sight words. Once students master the strategy use with monosyllabic words, multisyllabic words should be introduced. These words follow similar phonetic rules as the monosyllabic words; however, these are two syllables in length. As with the monosyllabic word phase, each session includes two to three multisyllabic nonsense words.

Word Identification Strategy

The word identification strategy was developed by Lenz, Schumaker, Deshler, and Beals (1984) and is meant to help students identify unknown words (Boyle, 2008). The key words are action words that prompt the student to perform a specific step. An important part of the strategy training involves teaching students extensive lists of affixes (prefixes and suffixes) and the meaning of each. Like other strategies from the University of Kansas Center for Research on Learning, this follows the eight-stage training process. The eight-stage process (Deshler, Alley, Warner, & Schumaker, 1981) consists of pretest and obtain commitment, describe the strategy, model the strategy, verbal rehearsal of strategy steps, controlled practice and feedback, advanced practice and feedback, posttest and make commitments, and generalization. Throughout the strategy training, as the child reads aloud the passages, the teacher records the number of word identification errors made and the student's level of comprehension.

The word identification strategy uses the mnemonic DISSECT (Discover, Isolate, Separate, Say, Examine, Check, Try; see Table 8.2) as a prompt for students to dissect or cut words apart to read them. The first step, *discover*, prompts the student to skip an unknown word, read the rest of the sentence, and then use the information to guess the unknown word. If the student still has difficulty, the student should proceed to the next step, *isolate*. In this step, the student should look at the first few letters to determine if they can identify a prefix. If a prefix is present, the student draws a

---

TABLE 8.2   Word Identification Strategy

DISSECT Strategy Steps

D—Discover the context.

I—Isolate the prefix.

S—Separate the suffix.

S—Say the stem.

E—Examine the stem using the "Rules of 3s and 2s".

    3s Rule: If the first letter in the stem begins with a consonant, underline 3 letters.

    2s Rule: If the first letter begins with a vowel, underline two letters (Repeat for each set of letters in the stem until all of the letters have been underlined and grouped).

    If you can't decode the stem using these rules, drop the first letter of the stem and then apply the rules.

C—Check with someone.

T—Try a dictionary.

box around the prefix. If not and the student still cannot identify the word, the student should go to the fourth step, *separate*. In the *separate* step, the child boxes off the suffix, if any. In the next step, *Say*, the student should try to say the stem. If recognized, the student should say all three parts (prefix, stem, and suffix) together. If unable to pronounce the stem, the student should move to the *examine* step of the strategy. In this step, the student examines the stem using the "Rules of 2s and 3s." If the stem can now be read using these rules, the student then combines the prefix, stem, and suffix together to pronounce the word. If, however, the student cannot pronounce the stem, the student should *check* with someone. The student is taught to check with either the teacher or, if appropriate, another student. If no one is available, the student should *Try* a dictionary. In this final step, the student looks up the word and uses the pronunciation guide to say the stem.

Research Evidence

PHONOLOGICAL AWARENESS STRATEGY.   This strategy was used with second- and third-grade students with either mild intellectual/cognitive disabilities or learning disabilities (LD) (Boyle & Seibert, 1998). The results indicated that from pre- to posttest, these children increased the number of monosyllabic words that they were able to pronounce, increased the number of multisyllabic words that they could pronounce, increased the correct pronunciation of words used during generalization, increased the correct pronunciation of nonsense words, and increased the correct pronunciation of unknown words.

WORD IDENTIFICATION STRATEGY.   This strategy was used with seventh-, eighth-, and ninth-grade students with LDs (Lenz & Hughes, 1990). The study results indicated that trained students were able to reduce the number of errors from baseline (range was 6.3 to 20.5 errors) to posttraining (range was 0 to 6.4 errors). In addition, the average baseline group score for reading on ability-level materials was 39% and increased to 88% after training, whereas the baseline average score for students on grade-level materials was 39% and increased to 58% after training. Still, in another article, by Bremer, Clapper, and Deshler (2002), the authors reported the results of two studies that were previously conducted. In the first study, ninth-grade students who were identified as struggling secondary readers were taught to use the word identification strategy. The results demonstrated that students trained in the Word Identification strategy showed greater gains compared to a comparison group of students. In another study, sixth-grade students with low achievement who received the strategy improved from pre- to posttest scores on measures of decoding and comprehension.

FLUENCY

Repeated Readings

Using *repeated readings* is a simple technique whereby the teacher has the student read one passage several times or until they reach a predetermined level of fluency. O'Shea, Sindelar, and O'Shea (1975) claim that four readings appear to be the optimal number because by the fourth reading, children have reached maximum gains in reading speed, error reduction, and expression. Repeated readings have been used since the late 1970s (Samuels, 1979) and have been proven effective for increasing fluency on passages that students read more than once, as well as on new passages. Repeated readings have been shown to be successful when the child's oral reading is monitored by the teacher or another higher level peer. In a review of repeated reading research, Therrien (2004) found that repeated readings are effective for increasing both fluency and comprehension. Moreover, it appears that repeated readings have transfer effects to new readings. In other words, increases in fluency and comprehension were found not only for the current passages that students were repeating, but for new passages as well. The effects were more pronounced for those new passages that contained common words from the previous passage. As with any skill, it appears that practice makes perfect (or at least improves reading skills).

Repeated reading works best when the text is matched with the child's reading level. Some (Clay, 1993, as cited by Kuhn & Stall, 2003) suggest that students practice repeated reading with texts that are at students' independent (easy) reading levels, and others (Dahl, 1979; Rasinski, 2000, 2004; Samuels, 1979) suggest that repeated readings be used with texts that are on students' current instructional reading levels (90% to 95% word recognition accuracy).

Teachers using repeated reading should prepare by allotting 15 to 30 minutes each day for repeated readings, using the same passage three to four times, and choosing short passages with reading levels that have been predetermined using a readability formula (Therrien, 2004). If the passages are too difficult, students will struggle to read them and read more slowly. If passages are too easy, students may not be practicing newly learned sight words or vocabulary words.

Once students are ready to read, Rasinski (2003) recommends the following guidelines: Use 50- to 500-word passages and have the student read the passage aloud until they reach a predetermined reading rate. The passages can come from a variety of sources including basal stories, newspapers, or textbooks. As discussed earlier, predetermined rates can be ascertained by using available reading rate charts, as well as past performance on curriculum-based measurements. Once a child achieves the criteria, move on to a new passage that is as difficult or slightly more difficult as the last. Finally, be sure to track the reading rate (as well as prosody) while the child is reading.

Research Evidence

REPEATED READINGS.   More than 100 studies have been conducted on repeated readings since Samuels first introduced it in 1979. Study findings have consistently shown that repeated readings lead to improvements in reading speed, word recognition, and comprehension (Samuels, 2002). In addition, Dowhower (1989) summarizes the findings from several studies and points out that, among students with reading problems, repeated readings result in decreases in word recognition errors, faster processing of text, and increased factual retention; foster more fluent reading for struggling word-by-word readers; encouraged deeper questioning and insights; and help students to remember pertinent content from passages, such as main ideas and vocabulary.

VOCABULARY

LINCS Vocabulary Strategy

The LINCS (List, Identify, Note, Create, Self-test) vocabulary strategy was designed by Edwin Ellis in 1992 to help students learn new vocabulary words through the use of memory-enhancement techniques. This five-part (step) strategy provides cues that assist students in focusing on the "critical elements of a vocabulary word, and then to use keyword mnemonic devices, mnemonic stories, visual imagery, associations with prior knowledge, and self-evaluation to enhance their memory of the meaning of the word" (Ellis, 2000, p. 1).

> Three instructional goals are associated with teaching students to use the LINCS Strategy: (a) increasing students' ability to independently learn key vocabulary, (b) providing students with a sense of empowerment or control over their learning, and (c) promoting students' motivation about learning new strategies. (p. 1)

TABLE 8.3   LINCS Vocabulary Strategy

LINCS Strategy Steps

L—List the parts.
I—Identify a reminding word.
N—Note a LINCing story.
C—Create a LINCing picture.
S—Self-test.

Like other strategies from the University of Kansas Center for Research on Learning, this follows the eight-step strategy process (Deshler, Alley, Warner, & Schumaker, 1981). Step one involves pretesting students to determine their ability to learn new vocabulary words and to see how they approach this task. Students are given a list of 10 vocabulary words to study on the first day, individually interviewed by the teacher to find out how they studied, and then tested on these words the second day. If students need the LINCS strategy, the teacher describes the strategy and acquires a commitment from the student to learn and use the strategy. The next two steps involve describing the strategy and modeling the strategy for the student (see Table 8.3 for the LINCS mnemonic). Next, students move on to verbal practice of the strategy steps. Upon mastery of the steps, students advance to controlled practice. In controlled practice, students use the strategy with specially designed nonsense words or real words and definitions to mastery level (applying the strategy to at least 80% of the words; 80% or above on quizzes; and explaining how reminding words, LINCing stories, and LINCing pictures aid in memory). After achieving mastery in the controlled practice stage, students move on to advanced practice and feedback. Students practice using the strategy on words that are similar to words they will encounter in their content-area classes. Once students reach mastery in the advanced practice stage, they proceed to the posttest and make commitments to generalize the strategy. In the generalization phase, students are instructed how to use the strategy in other situations and settings.

Research Evidence

LINCS VOCABULARY STRATEGY.   Research has shown the effectiveness of the LINCS strategy for students with and without learning disabilities at the middle- and high-school levels (Ellis, 1992, 2000). Further, research shows that this strategy has been taught to students in resource and mainstream classrooms with success. In the research reported by Ellis (1992, 2000), students with learning disabilities in a mainstream sixth-grade social studies classroom increased their mean scores from 53% at pretest to 77% at posttest. Students without learning disabilities in the same mainstream classroom increased their mean scores from 84% at pretest to 92% at posttest. Woodruff et al., 2002, studied the impact of a reading comprehension course that combines the LINCS strategy with three other strategies: visual imagery strategy (Schumaker, Deshler, Zemitzch, & Warner, 1993), paraphrasing strategy (Schumaker, Denton, & Deshler, 1984), and self-questioning strategy (Schumaker, Deshler, Nolan, & Alley, 1994). In this study, high school students who were considered two or more grades below level in reading comprehension showed significant gains after participating in the reading strategies course for 1 hour per day for one semester of the school year.

TEXT COMPREHENSION INSTRUCTION

Paraphrasing Strategy

The paraphrasing strategy is a reading comprehension strategy that asks children to find main ideas and details from each paragraph that is read, and then paraphrase that information aloud. The strategy aims to help students become actively engaged in reading through searching for main ideas and details in paragraphs and then transforming that information through paraphrasing to make it personally meaningful. The three steps of the paraphrasing strategy are represented by the acronym RAP (Read, Ask, Put; see Table 8.4).

Students use the strategy with short passages that are at least five paragraphs in length. For example, published reading materials such as *Timed Readings* are frequently used with this strategy. Similar to other strategies from the University of Kansas Center for Research on Learning, this follows the eight-step strategy process (Deshler, Alley, Warner, & Schumaker, 1981). Initially, the teacher pretests students to see if they qualify for the strategy. If students need the paraphrasing strategy, the teacher describes the strategy and acquires a commitment from students to learn and use the strategy. The next two steps involve describing the strategy and modeling the strategy for students. Next, students move on to verbal practice of the strategy steps. Upon mastery of the steps, students advance to controlled practice. In controlled practice, students begin reading passages that are on their current *reading ability level,* and upon reaching mastery (80% paraphrasing and 70% comprehension scores), they progress on to *grade level* passages in the advanced practice phase. Once students reach mastery in the grade-level phase, they proceed to the generalization phase. In the generalization phase students are instructed how to use the strategy with other materials and settings.

Throughout the strategy training, teachers keep records of students' paraphrasing and comprehension scores as they silently read passages, but paraphrase each paragraph aloud. This explicit comprehension strategy, once mastered, enables students with weak comprehension skills to read below-grade-level and grade-level materials.

Research Evidence

PARAPHRASING STRATEGY.   The paraphrasing strategy has been shown to be effective at increasing reading comprehension among students with disabilities. Ellis and Graves (1990) reported that teaching the paraphrasing strategy was effective at increasing reading comprehension among 68 fifth- through seventh-grade students with disabilities. Moreover, when they compared the effects of the paraphrasing strategy plus repeated readings with paraphrasing alone, they found that paraphrasing alone was just as effective. Similarly, Katims and Harris (1997) reported that the paraphrasing strategy was effective at increasing the reading comprehension for

---

TABLE 8.4 Paraphrasing Strategy

RAP Strategy Steps

R—*Read* a paragraph.

A—*Ask* yourself, "What were the main ideas and details in this paragraph?".

    Finding the main idea:

    1. Look in the first sentence of the paragraph.

    2. Look for repetitions of the same word(s) in the whole paragraph.

P—*Put* the main ideas and details in your own words.

---

middle-school students both with and without disabilities. Finally, Lauterbach and Bender (1995) conducted a study that trained three seventh-grade students with mild to moderate disabilities to use the paraphrasing strategy while reading passages. They reported that all three students improved their paraphrasing and reading comprehension.

SUMMARY

This section presented information on the five essential components of reading. It briefly addressed typical reading instruction in inclusion classrooms in elementary through high school settings. Additionally, this section described effective reading interventions for students with and without mild disabilities. Readers wishing to learn more about effective research-based instructional practices may access this information through a wide array of resources, including the Internet, library searches, professional journals, and textbooks.

WRITING

As is the case with teachers supporting reading instruction for students served in inclusive classrooms at the elementary through high school level, teachers instructing and supporting writing may observe and/or participate in multiple models of instruction for teaching and supporting student writing. Again, the instructional model employed by teachers and schools may be influenced by state mandates, school district initiatives, school-based decisions, enrollment issues, staffing patterns, scheduling problems, and teacher preferences. These issues also affect the instructional method or writing program selected (e.g., Writer's Workshop, Write Traits, direct instruction, language experience, guided writing). No matter what method or program is used, students with mild disabilities must master a minimal level of handwriting proficiency and spelling skills in order to demonstrate functional composition skills (Bos & Vaughn, 2006).

Written language has three main components: handwriting, spelling, and composing. Handwriting involves teaching children how to write manuscript and cursive letters. Spelling is a complex task that involves teaching students how to spell words from a list, spelling book, and/or vocabulary book. Composing involves teaching students how to write sentences, paragraphs, and essays.

Handwriting

Manuscript handwriting is an important skill for students to learn because most children and adults use manuscript handwriting as part of their daily life, and manuscript letters form the basis of the text that we read. Traditionally, manuscript has been taught first before cursive handwriting and is thought to be an easier form of handwriting for children to learn and produce (Bos & Vaughn, 2006). Cursive handwriting is typified by the use of letters that are connected together by flowing strokes. Some claim that cursive handwriting is easier for children with mild disabilities because the student has to see the entire word before writing it down as opposed to manuscript that uses a letter-by-letter approach (http://specialed.about.com/od/literacy/a/whycursive.htm). Others (e.g., Johnson & Mykelbust, 1967, as cited in Bos & Vaughn, 2006) believe that only one form of script should be taught: manuscript. The proponents of cursive handwriting feel that by viewing the word in its entirety, there will be fewer letter reversals. Yet, for some students with disabilities, cursive handwriting remains a struggle all their life, or at least until they are no longer required to write in cursive.

When teaching handwriting skills to students, teachers help students understand that proficient handwriting skills will enable students to convey messages to others. Activities should include not only practice with each letter, but activities that demonstrate to children the usefulness and practicality of writing. Early on, teachers should be concerned with the quality of letters before turning their attention to speed and fluency. Instruction should occur over distributed periods of time and under direct supervision. Furthermore, teachers need to provide immediate feedback to prevent students from practicing errors. Over time, students can begin to analyze their own handwriting by comparing their work with examples or models. Eventually, students should begin writing words and sentences using their newly developed handwriting skills.

Spelling

As mentioned previously, spelling involves teaching students how to spell words from a list, spelling book, and/or vocabulary book. The act of "traditional" spelling is an encoding process with which many students with and without mild disabilities struggle (Salend, 2008). Spelling entails the ability to remember and visualize words, to encode the letters represented by the sounds in words, and to apply knowledge of spelling rules and patterns (Hammeken, 2007).

Spelling is often an area of difficulty for students with mild disabilities. It is a problem that begins in elementary school and often deteriorates as students progress to older grades where words become longer and more complex (Dixon, 1991). Studies have found that students with disabilities typically misspelled two to four times as many words as their nondisabled peers, resulting in 10% to 20% misspelled words in writing (Deno, Marston, & Mirkin, 1982; MacArthur & Graham, 1987). Not only do these misspellings cause problems when students are spelling vocabulary words, but spelling difficulties slow down the writing process and interfere in the transcription and flow of getting ideas onto paper.

Over the years, a number of techniques have been developed that were proven to be effective in augmenting the spelling performance of students with mild disabilities. In typical classrooms, students are given between 15 and 20 words per week to study. In most of those classrooms, teachers use commercially prepared materials that often advocate a study–test method whereby students are given their spelling words on Monday and tested on Friday (Brown 1980). One of the problems with this approach is that students often postpone studying until the night before the test. This traditional approach, particularly for students with disabilities, may not be the most effective method of preparation (Murphy, Hern, Williams, & McLaughlin, 1990). Instead, teachers should use research-based spelling techniques that advocate changes in the way students with disabilities prepare for spelling tests.

Composing

In a 2003 article, Jean Schumaker and Don Deshler asked the question, "Can students with LD become competent writers?" Given the data that we know about students with disabilities, researchers have shown that they have many obstacles to overcome to gain competence at writing. Despite these concerns, research has consistently shown that, once students are taught strategies and techniques, they can improve their writing performance, in some cases to the point where their performance is comparable to nondisabled peers (McNaughton, Hughes, & Clark, 1997).

Graham and Harris (1988) recommend several principles that should serve as a framework for writing programs for students with disabilities. These principles, many of which reflect commonsense practical ideas, will enhance any teacher's writing program and are drawn from research. First, allocate time for writing. Second, good writing programs should expose students to a broad range of meaningful writing tasks. Third, integrate writing with other academic subjects. Fourth, automatize lower-level skills or disregard lower skills until the latter stages of writing. Fifth, expose students to different types of genre for writing. Sixth, help students develop goals for improving their written products. The seventh and perhaps most important area uses a *process approach* as a framework for writing. These principles should all be integrated into any writing program for students with mild disabilities.

PRODUCT VERSUS PROCESS.   For many years, writing was simply viewed as a product; writers would transcribe their thoughts on to paper to create end products such as essays or papers. Using this *product approach*, the product would be proofread, corrected, and turned in to the teacher for a grade. This product approach placed a great deal of pressure on students to produce a "perfect draft" that would allow them to meet the length requirement of the assignment and move on to the next paper. Additionally, according to Flower (1985), this approach may lead to students using weak writing strategies, including trial and error, perfect-draft, waiting for inspiration, and words looking for ideas. As you can see, the product approach is often a poor way to address writing assignments.

More recent views of writing have led to a *process approach* to writing that ultimately results in a better product. The Hayes–Flower model (Hayes & Flower, 1980) of writing strongly influenced this shift in thinking in the academic field. When students use a process approach, the quality of their products—completed essays or compositions—are typically much improved. In fact, some current views on writing look to incorporate both a process and a product approach. In fact, some elements of writing are more product oriented, such as correct spelling of words, grammatically correct sentences, proper paragraph structure, and punctuation (Gabrielatos, 2003) that teachers should focus on, particularly among young students. Therefore, writing may be viewed as both a process and product approach.

RESEARCH-BASED TECHNIQUES FOR TEACHING WRITING

This section describes instructional techniques and/or strategies designed to increase writing competency. Each technique is introduced, defined, and explained. Many descriptions also briefly summarize the research supporting the use of these techniques.

Handwriting

PROGRESSIVE APPROXIMATION APPROACH.   The progressive approximation approach to teaching letter formation was developed by Hofmeister in 1973. The steps are as follows:

1. The student copies the letter using a pencil.
2. The teacher examines the letter and, if necessary, corrects by overmarking with a highlighter.
3. The student erases incorrect portions of the letter and traces over the teacher's highlighter marking.
4. The student repeats steps 1–3 until the letter is written correctly (Graham & Miller, 1980, p. 11).

FAUKE APPROACH.   The Fauke approach to teaching letter formation was developed by. The Fauke approach uses the following steps:

1. The teacher writes the letter, and the student and teacher discuss the formational act.
2. The student names the letter.
3. The student traces the letter with a finger, pencil, and magic marker.
4. The student's finger traces a letter form made of yarn.
5. The student copies the letter.
6. The student writes the letter from memory.
7. The teacher rewards the student for correctly writing the letter (Graham & Miller, 1980, p. 11).

Study Techniques for Spelling

CLASSWIDE PEER TUTORING.   Classwide Peer Tutoring (CWPT) is a technique that has been shown to be effective at increasing the number of correctly spelled words for students with mild disabilities (Burks, 2004; Mortweet et al., 1999). During CWPT, students are assigned in pairs to be either the tutor or tutee for 10 minutes and then switch with one another for an additional 10 minutes (i.e., 20 minutes total). Each pair is given a list of spelling words, paper on which to write their spelling words, and a sheet to keep track of points earned. The tutors begin by reading the spelling words, one at a time, to the tutees who write the word. As tutees write each word, they also say the letters aloud. The tutors award the tutees two points for each correctly spelled word. If the word is misspelled, tutors tell the tutee how to spell the word correctly, and the tutees practice spelling the word correctly three times while saying the letters aloud. If the tutees spell the misspelled word correctly three times, the tutor awards one point. If the tutee still spells the word incorrectly, the tutors do not award any points. The tutors continue through the list of words and repeat them as necessary, until the timer sounds to end the first 10-minute session. Once the timer sounds, the students switch roles so that the tutees are now the tutors and the tutors are now the tutees. They proceed for 10 minutes spelling words from the same list. After the second 10-minute session ends, the teacher collects materials, and students report on the total number of points. The pair with the most points is rewarded with a prize or special privilege (e.g., 5 minutes extra library time, lining up first). Throughout the tutoring, the teacher circulates around the room and awards extra points for students who are working correctly and cooperatively.

FIVE-STEP WORD-STUDY STRATEGY.   Graham and Freeman (1986) researched and found that the five-step word study strategy was effective for use with elementary-aged students with learning disabilities. The steps of the strategy are as follows:

1. Say the word.
2. Write and say the word.
3. Check the word.
4. Trace and say the word.
5. Write the word from memory and check.
6. Repeat the five steps (Bos & Vaughn, 2006, p. 11).

When teaching this procedure to students, teachers should first model the steps. Next, students should practice the procedure with teacher support. Last, students should use the procedure independently to study spelling words.

Strategies for Composing Sentences, Paragraphs, Essays, and Monitoring Errors

SENTENCE WRITING STRATEGY.   The Sentence Writing Strategy (Schumaker & Sheldon, 1985) (see Table 8.5) was developed to assist students at writing a variety of sentence types. Because most students with disabilities rely on simple sentences for the majority of essays and compositions, the sentence writing strategy enables them to produce not only simple sentences, but also compound, complex, and compound-complex sentences (Schumaker & Deshler, 2003). This variety is not meant to make their writing more complicated, but to help them express their ideas more fully and to make the written product more readable.

Using the steps for the PENS (Pick, Explore, Note, Search) strategy (see Table 8.5), students *pick* a formula and *explore* (i.e., choose) words (subjects and verbs) that would fit the for-

TABLE 8.5 Sentence Writing Strategy

PENS Strategy Steps

P—Pick a formula.
E—Explore words to fit the formula.
N—Note the words.
S—Search and check.

mula. In the next step, *note*, students write down the sentence from the formula that they chose. In the last step, *search* and check, students examine the sentence to make sure that it is a complete sentence, identify the subject(s) and verb(s), determine whether the sentence has proper capitalization and punctuation, and read it to determine whether it makes sense.

Applying the PENS strategy to actual sentences, students first learn how to use the four formulas with simple sentences, next with compound sentences, then with complex sentences, and finally, with compound-complex sentences (Ellis & Colvert, 1996). Table 8.6 illustrates the four different types of simple sentences. Once students can successfully create the four types of simple sentences, they move on to compound sentences. As shown in Table 8.7, students create compound sentences by using a comma and a coordinating conjunction such as *and*, *so*, or *but* with two independent clauses. Variations of these sentences are created using one or two subjects and verbs from the formulas.

Once students master compound sentences using PENS, they move on to complex sentences and compound-complex sentences. A complex sentence is created by combining a dependent clause with an independent clause. Using the formula, students can create variations of these complex sentences. See Table 8.8 for examples.

TABLE 8.6 Formulas and Sample Simple Sentences

Simple Sentence Formulas and Example Sentences

S = subject and V = verb
S V = Tom ran home.
SS V = Tom and Judy walked home together.
S VV = Haja ran and kicked the ball.
SS VV = Yogi and Sevin ate three pizzas and drank soda.

TABLE 8.7 Formulas and Sample Compound Sentences

Compound Sentence Formulas and Example Sentences

S V = Tom ran home, *and* he rang the door bell.
SS V = Tom and Judy walked home together, *so* they could talk to each other.
S VV = Haja ran and kicked the ball, *but* it was caught by Tucker.
SS VV = Yogi and Sevin ate three pizzas and drank soda; *yet*, they were still hungry.
(*Note: And, so, or, for, nor, yet,* and *but* are coordinating conjunctions.)

TABLE 8.8	Formulas and Sample Complex Sentences

Complex Sentence Formulas and Example Sentences

S V = Tom ran home *because* he was afraid of the dog.

SS V = *After* the baseball game, Tom and Judy walked home together.

S VV = Haja ran and kicked the ball *as* he juggled his soda.

SS VV = *Before* leaving for the dance, Yogi and Sevin ate pizza and drank soda.

(*Note: Although, after, because, if, where, than, since, as, unless, before, though, whereas,* and *when* are the most frequently used subordinating conjunctions.)

Following student mastery of complex sentences using PENS, students move to compound-complex sentences. A compound-complex sentence is created by combining two independent clauses with a dependent clause. Using the formula, students can create variety of compound-complex sentences. See Table 8.9 for examples of these sentences.

In some cases, prior to using the PENS strategy, students may need to be taught prerequisite sentence-writing skills such as identification of subjects and verbs, use of proper punctuation, and rules for capitalization. Frequently, students need much practice to master these different types of sentences. Initially, students are taught to first identify a particular type of sentence before they are asked to create and write their own type (Ellis & Colvert, 1996).

RESEARCH EVIDENCE FOR THE SENTENCE WRITING STRATEGY. In one study, students who were taught the sentence writing strategy improved their performance on measures of sentence type and grammatically correct sentences. Before training, students exhibited mostly incomplete sentences and simple sentences; after training, students exhibited more sophisticated and complete sentences. Their sentences were more varied and included compound, complex, and compound-complex sentences (Ellis & Colvert, 1996). In another study (Kline, Schumaker, & Deshler, 1991), students who were trained in the sentence writing strategy not only reached mastery, but reached it faster when teachers provided elaborate feedback.

THE ERROR MONITORING STRATEGY. The purpose of the error monitoring strategy (Schumaker, Nolan, & Deshler, 1985) is to teach students to detect and correct errors in written products. The strategy stresses the importance of proofreading written products before handing them in. The error monitoring strategy uses the mnemonic WRITER (Write, Read, Interrogate, Take, Execute, Reread) and incorporates the COPS (Capitalization, Overall appearance,

TABLE 8.9	Formulas and Sample Compound-Complex Sentences

Compound-Complex Sentence Formulas and Example Sentences

S V = *Because* he was afraid of the dog, Tom ran home *and* he hid under his bed.

SS V = *After* the baseball game, Tom and Judy walked together *and* they enjoyed their conversation.

S VV = Haja ran and kicked the ball, *as* he juggled his soda, *but* he never scored a goal.

SS VV = *Before* leaving for the dance, Yogi and Sevin ate pizza and drank soda; *yet,* they came home on time.

TABLE 8.10	Error Monitoring Strategy

WRITER Strategy Steps

W—Write on every other line.
R—Read the paper for meaning.
I—Interrogate yourself using the COPS questions.
T—Take your paper to someone for help.
E—Execute a final copy.
R—Reread your paper.

Punctuation, Spelling) acronym within the strategy (see Table 8.10). Prior to the WRITER mnemonic being developed, the steps for the strategy included the following:

1. Use every other line as you write your rough draft.
2. As you read each sentence, ask yourself the COPS questions.
3. When you find an error, circle it and put the correct form above the error if you know it.
4. Ask for help if you are unsure of the correct form.
5. Recopy the paragraph neatly in a form for handing in to the teacher "(Schumaker et al., 1982)."

In the first step of the strategy, *write*, students are told that when writing a rough draft of a composition or essay they should write on every other line of the paper. Writing on every other line allows students to write corrections on the blank lines of the paper. Once the paper is written, students move on to the next step, to *read* the paper for meaning. While reading, students should check each sentence to make sure it relates to the topic of the paragraph and that the wording is correct. In the third step, *interrogate*, students review their paper, sentence by sentence, using the COPS questions (see Table 8.11). The COPS questions are, Have I *capitalized* the first word and proper nouns? Have I made any (*overall*) handwriting, margin, spacing, or careless errors? Have I used end *punctuation*, commas, and semicolons correctly? Do the words look like they are *spelled* right, can I sound them out or should I use a dictionary? (Schumaker et al., 1982)? Beginning with the first sentence, students ask all of the COPS questions and then move on to the second sentence, ask all of the COPS questions, and so on until they finish all of the sentences in the paper. The next step, *take*, instructs students to take their paper to someone if they have questions (or are unsure) about aspects of it or if they just want someone to double-check their paper. Once students are fairly certain that they have caught any mistakes, they move on to the *execute* step. In this step, students write a final copy on a new piece of paper (or they make corrections on a computer and print out a final copy). Before submitting the final copy, students need to complete the last strategy step: *reread* the paper. For students, this means making one final read of the paper to make sure that no errors were missed.

TABLE 8.11	COPS

COPS Strategy Steps

C—Capitalization
O—Overall appearance
P—Punctuation
S—Spelling

RESEARCH EVIDENCE FOR THE ERROR MONITORING STRATEGY. Schumaker & Deshler 2006, Schumaker et al. (1982), and Shannon and Polloway (1993) all conducted research supporting the use of the error monitoring strategy for students with mild disabilities. The studies showed that students improved their ability to detect and/or correct errors in writing.

SUMMARY

This section presented information concerning three areas of writing instruction: handwriting, spelling, and composition. It briefly addressed typical writing instruction in inclusion classrooms in elementary through high school settings. Additionally, this section described effective handwriting, spelling, and composition interventions for students with and without mild disabilities. Readers wishing to learn more about effective research-based instructional practices in these areas may wish to peruse the Internet, libraries, professional journals, and textbooks.

Conclusion

Reading is a multidimensional skill involving numerous factors from phonemic awareness to making sense of what is read. Teachers working with students with disabilities in inclusive classrooms must address not only the content for that particular class or grade level, but also have the skills to teach the students how to access the content as independently as possible. Included herein was an overview of the necessary skills to be taught and for students to master, as well as descriptions of research-based strategies for success.

As with reading, writing is a multifaceted process involving everything from graphomotor or handwriting skills, to spelling and, ultimately, creation of a written product that makes sense and can be used to inform the reader. A myriad of competencies constitute the writing process as delineated in this chapter. For teachers in inclusive classrooms, the strategies offered should serve as a guide for evaluation and instruction of students.

Reading and written-language instruction in the inclusive classroom requires knowledge of instructional practices and research-based strategies that allow all involved to progress successfully through the curriculum. This chapter was designed to provide the reader with a wealth of background information as well as practical ideas to help ensure each student has the opportunity to master skills and content.

References

Anderson, K. M. (2007). Differentiating instruction to include all students. *Preventing School Failure, 51,* 49–54.

Beers, K. (2003). *When kids can't read: What teachers can do: A guide for teachers 6–12.* Portsmouth, NH: Heinemann.

Berry, R. A. W. (2006). Beyond strategies: Teacher beliefs and writing instruction in two primary inclusion classrooms. *Journal of Learning Disabilities, 39,* 11–24.

Bhattacharya, A., & Ehri, L. C. (2004). Graphosyllabic analysis helps adolescent struggling readers read and spell words. *Journal of Learning Disabilities, 37,* 331–348.

Bos, C. S., & Vaughn, S. (2006). *Strategies for teaching students with learning and behavior problems* (6th ed.). Boston: Pearson/Allyn & Bacon.

Boyle, J. R. (2008). Reading strategies for students with mild disabilities. *Intervention in School and Clinic, 44,* 3–9.

Boyle, J. R., & Seibert, T. (1998). The effects of a phonological awareness strategy on the reading skills of elementary students with learning disabilities. *Learning Disabilities: A Multidisciplinary Journal, 8*(3), 145–153.

Bremer, C., Clapper, A., & Deshler, D. (2002). *Improving word identification skills using strategic instruction model (SIM) strategies.* National Center on Secondary Education and Transition, Minneapolis, MN.

Brown, R. (1980). New frontiers in writing assessment. In *Writing Assessment for the 80's.* (pp. 47–61). Washington, D.C.: National Institute of Education. (ERIC Document Reproduction Service No. ED195576)

Bryant, D. P., Smith, D. D., & Bryant, B. R. (2008). *Teaching students with special needs in inclusive classrooms.* Boston: Allyn & Bacon.

Burke, M. (2004). Effects of classwide peer tutoring on the number of words spelled correctly by students with LD. *Intervention in School and Clinic, 39,* 301–304.

Clay, M. M. (1993). *Reading recovery: A guidebook for teachers in training.* Portsmouth, NH: Heinemann.

Cunningham, P. (1980). Applying a compare/contrast process to identifying polysyllabic words. *Journal of Reading Behavior, 12,* 213–23.

Cusumano, C., & Mueller, J. (2007, March/April). *Leadership, 36*(4) 8–10.

Dahl, P. R. (1979). An experimental program for teaching high speed word recognition and comprehension skills. In J. E. Button, T. Lovitt, & T. Rowland (Eds.), *Communications research in learning disabilities and mental retardation* (pp. 33–65). Baltimore, MD: University Park Press.

Deno, S. L., Marston, D., & Mirkin, P. (1982). Valid measurement procedures for continuous evaluation of written expression. *Exceptional Children, 48,* 368–371.

Deshler, D. D., Alley, G. R., Warner, M. M., & Schumaker, J. B. (1981). Instructional practices for promoting skill acquisition and generalization in severely learning disabled adolescents. *Learning Disability Quarterly, 4,* 415–421.

Deshler, D. D., Palincsar, A. S., Biancarosa, G., & Nair, M. (2007). *Informed choices for struggling adolescent readers: A research-based guide to instructional programs and practices.* New York: Carnegie Corporation & the International Reading Association.

Dixon, R. C. (1991). The application of sameness analysis to spelling. *Journal of Learning Disabilities, 24,* 285–291.

Dowhower, S. (1989). Repeated reading: Research into practice. *The Reading Teacher, 42*(7), 502–507.

Ellis, E. S. (1992, 2000). *Learning strategies curriculum: The LINCS vocabulary strategy.* Lawrence, KS: Edge Enterprises.

Ellis, E. S., & Colvert, G. (1996). Writing strategy instruction. In D. D. Deshler, E. S. Ellis, & B. K. Lenz (Eds.), ·*Teaching adolescents with learning disabilities* (2nd ed., pp. 127–207). Denver, CO: Love Publishing Company.

Ellis, E. S. & Graves, A. W. (1990). Teaching rural students with learning disabilities: A paraphrasing strategy to increase comprehension of main ideas. *Rural Special Education Quarterly, 10,* 2–10.

Flower, L. (1985). *Problem-solving strategies for writing.* San Diego: Harcourt.

Friend, M., & Bursuck, W. D. (2006). *Including students with special needs: A practical guide for classroom teachers* (4th ed.). Boston: Allyn & Bacon/Pearson.

Friend, M., & Cook, L. (2007). *Interactions: Collaboration skills for school professionals* (5th ed.). Boston: Pearson/Allyn & Bacon.

Gabrielatos, C. (2003) Conditionals: ELT typology and corpus evidence. Paper presented at the 36th Annual BAAL Meeting, University of Leeds, UK, 4–6 September 2003.

Giangreco, M. F. (2007). Extending inclusive opportunities. *Educational Leadership, 64,* 34–37.

Graham, S., & Freeman, S. (1985). Teaching basic academic skills to learning disabled students: A model of the teaching and learning process. *Journal of Learning Disabilities, 18,* 528–534.

Graham, S., & Freeman, S. (1986). Strategy training and teacher- vs. student-controlled study conditions: Effects on LD students' spelling performance. *Learning Disability Quarterly, 9,* 15–22.

Graham, S., & Harris, K. R. (1988). Instructional recommendations for teaching writing to exceptional students. *Exceptional Children, 54*(6), 506–512.

Graham, S., & Miller, L. (1980). Handwriting research and practice: A unified approach. *Focus on Exceptional Children, 13*(2), 11.

Hammeken, P. A. (2007). *A teacher's guide to inclusive education: 750 strategies for success!* Thousand Oaks, CA: Corwin Press.

Hayes, J. R., & Flower, L. S. (1980). Writing as problem solving. *Visible Language, 14,* 288–299.

Iaquinta, A., & Hipsky, S. (2006). Practical bibliotherapy strategies for the inclusive elementary classroom. *Early Childhood Education Journal, 34*(3), 209–213.

Katims, D. S., & Harris, S. (1997). Improving the reading comprehension of middle school students in inclusive classrooms. *Journal of Adolescent & Adult Literacy, 41,* 116–118.

Kuhn, M. R., & Stahl, S. A. (2003). Fluency: A review of developmental and remedial practices. *Journal of Educational Psychology, 95*(1), 3–21.

Lauterbach, S. L., & Bender, W. M. (1995). Cognitive strategy instruction for reading comprehension: A success for high school freshmen. *High School Journal, 79,* 58–64.

Lenz, B. K., Deshler, D. D., & Kissam, B. R. (2004). *Teaching content to all: Evidence-based inclusive practices in middle and secondary schools.* Boston: Allyn & Bacon/Pearson.

Lenz, B. K., & Hughes, C. A. (1990). A word identification strategy for adolescents with learning disabilities. *Journal of Learning Disabilities, 23,* 149–163.

Lenz, B. K., Schumaker, J. B., Deshler, D. D., & Beals, V. L. (1984). *Learning strategies curriculum: The word identification strategy.* Lawrence, KS: University of Kansas.

MacArthur, C. A., & Graham, S. (1987). Learning disabled students' composing under three methods of text production: Handwriting, word processing, and dictation. *Journal of Special Education, 21,* 22–42.

McNaughton, D., Hughes, C., & Clark, K. (1997). The effect of five proofreading conditions on the spelling performance of college students with learning disabilities. *Journal of Learning Disabilities, 6,* 643–651.

Mortweet, S. L., Utley, C. A., & Walker, D. (1999). Classwide peer tutoring: Teaching students with mild mental retardation in inclusive classrooms. *Exceptional Children, 65,* 524–536.

Murphy, J., Hern, C., Williams, R., & McLaughlin, T. (1990). The effects of the copy, cover, and compare approach in increasing spelling accuracy with learning disabled students. *Contemporary Educational Psychology, 15,* 378–386.

National Reading Panel. (2000). *Reports of the subgroups: National Reading Panel.* Washington, DC: National Institute on Child Health and Development.

O'Conner, R., Jenkins, J., Leicester, N., & Slocum, T. (1992, April). T*eaching phonemic awareness to young children with disabilities: Blending, segmenting, and rhyming.* Paper presented at the American Educational Research Association annual conference in San Francisco.

O'Shea, L., Sindelar, P., & O'Shea, D. (1975). The effects of repeated readings and attentional cues on reading fluency and comprehension. *Journal of Reading Behavior, 17,* 129–141.

Rack, J. P., Snowling, M. J., & Olson, D. (1992). The non-word reading deficit in developmental dyslexia: A review. *Reading Research Quarterly, 27,* 28–53.

Rasinski, T. V. (2000). Speed does matter in reading. *The Reading Teacher, 54,* 146–151.

Rasinski, T. (2003). The fluent reader. New York: Scholastic.

Rasinski, T. (2004). Creating fluent readers. *Educational Leadership, 61,* 46–51.

Salend, S. J. (2008). *Creating inclusive classrooms: Effective and reflective practices* (6th ed.). Upper Saddle River, NJ: Merrill/Pearson.

Samuels, S. J. (1979). The method of repeated readings. *The Reading Teacher, 32,* 403–408.

Samuels, S. J. (2002). Reading fluency: Its development and assessment. In A. E. Farstrup & S. Samuels (Eds.), *What research has to say about reading instruction* (pp. 166–183). Newark, DE: International Reading Association.

Savage, R. (2006, July–September). Effective early reading instruction and inclusion: Some reflections on mutual dependence. *International Journal of Inclusive Education, 10,* 347–361.

Schumaker, J. B., & Deshler, D. D. (2003). Can students with LD become competent writers? *Learning Disability Quarterly, 26*(2), 129–141.

Schumaker, J. B., & Deshler, D. D. (2006). Teaching adolescents to be strategic learners. In D. D. Deshler & J. B. Schumaker (Eds.). *Teaching adolescents with disabilities.* NY: Corwin

Schumaker, J. B., & Sheldon, J. (1985). *The sentence writing strategy.* Lawrence, KS: Edge Enterprises, Inc.

Schumaker, J. B., Denton, P. H., & Deshler, D. D. (1984). *Learning strategies curriculum: The paraphrasing strategy.* Lawrence, KS: The University of Kansas.

Schumaker, J. B., Deshler, D. D., Nolan, S. M., & Alley, G. R. (1994). Learning strategies curriculum: The self-questioning strategy. Lawrence, KS: The University of Kansas.

Schumaker, J. B., Deshler, D. D., Zemitzsch, A., & Warner, M. M. (1993). Learning strategies curriculum: The visual imagery strategy. Lawrence, KS: The University of Kansas.

Schumaker, J. B., Deshler, D. D., Woodruff, S. K., Hock, M. F., Bulgren, J. A., & Lenz, K. B. (2006). Reading strategy interventions: Can literacy outcomes be enhanced for at-risk adolescents? *Teaching Exceptional Children, 38,* 64–68.

Shannon, T. R., & Polloway, E. A. (1993). Promoting error monitoring in middle school students with LD. *Intervention in School and Clinic, 28,* 160–164.

Therrien, W. J. (2004). Fluency and comprehension gains as a result of repeated readings: A meta-analysis. *Remedial and Special Education, 25,* 252–261.

Thurber, D. (1983). *D'Nealian Manuscript—An Aid to Reading Development. ERIC Document Reproduction Service (CS 007 057).* Arlington, VA.

Tomlinson, C. A. (1999). *The differentiated classroom: Responding to the needs of all learners.* Alexandria, VA: Association for Supervision and Curriculum Development.

Tomlinson, C. A. (2001). *How to differentiate instruction in mixed-ability classrooms* (2nd ed.). Alexandria, VA: Association for Supervision and Curriculum Development.

Tomlinson, C. A., & McTighe, J. (2006). *Integrating differentiated instruction & understanding by design.* Alexandria, VA: Association for Supervision and Curriculum Development.

Torgesen, J. K., Morgan, S., & Davis, C. (1992). Effects of two types of phonological awareness training on word learning in kindergarten children. *Journal of Educational Psychology, 84,* 364–370.

http://specialed.about.com/od/literacy/a/whycursive.htm

Woodruff, Deshler, and Schumaker (2002, as cited by Schumaker et al., 2006).

9

Cases About Teaching Reading Skills in Inclusive Classrooms

CASE 1

Fixing the Fluency of Frankie

Frankie Wilson is a student in Sandy Zachariah's fifth-grade class. Frankie was identified 2 years ago as having a learning disability (LD) because of poor reading skills. Sandy collaborates with Penny Mason, the LD teacher, during language arts and science classes. Sandy and Penny have been collaborating for about 3 years and are one of the best collaborative teaching pairs in the school. They frequently co-plan lessons prior to teaching them and meet the needs of all students in the inclusion classroom.

Frankie was first identified 2 years ago when he was evaluated for eligibility for special education because of his poor reading skills. In particular, on the Woodcock Reading Mastery Test–Revised, Frankie did poorly on the subtests Word Attack, Word Comprehension, and Passage Comprehension. Since being identified, he has received intense one-on-one from Penny and, as a result, has been able to remain in the fifth-grade class. During a recent reading activity, students were reading the story *Diary of a Wimpy Kid* by Jeff Kinney. As Frankie was reading, Sandy kept track of his miscues. In particular, on one page, he made six miscues. He said *horse* for *house*, *complementing* for *complaining*, *choose* for *chores*, *stuck* for *struck*, *expanded* for *explained*, and *patent* for *patient*. Unfortunately, as Frankie read, the other students in the class rolled their eyes and made faces when he read words incorrectly. When Frankie finished reading the paragraph, he exclaimed, "finally finished!" Reading is simply a struggle for Frankie and he often apologizes for reading so poorly. During DEAR (Drop Everything And Read) time, Frankie raises his hand and asks his teachers for help reading words or answering questions.

It is quite evident that Frankie's word attack problems interfere with his comprehension. Frequently, Frankie's mind drifts off when listening to other students read, and when asked questions about what was just read, Frankie can't answer them. In terms of his own reading comprehension, he seems to be able to answer literal comprehension questions, but has great difficulty answering higher level inferential comprehension questions. When he reads aloud, his "stop and go" reading is typical for a disfluent reader. Like other students who lack fluency, when Frankie comes across an unknown word, he uses word attack skills to try to pronounce it, and in the process, loses comprehension of what he read prior to the unknown word.

To help address his disfluency, Penny reviews vocabulary before and after reading and uses repeated readings. Interestingly, Frankie will often get most of the vocabulary words correct while reading aloud, yet misses easier sight words. For Frankie, some days are good with few errors, yet other days he struggles and misses quite a few words, as is typical with students who have word attack and fluency problems. Theses reading problems are not restricted to reading; in other content-area classes, such as science and social studies, Frankie also struggles while reading worksheets or his textbooks. These problems have resulted in lower grades in these subjects.

Discussion Questions

1. From the case, what skill(s) would you target for remediation? Or what skill(s) would you target for further assessment?
2. In the classroom, choose a skill area, and decide what modifications and/or supports could be used to help Frankie.
3. Outside the fifth-grade classroom, choose a skill area, and decide what remedial technique(s) and/or strategy(ies) could be taught to him to strengthen a weak skill area(s).
4. If you taught Frankie a student strategy or technique outside of the inclusion classroom, what could you do to ensure that it generalized to his classes or other settings?
5. How would you monitor his progress on the skill(s)? Describe how and when you would monitor progress.

CASE 2

Trina Needs Help!

Rita Wilson is a first-grade teacher in an inclusion classroom at Moonstruck Elementary School in North Carolina and works with Tracy Parsons, the special education inclusion teacher. Both teachers are still getting used to each other because both are new to the inclusion room. This particular inclusion classroom is comprises a heterogeneous mix of gifted, above-average, and average students with three students who are developmentally delayed, one student labeled as serious emotional disturbance (ED), and two students who qualified under the other health impaired (OHI) category because of attention deficit hyperactivity disorder (ADHD). The school has three other inclusion classes, and the principal would like each grade level to have at least one inclusion class. Within each class, students are not removed for special education services. The principal decided early on that all skills and specialized techniques should be taught to special education children within the inclusion classroom.

Trina is the only child of Kristen and Lucas Costas. Her parents first noticed problems when she was in preschool. Sent to Moon River Preschool because of its reputation in the community as a school that would prepare students with academic skills for public schools, Trina attended all-day sessions. Her teachers first noticed problems because of her inability to sit and pay attention. Her learning problems became apparent as she struggled to learn phonics and could not correctly say or write her letters. In addition to these problems, her speech was difficult to understand for both the teachers and other children. She has quite a few articulation errors that include deletion of consonant sounds in blends and clusters (*tuck* for *truck*) and substitution of consonants (*hop* for *stop*). Of course, these academic problems were exacerbated by her inattention and hyperactivity. These problems persisted through kindergarten, and the parents hoped that retaining her for 1 year would remediate the situation. Initially, it seemed to be a good idea, but as time passed, Trina continued to exhibit learning problems.

After undergoing some educational testing early in the school year, Trina was identified as having ADHD under the OHI category and has been the newest member of the "inclusion six" (the group with disabilities) in the class. Trina's main academic difficulties continue to occur in reading; however, her inattention and hyperactivity also affect other academic areas. In reading, her biggest weakness is with phonological awareness. Trina knows her initial letter sounds, but often cannot blend sounds together or makes mistakes with words with similar spelling (e.g., *hot* for *hat*). Her parents also noticed that Trina has difficulty completing seatwork, and parents in the neighborhood often send Trina home because she annoys them.

Unfortunately for Trina, she is one of the lowest-achieving students in the lowest-achieving reading group. Despite receiving extra "booster" sessions in reading, Trina still has difficulty reading sight words. For example, one day when students were playing the "Change the Word" game, Trina performed quite poorly. In this game, the teacher gives students a word (e.g., *hot*) and three phonemes (e.g., *p, n, c*). Students then have to replace the first phoneme in *hot* using one of the three given phonemes to form new words—*pot, not*, and *cot*. Although other students in her group are capable of completing this activity, Trina cannot form new words without teacher assistance.

Later that day as students left to go home, Rita and Tracy met privately and discussed Trina's problems with phonemic awareness. Rita mentioned that maybe Trina has auditory discrimination problems, and Tracy added that maybe they should refer her to speech and language services. Rita and Tracy then sat down and began to plan out the following day's lesson, which involved a rhyming game. Tracy wondered aloud if Trina would be able to successfully complete the activity.

Discussion Questions

1. From the case, what skill(s) would you target for remediation? Or what skill(s) would you target for further assessment?
2. In the inclusion class, choose a skill area, and decide what modifications and/or supports could be used to help Trina.
3. Outside of the inclusion class, choose a skill area, and decide what remedial technique(s) and/or strategy(ies) could be taught to her to strengthen a weak skill area(s).
4. If you taught Trina a student strategy or technique outside of the inclusion classroom, what could you do to ensure that it generalized to her classes or other settings?
5. How would you monitor her progress on the skill(s)? Describe how and when you would monitor progress.
6. What other phonological awareness activities or language activities would be appropriate for Trina?

CASE 3

Keeping Ruby Current

Ruby is a junior at Howell Senior High School. Ruby's homeroom teacher is Larry Kingman. Mr. Kingman teaches the current events class most of the morning and history in the afternoons. In current events, students discuss everyday news events. Mr. Kingman requires his students to read stories from the newspaper and *Newsweek* magazine prior to coming to class. Class discussion then centers on current news events from these materials. Because a presidential election is coming up in a few months, most of their discussions have been about candidates and their views.

Mr. Kingman has worked at Howell for 15 years and has only recently begun collaborating with the new special education teacher, Suzie Wetzman. Prior to that he and Terry Guntherson, the former special education teacher, collaborated. In his collaborative classes, Mr. Kingman has taught students with a variety of disabilities. However, it has often been difficult getting these students involved in discussions about current events because, for many, their poor reading skills prevent them from learning and remembering information that they read. In addition, Mr. Kingman has left the specialized instruction to the special education teacher. In most cases, he rarely diverts from a discussion format.

For Ruby, learning has been tough. Since being labeled ED in third grade, she has always been in classes for students with disabilities and has always struggled to learn new content and knowledge. Her emotional problems, anxiety, and depression, with resultant behavioral problems, have interfered with her learning. Despite these problems, her high IQ has kept her academically competitive in mainstream classes, in her younger days, and inclusion classes, more recently. Although she does have serious emotional problems, many of her teachers believe that she also has LD, particularly in the area of reading. To complicate matters, her psychotropic medications often leave her tired, further complicating her learning problems. Now in 11th grade, Ruby struggles with many of her reading assignments.

Despite her disability, Ruby has set high goals. She wants to attend Ben Franklin Community College (BFCC) to become a nurse's assistant. Ben Franklin offers a 2-year program and also has a Disability Services Center available for students with disabilities. Ruby is currently taking some college prep courses—current events, for example—to prepare her for college. Despite her borderline grades in some content classes, she excels in math and is often one of the top students in those classes.

Ruby's problems in her current events class stem from her inability to understand her reading assignments. In particular, she has a difficult time reading articles that use vocabulary beyond her comprehension. She often becomes frustrated and then either quits reading the materials or becomes angry and behaves inappropriately. Similarly, she also has problems reading her chemistry book. Her poor completion of reading assignments often puts her in jeopardy of failing classes. Her teachers have tried to help compensate for her reading problems by providing her with books on tape, but she refuses to use these. She claims that she will never be ready for college if she has to use taped books.

During one recent co-planning session, Mr. Kingman and Mrs. Wetzman discussed Ruby's problems. Mrs. Wetzman mentions her problems and offers to brainstorm with Mr. Kingman. "Hey, Larry," she starts. "Ruby really needs some help with her reading assignments. What would you think about sending home some scripted notes of the articles?" Mr. Kingman hesitant about taking on more work, responds, "Well, Suzie, the last time we tried modifying her assignments, she really didn't take advantage of it." "Yeah, but," Mrs. Wetzman continues, "she needs to pass as many courses as possible if she has any hopes of going to BFCC." Mr. Kingman remains quiet because he feels that he has given Ruby enough chances. Then he speaks: "If you develop these 'scripted notes,' then go ahead. But this year, I am already overwhelmed with the increased documentation that I have to do for the SFS [Standards For Success] and the new lesson plans that old man Varina (the new principal) has us doing." Mrs. Wetzman did not quite get the support that she wanted, but even half-hearted support was better than none, she thought. "Okay, I understand," she replied. She didn't want to push the conversation further, but thought she had better ask now. "Is there anything else that we could do to improve her grades in your class on the reading assignments?" Mr. Kingman exhausted from the long day, just gave her a backward glance as he packed up his materials to go home.

Discussion Questions

1. From the case, what skill(s) would you target for remediation? Or what skill(s) would you target for further assessment?
2. In the inclusion class, choose a skill area, and decide what modifications and/or supports could be used to help Ruby.
3. Outside of the inclusion class, choose a skill area, and decide what remedial technique(s)/strategy(ies) could be taught to her to strengthen a weak skill area(s).
4. If you taught Ruby a strategy or technique outside of the inclusion classroom, what could you do to ensure that it would be generalized to her classes or other settings?
5. How would you monitor student progress on the skill(s)? Describe how and when you would monitor progress.
6. Are there other accommodations that should be used for Ruby? Why or why not?

CASE 4

Smack You Upside Your Head!

As Gale read aloud from her sixth-grade social studies textbook at Saxton Elementary School, other students giggled as she tripped over words like *dilapidated* and *Ganges*. Gale was reading the chapter on India, which described the country and its people. Paul Rossini, the sixth-grade teacher, put off calling on Gale because he knew she struggled at reading, yet he wanted to treat all of his students in a similar fashion. When Gale came to a word that she couldn't pronounce, Mr. Rossini would pronounce it with her. Kelly Kapinski, the LD inclusion teacher, would also assist her, but she knew the textbook was written above Gale's comprehension level.

After her fifth mistake in the first three sentences, Gale's classmate, Forrest, shook his head and commented, "Dag girl, you need help." Upon seeing this, Mr. Rossini signaled to Forrest to quiet down. Meanwhile, Gale hit him with her pencil and said, "Boy, shut your mouth, or I'll smack you upside your head!" Gale was used to hearing comments like these from other students when she read. She knew that she had trouble reading and often did her best to avoid being called on to read aloud. Upon finishing the last few words, Mr. Rossini let out a "whew." It was exhausting to watch her read aloud. "Okay, Gale, what can you tell me about the Ganges River?" Gale looked up wearing a mysterious frown on her face and replied, "I don't know." Mr. Rossini pointed to another student in the class who answered the question. Kelly looked on, feeling helpless. She did not want to interfere with Mr. Rossini, but she also wanted to help Gale.

After class as students were filing out the door, Mr. Rossini motioned for Kelly to come over to him, and he remarked, "Kelly, I feel bad for Gale, but what can I do?" Mrs. Kapinski was also stymied by Gale's reading troubles and replied that she would have to think about it. She knew that part of the problem was the social studies textbook used in his class; the textbook was too difficult for the students and was written at an eighth-grade readability level. Even nondisabled students had a difficult time pronouncing certain vocabulary words and comprehending parts of it. But Mr. Rossini loved it. He loved the illustrations and diagrams. Besides, it was a perfect fit with the sixth-grade social studies standards set by the state.

As Mrs. Kapinski gathered her materials, she said to Mr. Rossini, "Let's try to get together tomorrow to discuss how we could help students during reading, especially for Gale and Willie." "Willie?" Mr. Rossini said with a surprised look on his face. "What's wrong with him?" "Haven't you noticed that whenever he reads the textbook, he too has a difficult time understanding what was read and a tough time with the vocabulary?" responded Mrs. Kapinski. "I guess," said Mr. Rossini as he directed students into his next class. "Don't you think that you can just pull them aside and spend more time on their reading skills?"

Before Mrs. Kapinski could respond, Mr. Rossini continued, "If you wanted to, you could probably pull them out of my class . . . to spend more time on reading." "Ah, it's interesting you mention that because 'gradewise,' they both seem to be holding her own—earning Cs on quizzes," Mrs. Kapinski replied. Mr. Rossini really felt that students who had problems keeping up in his class should not be pulled for additional instruction. However, in the past year, he had asked Mrs. Kapinski to pull three students with special needs from his other classes and made a formal referral for one other student.

Feeling frustrated and hurried for time, Mrs. Kapinski tried to cut to the chase and said, "Look Paul, maybe you could modify your teaching style so that kids like Gale and Willie don't have to read aloud." "The problem isn't with the way I teach, it's with their reading skills," Mr. Rossini shot back. "Paul, you know that they have reading problems that, in all likelihood, will never be fully remediated, but I'll look over their records and try to come up with some ideas," Mrs. Kapinski said walking backward down the hall. As she headed toward the office doors, she looked back to see Mr. Rossini still standing in the same spot, shaking his head in disbelief. "I'm not quite sure what he wants me to do," she said to herself.

As she pulled the files for both Gale and Willie, Mrs. Kapinski saw how thin they both were and remembered that new students, particularly transferees, had not yet accumulated a lot of documentation. As she poured herself a cup of coffee and sat down at the table, she recalled in a quiet voice, "That's right, Gale and Willie transferred here 6 weeks ago from the same school, Deer Park Elementary." Deer Park was located in the affluent end of town, far away from the problems of city life at Saxton Elementary. Mrs. Kapinski knew that Deer Park often had a higher referral rate for students with LD because their district had more money to address the learning problems of students, especially students with mild learning problems. She had reviewed both students' records when they first arrived at Saxton and felt confident that they would survive in the sixth-grade inclusion class, with minor services. Mrs. Kapinski had met with other teachers at Saxton who reported only minor reading problems with Willie and Gale. In fact, most reported that both had been earning Bs and Cs on tests and quizzes.

When Mrs. Kapinski came across the test scores, she saw that both students had earned overall reading scores in about the 40th to 50th percentile. "Ah, here it is. Woodcock Reading Mastery Test—overall score is a 4.3 grade equivalent for Gale and 4.8 for Willie. Not too bad," she thought. As she examined their records further, she noticed that both did have similar problems with reading comprehension, earning only grade equivalent scores of 4.0 for Gale and 4.2 for Willie (6 months ago). "Now I remember. There were some minor problems with comprehension that could be addressed," Mrs. Kapinski thought to herself. "Word attack looks better— a grade equivalent score of 4.7 for Gale and 4.9 for Willie," she commented to herself. Finally, Mrs. Kapinski saw some notes scribbled in their folders about "problems with gaining information from textbooks and short stories" and inability "to complete assignments independently" written about both of them by former teachers.

The next day before students arrived, Mrs. Kapinski caught up with Mr. Rossini, who was in the faculty lounge munching on donuts and drinking coffee. "Paul, I'm glad I caught up with you. I reviewed their records last night and saw that they both have similar problems with vocabulary and comprehension. Do you think we could come up with modifications in the way they read?" Mr. Rossini thought for a minute and then said, "Yeah, go on. What do you have in mind?"

Discussion Questions

1. From the case, what skill(s) would you target for remediation? Or what skill(s) would you target for further assessment?
2. In the inclusion class, choose a skill area, and decide what modifications and/or supports could be used to help Willie and Gale.
3. Outside of the inclusion class, choose a skill area, and decide what remedial technique(s)/strategy(ies) could be taught to them to strengthen a weak skill area(s).
4. If you taught these students a strategy or technique outside of the inclusion classroom, what could you do to ensure that it generalized to their classes or other settings?
5. How would you monitor students' progress on the skill(s)? Describe how and when you would monitor progress.
6. If teachers used textbooks written a level or two above students' comprehension, what could you do to assist them with reading problems? Explain specific remediation techniques or accommodations that could be used.

CASE 5

Jumpin' Judy

As Judy sat in her group reading the story "The Sly Fox," she was very fidgety. She bit her nails and nibbled at the skin on her fingers. She knew that it would soon be her time to read aloud and she hated it. Judy had trouble reading. She was quite clever and has always found ways to avoid it, but today she would not get a reprieve. "Judy, your turn," Mrs. Cronwell said. Judy jumped when she heard her name called. She was too busy watching her friend Sasha, who was in the back of the room dancing around. Noticing this, Mrs. Cronwell yelled out, "Sasha, stop fooling around and sit down." Again, Mrs. Cronwell signaled to Judy to read by saying, "Judy . . . let's go, get reading." Judy looked at Kyle's basal reader to see what page and line he was on. Mrs. Cronwell was stumbling who was not getting agitated, prompted Judy by saying, "Start with 'Timmy jumped.'" "Timmy," Judy began reading, "jump when he saw the moose." Oh, that's not *moose,* it's *mmmouse,*" said Judy as she sounded out the word. She continued, "The mouse sat up and carry clamed her paws. . . ." Mrs. Cronwell interrupted and corrected her: "The mouse sat up and carefully cleaned her paws. Keep going," Mrs. Cronwell urged Judy. Judy gave a big sigh and continued with, "She looked differed from most other kinds of mouses." Again, Mrs. Cronwell allowed her to finish the sentence before repeating it correctly: "She looked different from most other kinds of mice." This continued until Mrs. Cronwell finally called on another student.

Keisha Cronwell is the third-grade teacher. She works with Yolanda Lincoln, the special education teacher. Both teachers have been teaching collaboratively during language arts for the past 3 years. They decided that it was best to break down into four reading groups to teach the varying levels of third graders. "This group [of third graders] is like no other," Mrs. Cronwell would frequently comment when referring to the differing levels of reading skills. Judy is in the lowest group and often needs the most attention. She is scheduled to go through the formal testing process to see if she qualifies for special education services. Mrs. Lincoln feels certain that

Judy will qualify for LD, yet Mrs. Cronwell suspects that Judy might only be borderline and therefore may not qualify. Even though the three other students in the class with LD are in higher reading groups and much better readers than Judy, Mrs. Cronwell feels that Judy still might not qualify because she did well in many other academic areas.

As Mrs. Cronwell entered the room after finishing bus duty, the first words from her mouth were, "What are we going to do with that Judy if she doesn't qualify for LD services?" "Do we send her to the reading specialist, or is she considered 'one of ours' because you're special ed?" Mrs. Lincoln looked up from her papers and just shrugged. "Even if she does qualify, they probably won't move her from our room," Mrs. Lincoln remarked. "This kid can read words from the word list well, but she just can't read any of our stories fluently. Do you think I should move her down to a lower reader?" Mrs. Cronwell asked. Mrs. Lincoln just shrugged. She, too, was not quite certain what else to do with Judy.

Mrs. Lincoln has tried working one-on-one with Judy during reading, but nothing seems to work. Judy is the type of child who has processing problems. It is true that she can read most words in isolation, but she has poor fluency and poor comprehension. In addition to these problems, Judy hates to read. She frequently comments to her teachers how much she dislikes it and how it is a skill that she really doesn't need. Judy has splintered skills in reading and other subject areas. For some reason, she does well in phonological awareness, but poorly in word attack and vocabulary. Mrs. Lincoln and Mrs. Cronwell both tried sight words and word walls with Judy, but she still has problems reading fluently.

In addition to reading problems, her teachers also considered that Judy might have attention problems. Judy often has trouble keeping her mind on the task at hand. She is frequently off task, talking to other students or simply watching others in the class, particularly during independent seatwork. Mrs. Cronwell and Mrs. Lincoln have often debated whether these are avoidance behaviors or attention problems.

Discussion Questions

1. From the case, what skill(s) would you target for remediation? Or what skill(s) would you target for further assessment?
2. In the classroom, choose a skill area, and decide what modifications and/or supports could be used to help Judy.
3. Outside of the inclusion class, choose a skill area, and decide what remedial technique(s) and/or strategy(ies) could be taught to her to strengthen a weak skill area(s).
4. If you taught this student a strategy or technique outside of the inclusion classroom, what could you do to ensure that it generalized to her classes or other settings?
5. How would you monitor progress on the skill(s)? Describe how and when you would monitor progress.

10

Cases About Teaching Written Language Skills in Inclusive Classrooms

CASE 1

Who Should Take the Lead in Strategy Instruction?

Jasmine Jones is in her fourth year of teaching students with disabilities at the middle-school level. She works as the special education teacher who supports students receiving instruction in language arts in an inclusive model. This year, Jasmine will be working with four general education teachers in the sixth grade. Jasmine is happy about this assignment because she has worked with all of these teachers before. She is also excited to try out some of the strategies she learned over the summer.

During preschool, Jasmine sets up time to meet and plan with the sixth-grade language arts teachers. She wants to incorporate learning strategies into general instructional routines as well as a variety of organizational strategies to support all of the students' learning. Jasmine is prepared to support her suggestions with the research she learned over the summer and expects her colleagues to agree with her ideas.

Jasmine's planning meeting with her sixth-grade language arts team goes as she expects. Melissa Woods, the newest teacher on the team, agrees to do anything Jasmine recommends. John Elliott, the veteran teacher, agrees to "let" Jasmine have 20 minutes each day to teach and support the use of learning strategies in his class. Pam Jordan, certified in both English and special education, welcomes Jasmine's ideas for incorporating learning strategies and is excited about the possibility of updating her skills. Finally, Walter Phelps, a third-year teacher, agrees as well, as long as Jasmine takes the lead on this piece of instruction and planning.

The school year begins and the team decides to target organizational strategies first. They believe that organization is a priority area for all of the sixth-grade students whether or not they have a disability. The teachers agree to require all of their students to keep and maintain a three-ring binder for English language arts. The binder will be organized into sections and checked by either Jasmine or the general education classroom teacher every 2 weeks. Students will receive points during these checks, which over the grading period will be equivalent to one test grade.

After this system is established, Jasmine and the team will determine how they will support each student's writing skills.

Writing skills, along with reading proficiency, are a major focus in sixth grade. The teachers realize that each year their incoming sixth-grade students possess mixed abilities in English Language Arts. Even some of the gifted students seem to have a weak foundation in writing. Since Jasmine attended professional development in the Kansas Strategic Instruction Model (SIM) over the summer, the teachers want to determine the needs of their students so that they may in turn select the appropriate writing strategy to teach. Jasmine believes that they will most likely need to begin with *Proficiency in Sentence Writing*, but plans to wait to make this collective decision until after the writing assessments are completed.

The first month of school goes relatively smoothly for the group. The binder system for keeping students organized is established, and multiple writing assessments are given and scored. The teachers meet as a whole group to discuss common strengths and weaknesses of their students in the area of writing. They discover to no one's surprise that they will need to differentiate instruction in writing. Some of the students have really weak writing skills, and many are hesitant to write. The teachers decide to use the *Proficiency in Sentence Writing* strategy with Jasmine as the lead instructor and the other teachers as supporting instructors. Before they begin, Jasmine reviews the components of the strategy with her team and makes copies of the sentence-writing formulas for everyone. The teachers then practice as a small group teaching the strategy to each other. After this, they are ready to begin instruction with their students. Everyone, except John, is onboard with this plan. He wants Jasmine to take responsibility for strategy instruction, as this is not his area. She is the special education teacher. Jasmine hopes that once she gets going with the strategy and John sees how well it works, he will be more supportive.

One month later, Jasmine reflects on how things are going with writing. She is pleased to see that most of her students seem to have grasped the basic formulas for sentence writing. They apply these strategies when directed, and some even apply them without being prompted. Jasmine continues to take the lead on strategy instruction although Melissa, Pam, and Walter have started in a more active role. John is still not really onboard, but does seem happy with the progress students are making in their writing. Jasmine wonders what she can do to get John more actively involved in strategy instruction.

Discussion Questions

1. The teachers decide to use three-ring binders and binder checks as an organizational system for their students with and without disabilities. The binder checks will be equivalent to one test grade per grading period. Do you believe that this system is appropriate? Why or why not?
2. Jasmine convinces her sixth-grade team to use the *Proficiency in Sentence Writing* strategy. Which group of students would you target for instruction on this strategy, and why?
3. If you were going to work in an inclusive classroom, how would you set up strategy instruction?
4. It appears from the case study that Jasmine is going to teach sentence writing strategy to the whole group and receive support from everyone except John. What would you do to get John to support this strategy instruction?
5. What can special educators do to change the mindset of general educators concerning content area instruction and the responsibility for providing instruction to students with disabilities in the regular classroom?

CASE 2

Cursive Handwriting: The Nightmare

Ethel Perry has been a third-grade teacher at Winter Greene Elementary School for 22 years. During these years, she has witnessed many changes in education. One of the most noteworthy changes has been how her school meets the needs of struggling learners. Gone are the days when these children are kept in special classes and her school groups children based on levels of academic performance. Ethel misses the old days, but realizes that she needs to accept the new mandates or leave teaching before she gets her 30 years in.

Sunshine March is a recent college graduate with a degree in special education. She interviewed at Winter Greene Elementary School shortly after graduation and got a position as an inclusion teacher for third and fourth grade. Sunshine is excited about beginning her first year of teaching and hopes that the teachers she will work with at Winter Greene will welcome her. Sunshine learned about inclusion during her program at college, but has never taught in this model of instruction. She is a little nervous about it, but thinks that it will be easier than doing resource or self-contained. She's happy that she will have other teachers to support her during her first year of teaching rather than being solely responsible for student learning.

When preschool begins, Sunshine gets to meet the teachers with whom she will be working. She discovers that she will work with a very experienced teacher, Ethel, and a new teacher, Bryan Marshall. Sunshine is a little intimated by Ethel. She seems somewhat rigid and is not very happy about the news that her class will be the third-grade inclusion class this year. Bryan, on the other hand, seems like he will be a lot of fun to teach with. He is just as excited about teaching as Sunshine is and glad that he will have someone in his room to help out.

During preschool, Sunshine has some time to figure out which students receiving special education services she will support in her inclusion classes. She makes copies of her students' individualized education plans (IEPs) and reads their confidential files. She talks to the teachers of the students who were at Winter Greene last year and thinks about grouping for instruction. She also attempts to squeeze in time to plan with Ethel and Bryan. In addition, Sunshine familiarizes herself with the third- and fourth-grade curriculum. She realizes during this process that a week is a very short amount of time to get ready for students, and she hopes that she's ready.

School begins and Sunshine quickly realizes what her role is going to be in Ethel's classroom. Ethel seems to view her as a second set of hands and treats her like she is a paraprofessional, not a teacher. Because Sunshine is new and still learning the third-grade curriculum, she doesn't say anything. She does what Ethel asks her to do and pretty much keeps her mouth shut. Sunshine and Ethel meet after school on Thursdays so that Ethel can tell Sunshine what she will be teaching the next week. After a few weeks, Sunshine begins to wonder if Ethel uses recycled lesson plans and just updates the books based on what's available in her classroom at the time. Everything seems so programmed, boring, and not differentiated to meet the needs of all of the students. Ethel doesn't believe in dynamic grouping for instruction. Actually, she doesn't like grouping for instruction at all. She teaches whole group for everything. If students don't get a concept, Ethel just keeps on going. Sunshine is not happy about the situation, but is at a loss of what to do.

The atmosphere in Bryan's classroom is like night and day from Ethel's. Bryan likes teaching most content in small groups. He pretests his students before introducing new content, and then creates groups accordingly. If students don't understand what he is trying to teach them, he tries another way of teaching. His classroom is fun to be in and the students respond accordingly. He values Sunshine's input, and they plan all student instruction together. They take turns leading whole group instruction and rotate between groups for small group instruction. Bryan feels that it is essential that he know how all of his students are doing and doesn't want his classroom to be a class within a class when Sunshine is there to support inclusion.

About halfway into the first grading period, Ethel tells Sunshine that she will be introducing cursive handwriting to "their" class. Ethel likes teaching cursive handwriting and takes great pride in her students going to fourth grade with this skill. Sunshine is concerned about beginning this now. She doesn't understand how the students who are struggling with writing in manuscript and reading manuscript are going to make the leap to writing and reading text in cursive. She relays this concern to Ethel, who dismisses her concern. Sunshine is not happy!

Ethel begins cursive writing instruction by introducing five letters of the alphabet at a time, upper- and lowercase. She models writing each letter and then directs students to write the letters five times each until mastery is achieved or time runs out. After only 6 days, all of the letters of the alphabet have been introduced, so Ethel models how to write words in cursive writing. She uses words from the spelling curriculum and informs the students that they will be expected to write and/or spell their spelling words on the weekly tests in cursive handwriting. This announcement is met with many groans. Sunshine is beside herself. The handful of students receiving inclusive support is not showing success with this model of instruction. There are many issues: They can't read the words in manuscript, they can't spell the words in manuscript, they are having trouble forming the letters of the alphabet in cursive and connecting letters appropriately in cursive, and they are totally frustrated. Sunshine feels that they are being set up to fail. She tries speaking with Ethel again about this issue and is told that this is the way that she has always taught cursive writing and that she is not going to change now. Sunshine doesn't know what to do or who to talk to about this situation, but she knows she has to do something.

Discussion Questions

1. Sunshine is beginning her first year as a special education teacher. She will be working with Ethel, a veteran teacher who is not happy to discover that her classroom will be the inclusion class for third grade. If you were in this situation, what would you do?
2. If you were the inclusion teacher working with Ethel, how would you address her using you as a paraprofessional? How would you deal with the fact that she teaches everything whole group and just keeps on going when students don't learn a concept?
3. When Ethel decides to introduce cursive handwriting and dismisses Sunshine's concerns, what do you think that Sunshine should have done?
4. Do you believe that it is appropriate to teach cursive handwriting to students who are still learning to form and read letters in manuscript? Why or why not?
5. If you were to teach cursive handwriting to students in third grade, what pacing for instruction would you use? How would you support writing and reading in cursive?
6. What do you think that Sunshine should do to address the issue with Ethel?
7. Compare and contrast the teaching situation and learning environment in Ethel and Bryan's classrooms.

CASE 3

Spelling the Fernald Way

Dale Skiles is a special education teacher who has taught in resource and self-contained models of instruction for several years. This year she is going to try teaching students with mild disabilities in an inclusion classroom in second and fifth grades. Dale is happy about the change and looks forward to the new experience. Because she has worked at her school for five years, she feels that she has a good idea of which teachers she will have a good working relationship with when co-teaching. Dale's principal has a lot of respect for her, and has given her the responsibility for deciding which second- and fifth-grade classroom teachers will be doing inclusion this year.

Before meeting with the second- and fifth-grade teachers, Dale meets with the special education coordinator of her school. They determine how many students will need inclusive services this year in second and fifth grade. They review their individual education programs and confidential files so that they may match students to teachers. After this process is completed, Dale sets up a meeting with the teachers who will be teaching second and fifth grades. She does this so that she will have buy-in from the teachers and so that the teachers will feel as though they have a choice in the process. At the meeting, it is decided that Dale will work with Sally Wilson, a second-grade teacher, and Bonnie Sullivan, a fifth-grade teacher. Sally and Bonnie have worked with Dale in the past and have a good relationship with her.

Once this decision is made, Dale sets up other appointments to meet individually with Sally and Bonnie. She wants to meet with them both so that they may begin the school year on the same page. Dale will be supporting each teacher in the area of language arts instruction. She will not only teach reading skills but also writing. The school district wants to see a significant increase in test scores in the area of writing this year.

Dale, Sally, and Bonnie collectively decide that they want to emphasize vocabulary, spelling, and writing in context. They wish to do this by selecting important grade-level vocabulary from literature they will be reading and then infusing spelling and writing across the content areas. The teachers realize that they will need to receive permission from the school's principal to abandon the stand-alone spelling book that the school uses. They believe that if they can support their argument for this approach with the research literature on reading, spelling, and writing that their principal will agree with their recommendation. They are tired of teaching spelling in isolation and don't see the benefit of doing so. The teachers meet with the principal, present their instructional plan with its rationale, and receive permission to proceed.

The next step in incorporating their instruction plan is to first determine which piece of literature to begin the school year with and what vocabulary to emphasize. Dale and Sally and Dale and Bonnie meet to decide on where to begin. Each team reviews the piece of literature selected and then examines how it fits into the curriculum as a whole. They plan how they can support vocabulary development, spelling, and writing across each curriculum area. Dale recommends that they use Fernald's multisensory approach to spelling, modifying the approach slightly. She explains that this approach involves having the teacher writing and saying a word while students watch and listen. Depending on the word, teachers may provide a definition or elicit definitions from students. Next, students trace the word while simultaneously saying it (this step is optional for older children). Then students copy or write the word while saying it. Finally, the word is written from memory. If students spell the word incorrectly, the step where students copy and/or write while saying the word is repeated. If the word is

Explicit Instruction

spelled correctly, students place it in individual student word boxes for later use in writing. Dale recommends that teachers pretest students on words in their reading and spelling vocabulary prior to using the Fernald method. She states that this will save time teaching students to read and spell words already in their repertoire. It will also allow for differentiation of instruction. The group agrees to try this approach. They also agree to emphasize meaning and relevance and to promote multiple opportunities for practice in using spelling words across the content areas.

The new school year begins and along with it the partnerships between Dale, Sally, and Bonnie. At first, Dale models use of the modified Fernald method for teaching students to spell new words, and then later, all of the teachers use the system. They find that the method supports reading, spelling, vocabulary development, and writing as well as allowing for individualized instruction. They are pleased, and their students are all making adequate progress.

Discussion Questions

1. Describe the steps that Dale takes to develop a positive inclusion experience for the teachers working in second and fifth grades.
2. What would you do if you were to approach grade-level teachers about doing inclusion, and no one wanted to do it?
3. If you are required to use a stand-alone textbook for spelling, how would you work to incorporate these words across students' reading, writing, and content-area instruction?
4. The Fernald method for teaching spelling uses multiple modalities. If you were to use this method, would you use it as described, or would you modify the method? Why?
5. What suggestions, if any, would you give to Dale, Sally, and Bonnie concerning spelling instruction for students with and without disabilities?

CASE 4

Assistive Technology: Is It the Answer?

Justin Armstrong, a 10th-grade English teacher, works with Beth Warren, a special education teacher, at Valley High School. This is the third year that Justin and Beth have worked together to provide inclusion services to students with disabilities. They have a good relationship that has grown even better over the years. Justin and Beth work as a team. They take turns leading instruction and plan extensively together. On occasion they attend professional conferences together to enhance their teaching techniques and to build their individual knowledge base concerning instructional practices for students with and without special needs.

Justin and Beth teach four periods of English per day with two scheduled planning periods. They try to meet daily to plan instruction, but sometimes meet less than this due to IEP meetings and/or competing demands on their time. They have about 25 students in each class, with approximately three to five students receiving special education support services in each. The students who are eligible for special education services mainly have mild disabilities that include learning disabilities, emotional/behavioral disorders, attention deficit with and without hyperactivity, Asperger syndrome, and traumatic brain injury. Each student brings different strengths and needs to the classroom. Justin and Beth work hard to address the strengths and needs of all of their students by differentiating instruction.

Like every teacher, Justin and Beth lose and receive students throughout the school year. Sometimes they experience a shift in the number of students receiving inclusion services by class. This year, Justin and Beth discover that they will get a student named Aaron in their second period English class. The guidance counselor, Brandy Wellington, has little information to provide before Aaron is placed in their class. Aaron is moving to Valley High School from a school located out of state. His mother registered him at Valley High the day before he is scheduled to begin school and didn't have a copy of his current IEP. She told Brandy that Aaron has a neurological disorder with hemiparesis. He functions slightly below grade level in reading and writing. With accommodations, he is at grade level in his content-area classes. Aaron uses a battery-operated wheelchair for mobility and is able to take care of his own personal-care needs with minimal assistance in the school environment. His mother reported that Aaron is able to write successfully using specialized computer technology. She couldn't remember what this technology was.

After meeting with Brandy about Aaron, Justin and Beth decide to contact the school district's assistive technology (AT) contact for their school. They realize that a new IEP will need to be developed for Aaron after he begins school, and they wish to alert their AT contact of his arrival. They want to get all of their ducks in a row and be ready to request permission to reevaluate Aaron at this first formal planning meeting. Justin and Beth are eager to learn more about the technology available to meet the needs of students like Aaron and hope that they might be able to use it with other students in their classes.

Aaron begins school the next day as expected. Brandy escorts him from the drop-off area of the school (car riders) to his classes and introduces him to his new teachers. At the end of the day, she will escort him back to the pick-up area of the school. She plans to serve as Aaron's personal escort until he learns where all of his classes are and until special transportation may be arranged. Upon meeting Aaron, Justin and Beth get the impression that he is a pleasant young man who appears well groomed and articulate. They notice that his hemiparesis affects the right side of his body (arm and leg) and that he appears to compensate well for this deficit. Justin and Beth introduce him to the other students in second-period English and continue their instructional plan as usual. They decided to use Aaron's first day of school as an observation day to see what, if any, assistance he might need in their class.

Justin and Beth's students are in the middle of a unit concerning the novel *To Kill a Mockingbird*. The students are about halfway through reading the book and are planning their documentaries. The students are placed in four heterogeneous groups and are expected to work cooperatively. Aaron is assigned to a group and given a copy of the novel. He has never read the book, but has seen the movie. Beth reviews what each group will be doing to create their documentaries after reading the book so that Aaron understands the task. Students are provided with guiding questions for reading, given some class time to read, and then discuss the section of the book read daily in class. The documentary assignment will require students to read the book, determine an appropriate community representative to interview, develop interview questions, conduct and videotape an interview, and finally present their findings to the class. Each group member has a role in the process. Justin and Beth realize that Aaron is going to need some time to catch up to his peers on this assignment and may require support in doing so. For right now, they want to see how independent he is and how he compensates for being behind. They also wish to see how his physical disability hinders his academic performance so that they will be able to discuss this with the AT contact for their school.

Aaron joins his assigned group willingly. He appears to listen attentively to Beth's description of the documentary assignment and asks questions to ensure understanding. His group reviews what they did the day before and what they are expected to do today. One student reads aloud the guiding questions for the chapter, and then everyone reads the assigned section of the book. Justin has a little trouble holding the book independently and turning the pages. This difficulty hinders his reading speed. When time is up, the students orally discuss any answers they found to the guiding questions. Aaron is able to accurately answer one question concerning a portion of the chapter he read during the allotted time. All students are expected to take notes of their discussion. Aaron has trouble holding a pencil and writing while positioning his paper on the lap tray of his wheelchair. He is able to form letters and spell adequately, but his speed in writing is a significant issue. Writing in this manner does not appear to be an efficient use of his time.

Justin and Beth discuss their observations of Aaron after he leaves class. They decide to see if they can borrow a notebook computer from the media center of the school for Aaron to use tomorrow in English. They want to see if he can type using one hand and, if so, how efficient he is. If his typing speed is too slow, they may wish to recommend word prediction or voice-activated software or both for him for writing. Beth has heard about word prediction software, but has never used it. She has also heard that voice-activated software requires a quiet environment and takes time to get going. Beth and Justin believe that a personal notebook computer for Aaron may be the answer. It would allow him independence in all of his classes, and he could take it home with him to complete his homework assignments. He might need the support of a personal assistant to set it up for each class; they will have to see. Tomorrow, Justin and Beth will see how Aaron performs with a notebook computer. Beth will also talk to him about what type of technology he used at his last school. After this, Justin and Beth will phone the AT contact for more information so that everyone will be ready for Aaron's IEP meeting next week.

Discussion Questions

1. Justin and Beth decide to observe Aaron on his first day in their classroom to see his level of independence. Do you agree with this decision? Why or why not?
2. Aaron uses a battery-operated wheelchair for mobility. These chairs tend to be very heavy and take up a lot of space. They also don't tend to be height adjustable. How should Beth and Justin set up their classroom so that Aaron is able to access instructional materials and maneuver his chair around the classroom?
3. Based on your current knowledge of assistive technology and the information presented in this case study, what technology do you think Justin and Beth should explore for Aaron, and why?
4. Because Aaron's wheelchair has a lap tray, would you set up a notebook computer on it or create a separate workstation for him? Why?
5. What other information do you believe that Justin and Beth should obtain prior to Aaron's first IEP meeting at their school?

CASE 5

To Scribe or Not to Scribe, That Is the Question

Ann Hamilton is a fourth-grade teacher at Black Swan Elementary School. She has taught fourth grade for 7 years. During these years, her classroom has been used as the inclusion class twice. Ann doesn't mind having students with disabilities in her classroom, but the school district is now basing teacher raises on student test scores on the end-of-the-year state assessments. Since this initiative passed, Ann and the other teachers in her school are less eager to have students with disabilities in their classes. No one has a problem having the gifted children.

Rita Law is a special education teacher assigned to support inclusion in third and fourth grade. Rita has been an inclusion teacher at Black Swan Elementary School for 3 years. She has never worked with Ann, but knows her. Rita has mixed emotions about working with Ann. She has heard from the other special education teachers that Ann is resistant to providing accommodations for students with disabilities in her classroom. She doesn't think that they are fair. She apparently doesn't care if students receive accommodations outside of her classroom for testing, but she doesn't want them to receive them routinely in her classroom. Based on this information, Rita decides to meet with Ann before the school year begins to discuss this issue as well as how they will plan instruction together for the year.

Rita prepares a brief agenda for their meeting and asks Ann to add any items she might like to discuss. During their meeting, they talk about the students they will have in their classroom this year. As of now, they have 24 students. Of these students, five are eligible for special education services in reading and writing. All of these students have accommodations listed on their IEPs in the area of testing and writing. The accommodations include small group setting, flexible time, directions and items read aloud other than reading passages, and a scribe for writing. Rita explains to Ann that students receiving accommodations must receive them consistently, not just during testing. To do this, students must practice taking tests and completing assignments with their designated accommodations. This is especially important in the area of writing as students learn to dictate to a scribe and then are required to tell the scribe where to place punctuation marks and capital letters. This skill takes extensive practice. Rita volunteers to demonstrate how to teach whole and small group using the students' designated accommodations. She notes that although the accommodations are designed for students with disabilities, they are also beneficial for students without disabilities. Ann agrees to "allow" her to do this. Rita and Ann also discuss how they wish to set up the language arts block for instruction. They agree to use a three block model of instruction (see Fountas & Pinnell, 2001, *Guiding Readers and Writers Grades 3–6: Teaching, Comprehension, Genre, and Content Literacy** for more information) using dynamic grouping. They will split the students into four groups and assign students to groups based on individual strengths and weaknesses. Ann will teach the high groups and Rita the low groups. They will meet weekly to plan and modify group assignments. After the meeting, Rita is hopeful that the year will go well.

The school year begins, and initial assessments are conducted. Ann and Rita meet weekly as planned and are developing a good working relationship. The concerns that Rita had initially are gone. The pair has created a daily activity where all of the students are able to practice adding capital letters and punctuation marks to sentences. Ann has noticed that this activity helps all of the students with writing sentences correctly and is pleased. Rita works with the students in her assigned groups on dictating to a scribe. At this point in the school year, she still has all of the students receiving special education services in her groups. The students who are not eligible for special education support are progressing well, although Rita has to make sure that they also write independently so they will be ready for the state assessment without accommodations.

As the school year progresses and the state writing assessment draws near, Rita realizes that a couple of "her" students are now in Ann's group for the language arts block. She also realizes that Ann is not having them practice dictating their writing as they had discussed previously. Rita plans to mention this to Ann at their weekly planning meeting. Her students really need to practice dictating now so that they will be ready for the assessment.

---

*Fountas, I. C. & Pinnell, G. S. (2001). Guiding readers and writers grades 3–6: Teaching, comprehension, genre, and content literacy. Portsmouth, NH: Heinemann.

Rita and Ann meet on Friday afternoon after school as scheduled. Rita carefully brings up the subject of their students practicing writing with a scribe. Ann admits that she has stopped practicing. Rita asks, "How are the students doing without a scribe?" Ann reports, "They are not doing very well." Rita asks, "What do you see as being the students' primary issue with writing?" Ann states, "The students seem to have good ideas, but have trouble getting those ideas on paper. They just seem to get hung up on spelling and then stop writing." Rita tells Ann, "This is why they have a scribe as an accommodation on their IEPs. We know that they have good ideas; they just can't seem to get those ideas down on paper. With a scribe, the students don't have to worry about spelling. They can just let their ideas flow and then worry about revising and editing later." Ann and Rita agree that Ann will initiate practice again with the couple of students she is working with in her language arts groups. They also agree to discuss whether or not a scribe continues to be necessary for next year before the students' next IEP meeting.

Discussion Questions

1. How do you believe that district mandates concerning teacher pay for student performance on state assessments will impact inclusive practices?
2. When do you feel it is appropriate for a student with a disability to have a scribe for writing? Should this be a "standard" accommodation for students with disabilities? Why or why not?
3. What steps would you take to show Ann that accommodations are "fair" for students with disabilities so that they may be successful in the general curriculum?
4. Do you believe that it is appropriate for Ann and Rita to use dynamic grouping in their language arts block? This type of grouping may lead to students with disabilities receiving their primary reading and/or writing instruction from Ann instead of Rita. And students without disabilities may receive their primary instruction from Rita. Is this legal?
5. What is your opinion on how Rita handled the situation of Ann not providing practice in using a scribe for students with disabilities in her language arts group?

11

Effective Techniques for Teaching Math

Mary Little

Mathematics is used on a daily basis throughout our lives. The ability to compute, problem solve, and apply concepts and skills in mathematics influences multiple decisions. From personal, professional, and societal perspectives, the mastery of mathematical skills of number sense, computation, and problem solving are necessary. Calculating expenditures, interpreting student progress data, and developing personal financial plans all require skills in mathematics. The National Research Council (1989) reported that mathematics is the invisible culture of our age and emphasizes that mathematics is embedded in our lives in many ways: practical, civic, professional, recreational, and cultural. This is especially evident in our technology-rich society, where number sense and problem-solving skills have increasing importance, as technology (e.g., calculators, computers, software programs, etc.) enhances both the opportunities for, yet the demands of, advanced levels of proficiency in mathematics.

Despite the need to be proficient in mathematics, it is often challenging for students with and without disabilities to master. Students who have learning difficulties that affect their ability to do well in mathematics come from a variety of backgrounds and experiences. Some similar characteristics include memory or attention difficulties, math anxiety, and incomplete or inaccurate prior knowledge. Whatever the reasons, comparative assessment results continue to illuminate the current needs of students in mathematics. In both 2007 and 2009, U.S. fourth graders showed no measurable gain in mathematics (NCES, 2009). In fact, in the 2009 National Assessment of Educational Progress (NAEP) report, eighteen percent of grade four students and twenty-seven percent of grade eight students scored below the "basic" level. Additionally, only three percent of U.S. students attained advanced levels of mathematics achievement by grade 12 (NCES, 2009).

CHANGING STANDARDS

It is important to look at possible reasons for the decline of student performance in mathematics, as well as consider the new federal requirements and mandates related to increased rigor and accountability for results for all students, including students with disabilities. One explanation is that mathematics curriculum in the United States focuses on too many superficially taught topics in a given year. More successful approaches, found particularly in Asian countries, tend to focus on a few topics. The lessons are often devoted to the analysis of a few examples, and teachers encourage students to share different solutions to problems (Lee, Grigg, & Dion, 2007).

The National Council of Teachers of Mathematics (NCTM) is the largest organization for mathematics educators in the United States. Their published national standards plan is highly influential; almost every state has incorporated the NCTM national standards into their state standards (Woodward & Montague, 2002). When considering issues related to reported student results and recent revisions to federal legislation, the NCTM initiated reform efforts in math education, including a revision of the suggested math standards. As a result of published concerns about student achievement, NCTM recently revised their curriculum standards to include an increased process approach for a deeper understanding of a decreased amount of standards (NCTM, 2000). NCTM highlights the importance of giving students opportunities to use and discuss multiple representations during problem solving (NCTM, 2000). The continued focus of the revised standards (2000) on high-level conceptual learning and problem solving (Jitendra et al., 2005; Maccini & Gagnon, 2002) has been cited as being responsible for the instructional shift away from procedural practice (Gersten et al., 2009). Concerns regarding these new curriculum standards (www.nctm.org) as related to the successful inclusion of students with disabilities have been raised, because there is little mention of students with disabilities in the standards (Woodward & Montague, 2002) and the process approach to teaching math may not meet the needs for explicit instruction needed by some students, especially students with disabilities (Miller & Hudson, 2007). Researchers in special education have expressed concern regarding the applicability of the mathematics standards (Jackson & Neel, 2006). Despite the conceptual push by NCTM, special education has kept its emphasis on its behavioral tradition in mathematics instructional interventions (Woodward, 2004).

As a response to the overwhelming number of grade-level mathematics standards required in some states, NCTM recently presented the Curriculum Focal Points. The Focal Points serve to narrow the emphasis to what is essential at each grade level. Although NCTM claims that the Focal Points are designed to give school districts guidance in delivering the standards, many others claim differently (Cavanagh, 2006). The Focal Points address a shift in curriculum rather than recommended instructional pedagogy. One of the largest changes to the 15-year-old suggested mathematics standards is the shift in importance to memorizing certain computational facts, one of the most profound areas of mathematical weakness for students with disabilities (Gersten, Jordan, & Flojo, 2005). A focus of the recently formed National Mathematics Advisory Panel is to improve the performance of students with disabilities in mathematics.

Students with Disabilities

In terms of the academic performance of students with disabilities, researchers have found that math difficulties emerge in elementary school grades and continue as students progress through secondary school grades (Cawley, Parmer, Yan, & Miller, 1998). It is currently estimated that between 4 – 7% of the school-age population experience some form of mathematics-focused disability (Gross-Tsur, Monar, & Shalev, 1996). Approximately one-fourth of the students identified with learning disabilities were identified because they underperformed in mathematics (Lee, Grigg, & Dion, 2007). Students with learning disabilities in mathematics perform several grade levels below their general education peers (Gersten et al., 2009), struggle in basic mathematics skills (Hudson & Miller, 2006), and have difficulty in problem-solving situations (Maccini & Hughes, 2000). Specifically, students with disabilities often fail to achieve a sufficient conceptual understanding of the core concepts that underlie operations and algorithms used to solve problems that involve whole and rational numbers (Fuchs & Fuchs, 2001).

Difficulties in mathematics are part of a larger educational concern. Students with learning disabilities are frequently characterized as having perceptual and neurological concerns that impact learning. Students with difficulties in math often have other related difficulties, such as in memory, poor calculation skills, number reversals, and difficulty understanding conceptual and/or procedural processes, especially as represented through symbols and signs (Bryant, Bryant, & Hammill, 2000; Bryant, Hartman, & Kim, 2003).

Several factors may interfere with learning and the subsequent mastery of concepts and skills in mathematics for students with disabilities, especially learning disabilities (Ginsburg, 1997). These include:

1. *Perceptual skills.* By definition, students with learning disabilities have difficulty with spatial relationships, distances, and sequencing. These difficulties may interfere with the acquisition of and demonstration of math concepts and skills, such as estimating size and distance, and problem solving.

2. *Language.* The vocabulary and language of mathematical concepts is not only varied, but also abstract. Students with difficulties and/or disabilities in the area of language may also have difficulties with understanding such mathematical concepts as *first, second, greater than, less than*, as well as associated vocabulary terms such as *vertex, complimentary, acute,* and so on. For students who have deficits in reading and mathematics, the difficulty with word problem solving is accentuated (Jitendra, DiPipi, & Perron-Jones, 2002). These language skills, in both oral and written language, may hinder the understanding, solving, and explaining of word problems (Kroesbergen & Van Luit, 2003; Monroe & Orme, 2002).

3. *Reasoning.* Students with disabilities may not possess the abstract reasoning skills necessary for higher-level math skills development. These skills in reasoning may also present difficulties if instruction in mathematics is at the conceptual, abstract level.

4. *Memory.* Many students with learning and behavioral problems have difficulties remembering information that was presented. This is especially evident with the abstract symbols used in mathematics (e.g., minus, greater than, less than, etc.).

Given these characteristics, researchers have identified considerations for lesson planning and design as well as comprehensive teaching methods for students with disabilities.

MEETING THE INSTRUCTIONAL NEEDS OF ALL STUDENTS IN MATHEMATICS

Difficulties with learning mathematics occur in one or more domains and on a continuum of needs, from temporary to severe, which may manifest at different points in a child's learning. Given that difficulties may be encountered at different ages and in different mathematical domains, research and interventions may be appropriate at different levels and in different domains (Bryant et al., 2008). Students who continue to experience a lack of success in math may develop negative feelings about math, have math anxieties, or develop learned helplessness. Students who experience continuous failures expect to fail, resulting both in reticence to try something new and reliance on others to help them.

At the outset of teaching mathematics to struggling students, it is important to promote a positive attitude and develop a rationale for learning math. Attitudes, beliefs, and motivation play important roles in learning math. Considering that students may have already not had many successes in mathematics, the teacher should promote a positive attitude about math by providing an accepting, stimulating, and encouraging classroom environment. It is important to involve students in goal setting in math and discuss the relevance of learning math to real-life experiences. This can be done by making connections between student needs and interests in math with the goals and skills within the math curriculum.

To meet the curricular goals in mathematics, it is important to review current research and teach students using research-based instructional techniques. There are numerous sources of information about the most current research. For example, the U.S. Department of Education sponsors a web site, *What Works Clearinghouse* (www.whatworks.ed.gov/). It offers a range of publications that evaluate math curricula, which are designed to increase student outcomes related to mathematics achievement. Programs are reviewed using criteria as a research-based program.

In addition, research has shown that the use of various mathematical and metacognitive approaches to scaffold instruction of abstract concepts enables students to master mathematical problems that otherwise would not be mastered (National Research Council, 1989, 2001). Current research-based, instructional, and metacognitive strategies can be implemented to address the needs of students with and without disabilities to master content in math classes (McLeskey, Hoppey, Williamson, & Rentz, 2004). To meet the diverse needs of students with disabilities in math, the following effective instructional practices are recommended:

1. Instructional design and lesson planning features are effective ways to differentiate presentation methods, levels of learning, and feedback and demonstration of mastery to meet the students' individual needs. It is important to set clearly defined curricular goals aligned with standards.
2. Instructional routines and metacognitive strategies that focus on cognitive behavioral techniques benefit students with learning and behavioral problems and actively engage the students in the learning process.
3. Monitor progress and provide effective feedback through formative assessment procedures throughout instruction. Make adjustments in teaching, materials, grouping, or other features of instruction or accommodations if students are not making adequate progress.

LESSON PLANNING TO DIFFERENTIATE INSTRUCTION

Differentiated instruction is a philosophy or approach to planning and teaching based on the premise that teachers must consider *who* they are teaching as well as *what* they are teaching. The principles of differentiation include on-going assessment and adjustment, clarity of the big ideas of the curriculum, use of flexible grouping, tasks that are respectful of each learner, and instruction that stretches the learner. Differentiating the content refers to what is being taught, as well as how students gain access to a body of knowledge. Development of a differentiated classroom occurs along a continuum. A lesson or a unit may be differentiated as teachers gain proficiency using a broader range of effective teaching methods and techniques.

To enact differentiating instruction in the mathematics classroom, teachers need to be efficient at several types of instruction. For example, many general mathematics educators are being prepared for investigation-oriented mathematics instruction whereas special education teachers are being prepared for more explicit behavioral approaches to teaching mathematics. Hudson, Miller, and Butler (2006) suggested a combination of the two approaches. To differentiate instruction, either in co-taught or individual classrooms, requires thorough knowledge of each student, the content, and how that student learns. Teachers differentiate classroom instruction by implementing the most effective instructional methods. Learning to differentiate instruction requires knowledge of the multiple variables that must be considered when planning lessons, implementing content, and monitoring for continuous progress and assessment. Incorporating these components into the lesson increases the learning opportunities for all students (Mastropieri & Scruggs, 2007). The critical components of lesson design include:

- State standards and objectives
  - Should be written in terms of the students (not in terms of the teacher).
  - Indicate the specific observable behavior.
  - Indicate the mathematics (skill or concept) to be learned by the students (e.g., students will subtract a two-digit number from a two- or three-digit number with and without renaming).
- Prerequisite skills and concepts needed by the students.
- Materials needed for the lesson: List the materials needed for the teacher and for the students.
- Cognitive levels of learning or combination of levels involved in the lesson: concrete, representational, abstract, concrete-representational, representational-concrete, concrete-abstract, abstract-concrete, representational-abstract, abstract-representational, and concrete-representational-abstract (all cognitive levels at the same time).
- Instructional procedures for the lesson
  - *Introduction (setting the stage):*
    - All procedures should be detailed to implement them.
    - Include example questions, items, and/or exercises to clarify your ideas, and include copies or drawings of assigned handouts, exercises, and/or homework.
    - Critical elements: Motivate the students, communicate learning objectives, relate to prior knowledge, and read children's books.
  - *Instructional input and modeling (development of main idea):* This section should include an explanation of the procedures to be used when teaching the lesson. What will the students do and what will the teacher do? This could include demonstrations, experiments, explorations, games, and/or others.
  - *Guided practice and check for understanding:* Students demonstrate a skill or concept, extend a concept (or apply it), complete some problems/activities/samples, and then repeat operations. Teachers check for students' understanding by asking questions, observing operations, and/or adjusting problems (continuous progress monitoring).
  - *Independent practice:* Students complete follow-up activities or practice activities. Possible activities include learning centers, experiments, explorations, games, seatwork, computers, or calculators.
  - *Concluding activity:* Closure or closing remarks to summarize the lesson objective, review independent work, and set expectations.

Researchers have noted that math difficulties emerge in elementary school grades and continue as students progress through secondary school grades (Maccini & Gagnon, 2002; Miller & Hudson, 2007). Specifically, students often fail to achieve a sufficient conceptual understanding of the core concepts that underlie operations and algorithms used to solve problems that involve whole and rational numbers (Bryant, Smith, & Bryant, 2008). Devlin (2000) stated that for students to understand abstract concepts more easily, it is important for them to learn precursor concepts concretely first. The National Council of Teachers of Mathematics (NCTM, 2000) has emphasized the importance of representations in the development of students' communication of mathematics ideas:

> Young students use many varied representations to build new understandings and express mathematical ideas. Representing ideas and connecting the representations to

mathematics lies at the heart of understanding mathematics. Teachers should analyze students' representations and carefully listen to their discussions to gain insights into the development of mathematical thinking and to enable them to provide support as students connect their languages to the conventional language of mathematics. (p. 135)

One way to simplify students' understanding of abstract concepts is to transform such complex concepts into concrete manipulations and pictorial representations. Such instruction is known as the concrete-representational-abstract sequence of instruction (CRA) (Miller & Mercer, 1993). (See Figure 11.1.)

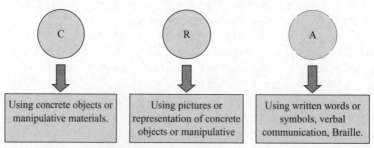

Note: Concrete (C), Representational (R), and Abstract (A)

FIGURE 11.1 Learning Levels

CRA involves using manipulatives (concrete). Once a student masters the math concept using manipulatives, the objects are replaced with pictorial representations, such as a picture of the object (representational). This level is a critical bridge between the manipulatives and the abstract symbols (e.g., equations, algorithm, etc.) because this step builds the mental schema bridging these two levels. It is critical to develop mathematics conceptual knowledge during the representational level of learning. Finally, once the student is able to comprehend representational figures and designs, the concept uses Arabic symbols and explanation (abstract). Successful performance at the abstract level is the goal and purpose of using CRA, because mathematics is most often expressed at this level (e.g., within text materials and assessments).

Within CRA, each level is designed to build on the previous level to promote overall improved mathematical performance. The three levels of CRA are sequentially interrelated. They are not independent activities but interconnected and should not be treated as separate activities that are either hands-on, pictorial, or use abstract notation. Instead, each level prepares the student for the next level of learning (Witzel, Ferguson, & Brown, 2007). The connections between the levels of learning are critical to bring the student from one level to the next. For example, a concrete lesson must be designed to be easily represented pictorially and described abstractly. If the levels are not connected or designed in sequence, then the student must learn multiple ways to solve a problem without mastering any of the steps along the way.

METACOGNITIVE STRATEGIES AND INSTRUCTIONAL ROUTINES

Metacognition refers to higher order thinking that involves active control over the cognitive processes engaged in learning (Montague et al., 2000). Planning how to approach a given learning task, monitoring comprehension, and evaluating progress toward the completion of a task are metacognitive in nature. Metacognitive strategies include mnemonic devices, problem-solving routines, self-monitoring skills, and the use of graphic organizers. Graphic organizers are designed to assist students in representing patterns, interpreting data, and analyzing information relevant to problem solving.

Numerous research-based metacognitive strategies are used when teaching mathematics to assist students who struggle with mathematics due to memory or perceptual difficulties. One is a mnemonic to help students remember algorithms or problem-solving procedures, and uses the acronym DRAW, as described by Miller and Mercer (1993) and used in the Strategic Math Series. The Strategic Math Series features seven phases to teach basic math facts: pretest; teach concrete application; teach representational application; introduce a DRAW strategy (see below); teach abstract application; posttest; and provide practice to fluency and develop problem-solving strategies.

EXAMPLE   **Draw**

D-*Discover* the sign $(+, -, \times, \div)$.

R-*Read* the problem ("four plus three equals blank").

A-*Answer*, or "DRAW" a conceptual representation, using lines

///   ///

and tallies, and check $(4 + 3 = \underline{})$.

///   ///

W-*Write* the answer $(4 + 3 = \underline{7})$

Using the Strategic Math Series, students with learning problems were able to acquire computational skills, solve word problems, apply a mnemonic strategy to difficult problems, increase their rate of computation, and generalize math skills across examiners, settings, and tasks (Mercer & Mercer, 2005).

There is another metacognitive strategy that uses sequential steps to explicitly identify key components of word problems. RIDE is a mnemonic strategy that identifies the steps needed to successfully solve word problems:

EXAMPLE   **Ride**

R-*Read* the problem correctly

I-*Identify* the relevant information

D-*Determine* which operations and unit are needed for expressing the answer

E-*Enter* the correct numbers and calculate and check the answer (Mercer & Mercer, 2005)

Numerous research-based metacognitive strategies have been validated for use in math lessons. One final example included here was used as an intervention to teach algebra to adolescents with learning disabilities by Hutchinson (1993). This intervention to help students solve equations in algebra involves the use of the mnemonic CAP:

EXAMPLE **Cap**

C-*Combine* like terms

A-*Ask* yourself, "Have I isolated the variables?"

P-*Put* the values of the variable in the initial equation to check if equation is balanced (Hutchinson, 1993)

The introduction of metacognitive strategy instruction into mathematics lessons should not be considered an addition to the required content, but rather an array of research-based tools developed to facilitate the understanding, retention, and use of required course content. Metacognitive strategies allow a teacher to teach students *how to think* about what they are doing and learning. As developing learners, students should be taught these strategies in order to realize how they learn best. Metacognitive strategies are not only related to teaching mathematics. These strategies can be used in all areas and subjects. Examples of additional strategies include prior knowledge prompts, advance organizers, mnemonics, and graphic/visual organizers.

INSTRUCTIONAL STRATEGIES AND TECHNIQUES FOR STUDENTS WITH DISABILITIES

Lesson design begins with the state standards for all students in the content area of mathematics. State content standards are usually based on the theoretical frameworks and content continuums of the knowledge and skills needed to master, use, and generalize mathematics. Although the continuum may vary among states, the developmental continuum in mathematics is similar: pre-number skills, numeration and place value, computation, fractions/decimals/percents, and problem solving. The next section describes the content and offers several instructional methods and/or activities to use during instruction.

PRE-NUMBER SKILLS.   Skills are needed prior to formal mathematics, including the conceptual development of pre-number skills such as classifying objects, one-to-one correspondence, and recognizing a series. Although these important skills are precursors, students often do not possess these skills and need further skills development. Specific activities include:

1. Ask the students to sort various materials into categories. Then ask them to develop the categories based on the materials provided.
2. With pictures of items (e.g., animals, toys, people, etc.) sorted into categories, ask the students to name the category. Then ask the students to re-arrange the pictures to new categories.
3. Use familiar objects and cards with designated numbers (e.g., five). Ask the students to point, and count the number of items, to the designated number. This can be revised as the students learn the designated numbers.
4. Use every opportunity (e.g., lining up for lunch, musical songs, etc.) to associate the number, the number word, and the associated amount to build relationships among the number concepts (e.g., 3, three, and ***).
5. Give the students some objects of various lengths and types. Then ask them to put the objects in order from shortest to longest.
6. Ask the students to stack objects (e.g., books, pens, etc.) from shortest to tallest.

7. Fill same-size jars with sand of varied amounts, and ask the students to sequence them in order.

8. Ask the students to stand in a line, from shortest to tallest.

NUMERATION AND PLACE VALUE.   Often, students can count and can name the number when shown, but may have limited or incorrect understanding of the underlying numerical concept or place value. Students may be able to add single digits, but may demonstrate little knowledge of numerals when asked to add using regrouping.

Understanding numeration and place value is necessary as a framework to progress through computation (especially re-grouping), understanding types of errors (especially when using calculators), and applying math computation to everyday problems and word problems. Current research related to teaching mathematical concepts supports the use of concrete and abstract examples to facilitate basic skill development. Furthermore, various numeration readiness concepts are necessary as foundations for scaffolding future skills; several activities to consider include:

1. Cardinality: Identify, write, and/or name the numeral that is represented by a picture of multiple items (e.g., six cats).

2. Grouping and patterning: Given some items (e.g., wiki sticks, popsicle sticks, etc.), ask the students to form items of ones, tens, and so on.

3. Base 10: On a T-Chart (See Figure 11.2 below), ask the students to write the supplied numbers in each of the correct places and describe the amounts.

4. Place value for regrouping: Show, name, and identify the value of a specific digit within a multi-digit number. For example, use a deck of cards and ask the students to create specific multi-digit numbers from the cards.

5. Verbal names: Using index cards with number names printed (e.g., hundreds, tens, seven, etc.), base 10 blocks, and erasable white boards, have the students match and/or write the numbers, the names or numbers on the white board, varying the amount and types of numbers to assure continued learning.

As students master the skills of numeration and place value with single digit and double digit numbers, introduce them to three- and four-digit numbers using similar activities. Many of the principles and concepts that the students learn with single- and double-digit numbers will apply when generalized to three-digit numbers and beyond. If these skills need to be taught or reviewed for older students, the following sources of numbers may be useful for teaching place value: an odometer, charts and graphs, mileage charts, population data, and the financial data page from the newspaper.

100s	10s	1s

FIGURE 11.2   T-Chart of Place Value—Base 10 Numbers

COMPUTATION. Memorizing math facts and mastering the four basic operations (addition, subtraction, multiplication, and division) are important skills in mathematics. Computing math problems, with or without a calculator, is made much easier if the students understand numeration and place value, as well as given frequent practical applications of the math problems. Teachers can improve students' conceptual knowledge of computation by scaffolding the students' learning of the key skills with computation. Students may have difficulty with math computation if they do not have an understanding of numeration and/or place value. Teachers should use manipulatives (e.g., base 10 blocks, counters, etc.) with students to teach the concepts of computation in a concrete manner. Teachers should use multiple methods, such as representing the problem with tally marks, pictures, and so on. If students have not yet mastered the one-to-one correspondence of the abstract written number (e.g., 3) with the amount (***), there are strategies and programs that build on that skill. For example, the *Touch Math* procedure teaches students to actually touch the number to represent the amount and provides dots on the numbers to associate the amount with the abstract number. The following example lesson (see Figure 11.3) clearly shows a progression of teaching computation from initial instruction to generalizing the skills to word problems and additional applications.

Students who struggle in math may also have difficulties with the language of math, especially as they apply math to real life problems and word problems. It is important to introduce and use accurate mathematical terms when teaching students. The following example (see Figure 11.4) shows the use of math terms while teaching computational skills.

Finally, students may have difficulty learning their basic math facts in computation at the automatic level; that is, students cannot accurately and fluently demonstrate their math facts without the use a multiplication chart, *Touch Math* procedure, calculator, and so on. Practicing math facts with flash cards, computer-assisted programs, timed math tests, and other practice opportunities with the teacher, peers, and in small groups improves student mastery. Some web-based technology software in the areas of computations includes:

FASTT Math and Go Solve—http://tomsnyder.com

Super Kids Math Worksheet Creator—http://www.superkids.com/aweb/tools/math

Awesome Library in Math—http://www.awesomelibrary.org/Classroom/Mathematics/
Mathematics.html

FRACTIONS/DECIMALS/PERCENTS.   The concepts of fractions, decimals, and percentages are difficult math concepts to teach to mastery. Conceptually, students should be introduced to the concepts and relationships of "parts" to the "whole" before tackling grade-level standards and textbook problems including fractions, decimals, and percentages. Many manipulatives, such as measuring cups, fraction circle wheels, cardboard strips, and so on, can be used to teach fractions, even to very young students. A sequence for teaching fractional concepts (as expressed as fractions, decimals, or percentages) includes the following activities. The student will:

1. Manipulate concrete objects (e.g., fraction blocks)
2. Match fraction models (halves, thirds, etc.) with terms
3. Point to the fractional model when its name is identified
4. Draw diagrams or use manipulatives to represent the fractional part
5. Write the fraction name when given fractional drawings
6. Use fractions to solve problems

Teachers reinforce the concepts of the multiple ways to represent the relationships of "parts" to the "whole," interchanging fractions, decimals, and percentages. The use of number lines

1. Provide concrete experiences to promote understanding.
   Example:

   □ □   +   □   =

   □ □   □ □

      4   +   3   =_____

2. Provide semiconcrete experiences to promote understanding.
   Example: //// + ///
   4 + 3 = _____

3. Provide abstract activities and practice to promote mastery.
   Example: 4 + 3 = _____

4. Teach rules that show patterns and relationships.
   Example: *Zero rule:* Any number plus zero equals the number.
   4 + 0 = 4
   Order rule: Addends yield the same sum regardless of their order.
   4 + 3 = 7   3 + 4 = 7

5. Teach algorithms for solving problems.
   Example: *Fact:* 7 + 2 = _____ *Algorithm:* Start BIG and count on.

6. Use mnemonics to help students remember algorithms or problem-solving procedures.
   Example: DRAW
   D–*Discover* the sign (+, −, ×, ÷)
   R–*Read* the problem ("four plus three equals blank").
   A–*Answer,* or "DRAW" a conceptual representation of the problem, using lines
         //// ///
   and tallies, and check (4 + 3 = __).
         //// ///
   W–*Write* the answer (4 + 3 = _7_).

7. Provide a variety of practice activities to promote mastery and generalization.
   Example: Provide vertical and horizontal problems.
        Use self-correcting materials, instructional games, peer tutoring, and computer-assisted
        instruction for seatwork.
   Provide activities to improve the rate of responses (e.g., one-minute probes).

8. Teach problem solving.
   Example: Have students solve a variety of word problems.
        Have students create their own word problems.
   Provide students with strategies for solving problems.

FIGURE 11.3   Instructional Components for Teaching Computation

can display decimals and their fractional equivalents. In addition to using the number lines as an aid in computing decimal-fraction problems, the student can be instructed to fill in blank sections of number lines, as the example below shows:

Fraction	_____	_____	1/2	3/5	_____
Percent	_____%	33%	_____%	_____%	_____%
Decimal	.25	_____	_____	_____	.67

Operation	Terms
Addition	8←addend + 4 ←addend 12 ←sum
Subtraction (take away)	9 ←minuend − 4 ←subtrahend 5 ←difference
Multiplication	8 ←multiplicand or factor × 5 ←multiplier or factor 40 ←product
Division	8 ←quotient or factor 6) 48 ←dividend or product ↑ divisor or factor

FIGURE 11.4 Math Terms in Basic Computations

Once students demonstrate conceptual understanding of these critical concepts of "parts" to "whole" and the multiple ways to represent each, the teacher can build upon the conceptual understanding in computation. The following example (see Figure 11.5) shows the use of the levels of learning in the addition of fractions.

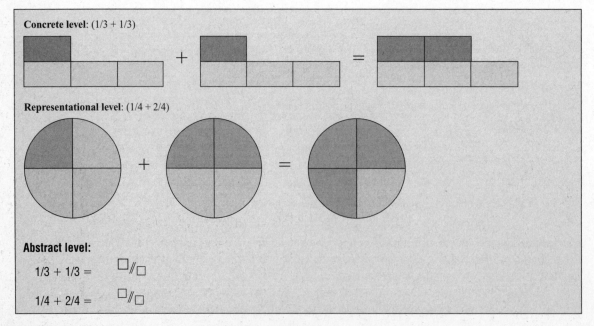

FIGURE 11.5 Addition of Fractions with Same Denominators

When teaching these concepts, real-life applications using money, measurements, weight, distances, and time often improve student motivation and interest in learning the more difficult skills of fractions, decimals, and percentages. There are also excellent computer-assisted programs to introduce and reinforce skills such as:

Visual Fractions—http://www.visualfractions.com

Cuisenaire Rods—http://en.wikipedia.org/wiki/Cuisenaire.rods

PROBLEM SOLVING.   Students with learning problems often find problem solving one of the most difficult skills in mathematics to learn because of their difficulties with reading and logical reasoning, as well as insufficient instruction in mathematics. Therefore, building an understanding for word problems begins early in students' learning of math because students must understand vocabulary and concepts in mathematics. Vocabulary is often considered as a separate language, and must be treated much like learning any foreign language. Although there is growing discussion of using mathematics terminology in everyday language for early childhood ages (Witzel, Ferguson, & Brown, 2007), discussion continues for students at the secondary levels (see Mastropieri & Scruggs, 2007). Explicit instruction in specific mathematics terminology is essential for students learning terms in mathematics such as polyhedron or quadratic equation. Teachers should teach terms explicitly along with incorporating terms into modeling and guided practice activities until they become part of the students' vocabulary.

Despite its difficulties, problem solving may be the most important skill we teach students who have learning or behavioral problems. Whereas most students can generalize and apply the operations to real-life situations with little explicit instruction or strategy instruction, students who struggle in math or with learning problems will be less likely to apply these skills without instruction, rehearsal, and practice. Students who are taught strategies for problem solving are more likely to be successful than students who are taught the sequence of solving problems (Fuchs et al., 2003; Jitendra, 2002).

Montague and Bos (1996) integrated cognitive strategies into an eight-step problem-solving process (see Figure 11.6).

Each word problem has essential elements that students should be explicitly taught to identify in order to master problem solving. By essential elements, Jitendra (2002) described word problems as having one of three types: change, group, or comparison. A student recognizes a change strategy by a beginning set, a change set that has been lost or added, and that the final set

---

Step 1: *Read the Problem*—Read orally, asking for assistance with the terms, as needed.

Step 2: *Paraphrase the Problem*—Underline the important facts in the word problem.

Step 3: *Visualize*—Graphically display the facts, and show their relationship to the question.

Step 4: *State the problem*—State what is known, and underline the key words in the question.

Step 5: *Hypothesize*—Determine the operation, based on what is known and the question.

Step 6: *Estimate*—Consider and write an estimated answer.

Step 7: *Calculate*—Show the calculation.

Step 8: *Self-check*—Refer back to the problem to check and make sure the answer is reasonable.

FIGURE 11.6   Steps in Problem-Solving Process in Math

Step 1. **F**—*Find* the problem type

- Did I read and retell the problem to ask the type of problem?

Step 2: **O**—*Organize* the information according to the problem type

- Did I underline the question?
- Did I find the numbers/parts that are compared in the word problem?
- Did I draw a diagram of the question, the numbers/parts compared, and the relational statement (e.g., more, less, difference, etc.)?

Step 3: **P**—*Plan* to solve the problem

- Did I transfer the information in the diagram to a math sentence or an equation?

Step 4: **S**—*Solve* the problem

- Did I solve for the missing number in the math sentence of the equation?
- Did I write the complete answer?
- Did I check to see if the answer makes sense?

FIGURE 11.7   Self-Monitoring Checklist for Solving Word Problems

being asked for reflects the change. The group problems show a larger set in the problem and the other smaller sets are deduced from the problem. The comparison sets of problems present one number set and a difference, more or less, and ask for a referent set. Even if the problems in a textbook extend these three types, it is important for students to recognize what is being asked in the problem and to have a strategy to approach the problem.

Montague and Jitendra (2006) developed a four-step strategy (FOPS) self-monitoring checklist to assist students' approach to solving word problems. This strategy can be applied to any type of problem encountered (see Figure 11.7).

PROGRESS MONITORING AND ASSESSMENT

Assessment is "the process of gathering evidence about a student's knowledge of, ability to use, and disposition toward mathematics and of making inferences from that evidence for a variety of purposes" (NCTM, 1995, p. 3). Furthermore, assessment tasks should match the student's prior knowledge, and the mathematics curriculum, and any instructional strategies as an ongoing process. In other words, the teacher should not teach one way and assess another way. These considerations are reflected in the five shifts recommended by the National Council of Teachers of Mathematics (NCTM, 1995):

- Shift in content toward a rich variety of mathematical topics and problem situations and away from just arithmetic;
- Shift in learning toward investigation problems and away from memorizing and repeating;
- Shift in teaching toward questioning and listening and away from telling;
- Shift in evaluation toward evidence from several resources and away from a single test judged externally; and
- Shift in expectation toward using concepts and procedures to solve problems and away from just mastering isolated concepts and procedures.

There are different useful types of assessment. Various types of assessment may be used in isolation or in combination with others for the purpose of providing important information to use in instructional planning. The following list provides a brief description of objective, alternative, authentic, performance, naturalistic, achievement, standardized, and diagnostic assessment:

1. *Objective assessment* refers to testing that requires the selection of one item from a list of choices provided with the question. This type of assessment includes true-false responses, yes-no answers, and questions with multiple-choice answers.

2. *Alternative assessment* refers to other (nontraditional) options used to assess students' learning. When using this type of assessment, the teacher is not basing student progress only on the results of a single test or set of evidence. Some forms of this type of assessment include portfolios, journals, notebooks, projects, and presentations.

3. *Authentic assessment* is a form of alternative assessment that incorporates real-life functions and applications.

4. *Performance assessment* (often used interchangeably with authentic assessment) requires the completion of a task, project, or investigation; and the ability to communicate this information, or construct a response that demonstrates knowledge or understanding of a skill or concept.

5. *Naturalistic assessment* involves evaluation that is based on the natural setting of the classroom. It involves the observation of students' performance and behavior in an informal context.

6. *Achievement test battery* is composed of subtests of mathematics concepts and skills and usually includes technical aspects of mathematics.

7. *Standardized tests* include content areas, and provide useful information about students' mathematics skills. Their validity and reliability depends on three basic assumptions: Students have been equally exposed to the test content in an instructional program, students know the language of the test directions and the test responses, and students similar to those taking the test have been included in the standardization samples to establish norms and make inferences.

8. *Diagnostic tests* are used within the diagnostic-prescriptive teaching of mathematics. The diagnostic-prescriptive teaching of mathematics is an instructional model that consists of diagnosis, prescription, instruction, and on-going assessment. The tests can be teacher-made or commercially developed.

Deciding on instructional adjustments and implementing interventions can be difficult. Riccomini (2005) found that general and special education elementary teachers were able to accurately identify the mathematical error pattern of students who made repeated errors. However, they did not develop interventions based on the identified error pattern or needs of the students. Thus, teachers were able to determine the mathematical error but they did not design an appropriate correction procedure to the help the student succeed. One thing that may help is frequent progress monitoring using the various types of assessments described in the above list. Safer and Fleishman (2005) found that student performance increased when teachers made instructional adjustments based on individualized curriculum-based measurement data. Frequent assessment and linked instructional interventions are essential to increasing student mathematics performance.

To use curriculum-based measures (CBM) for instructional decision making, teachers gather data on student performance (often referred to as progress monitoring), and then use this information to set goals for instruction. Deno identified four essential characteristics for CBM measures: (a) reliable and valid, (b) simple and efficient, (c) easily understood, and (d) inexpensive (Deno, 1985). CBM probes can be developed by the teachers based on their curriculum, located on-line (e.g., www.interventioncentral.org), or purchased from a publisher. Screening and continuous progress monitoring in mathematics provides important information for both planning and intervening in student instruction in mathematics (Fuchs et al., 2007; Safer & Fleishman, 2005). As teachers face increasing pressures to demonstrate the effectiveness of their math instruction, there is a growing need for assessment tools that can track the continuous progress of their students.

Summary and Discussion

Accountability for improved student learning in mathematics classrooms is based on student learning through the multiple considerations used when planning and implementing instruction, as well as interventions and continuous progress monitoring through various types of assessments. Students with disabilities and/or who struggle to learn mathematics are actively engaged through the use of the revised mathematics standards, effective instruction, metacognitive strategies, accommodations, and technology, which serve to improve students' achievement in mathematics understandings, concepts, and skills. Carefully designed lessons—incorporating differentiated instructional approaches, levels of learning, and metacognitive strategies—provide the scaffolded support for students who struggle learning math. Various examples of instructional strategies and activities were provided for each major mathematical concept. Lastly, continuously monitoring student performance through various, and curriculum-based, progress monitoring assessments by teachers provides results of student learning which can be used to address instructional decisions and school accountability. Most importantly, however, actively engaging students through various research-based instructional methods, resources, metacognitive strategies, accommodations, and technology, and actively engaging teachers to continuously monitor student achievement and performance related to the curriculum standards, will have the greatest impact on those most directly affected—teachers and their students.

References

Bryant, B. R., Bryant, D. P., Kethley, C., Kim, S., Pool, C., & Seo, Y-J. (2008). Preventing mathematics difficulties in the primary grades: The critical features of instruction in textbooks as part of the equation. *Learning Disabilities Quarterly, 31,* 21–35.

Bryant, D. P., Bryant, B., & Hammill, D. (2000). Characteristic behaviors of students with LD who have teacher-identified math weaknesses. *Journal of Learning Disabilities, 33,* 168–177, 199.

Bryant, D. P., Hartman, P., & Kim, S. A. (2003). Using explicit and systematic instruction to teach division skills to students with learning disabilities, *Exceptionality, 11*(3), 151–164.

Bryant, D. P., Smith, D. D., & Bryant, B. R. (2008). *Teaching students with special needs in inclusive classrooms.* Boston: Allyn & Bacon.

Cavanagh, S. (2006). Math organization attempts to bring focus to subject. *Education Week, 26*(4), 1–24.

Cawley, J. F., Parmer, R. S., Yan, W., & Miller, J. H. (1998). Arithmetic computation performance of students with learning disabilities: Implications for curriculum. *Learning Disabilities Research & Practice, 13,* 68–74.

Deno, S. L. (1985). Curriculum-based measurement: the emerging alternative. *Exceptional Children, 52,* 219–232.

Devlin, K. (2000). Finding your inner mathematician. *Chronicle of Higher Education, 46,* B5.

Fuchs, L. S., & Fuchs, D. (2001). Principles for the prevention and intervention of mathematics difficulties. *Learning Disabilities Research & Practice, 16,* 85–95.

Fuchs, L. S., Fuchs, D., Compton, D. L., Bryant, J. D., Hamlett, C. L., & Seethaler, P. M. (2007). Mathematics screening and progress monitoring at first grade: implications for responsiveness to intervention. *Exceptional Children, 73*(3), 311–330.

Fuchs, L. S., Fuchs, D., Prentice, K., Burch, M., Hamlett, C. L., & Owen, R. (2003). Enhancing third grade students' mathematical problem solving with self-regulated learning strategies. *Journal of Educational Psychology, 95,* 306–315.

Gersten, R., Baker, S., Jordan, N. C., & Flojo, J. R. (2009). A Meta-analysis of instruction and interventions in mathematics. Instructional Research Group. Washington, DC: U.S. Government Printing Office.

Gersten, R., Jordan, N. C., & Flojo, J. R. (2005). Early identification and interventions for students with mathematics difficulties. *Journal of Learning Disabilities, 38,* 291–292.

Ginsburg, H. P. (1997). Mathematics learning disabilities: A view from development psychology. *Journal of Learning Disabilities, 30*(1), 20–33.

Gross-Tsur, V., Manor, O., & Shalev, R. S. (1996). Developmental dyscalculia: Prevalence and demographic features. *Developmental Medicine and Child Neurology, 37,* 906–914.

Hudson, P., & Miller, S. P. (2006). *Designing and implementing mathematics instruction for students with diverse learning needs.* Boston: Allyn & Bacon/Pearson.

Hudson, P., Miller, S. P., & Butler, F. (2006). Adapting and merging explicit instruction within reform based mathematics classrooms. *American Secondary Education, 35*(1), 19–32.

Hutchinson, N. L. (1993). Second invited response: Students with disabilities and mathematics education reform–Let the dialog begin. *Remedial and Special Education, 14*(6), 20–23.

Jackson, H. G., & Neel, R. S. (2006). Observing mathematics: Do students with EBD have access to standards-based mathematics instruction? *Education and Treatment of Children, 29*(4), 593–614.

Jitendra, A. (2002). Teaching students math problem-solving through graphic representations. *Teaching Exceptional Children, 34*(4), 34–38.

Jitendra, A. K., DiPipi, C. M., & Perron-Jones, N. (2002). An exploratory study of schema-based word-problem solving instruction for middle school students with learning disabilities: An emphasis on conceptual and procedural understanding. *Journal of Special Education, 36*(1), 23–38.

Jitendra, A. K., Griffin, C., Deatline-Buchman, A., Dipipi-Hoy, C., Sczesniak, E., Sokol, N. G., & Xin, Y. P. (2005). Adherence to mathematical professional standards and instructional criteria for problem-solving in mathematics. *Exceptional Children, 71*(3), 319–337.

Kroesbergen, E., & Van Luit, J. E. H. (2003). Mathematics interventions for children with special needs *Remedial and Special Education, 24*(2), 97–114.

Lee, J., Grigg, W., & Dion, G. (2007). *The nation's report card: Mathematics 2007* (NCES 2007-494). Washington, DC: National Center for Educational Statistics, Institute of Education Sciences, U.S. Department of Education.

Maccini, P., & Gagnon, J. (2002). Perceptions and application of NCTM standards by special and general education teachers. *Exceptional Children, 68,* 325–344.

Maccini, P., & Hughes, C.A. (2000). Effects of a problem-solving strategy on the introductory algebra performance of secondary students with learning disabilities. *Learning Disabilities Research & Practice, 15,* 10–21.

Mastropieri, M. A., & Scruggs, T. E. (2007). *The inclusive classroom: Strategies for effective instruction* (3rd ed.). Upper Saddle River, NJ: Merrill/Pearson.

McLeskey, J., Hoppey, D., Williamson, P., & Rentz, T. (2004). Is inclusion an illusion? An examination of national and state trends toward the education of students with learning disabilities in general education classrooms. *Learning Disabilities Research and Practice, 19*(2), 109–115.

Mercer, C., & Mercer, A. (2005). *Teaching students with learning problems* (7th ed.). Upper Saddle River, NJ: Pearson/Merrill-Prentice Hall.

Miller, S. P., & Hudson, P. (2007). Using evidence-based practices to build mathematics competencies related to conceptual, procedural, and declarative knowledge. *Learning Disabilities Research & Practice, 22*(1), 47–57.

Miller, S. P., & Mercer, C. D. (1993). Using data to learn about concrete-semiconcrete-abstract instruction for students with math disabilities. *Learning Disabilities Research & Practice, 8,* 89–96.

Monroe, E. E., & Orme, M. P. (2002). Developing missing vocabulary. *Preventing School Failure, 46*(3), 139–142.

Montague, M., & Jitendra, A. (2006). *Teaching mathematics to middle school students with learning difficulties.* New York: Guilford Press.

Montague , M., Warger, C., & Morgan, T. H. (2000). Solve It! Strategy instruction to improve mathematical problem solving. *Learning Disabilities Research and Practice, 15,* 10–16.

Montague, M., & Bos, C. S. (1996). The effect of cognitive strategy training of verbal math problem solving performance on learning disabled adolescents. *Journal of Learning Disabilities, 19,* 26–33.

National Center for Education Statistics. (2009). *Highlights from the Trends in International Mathematics and Science Study (TIMSS) 2009.* Washington, DC: U.S. Government Printing Office.

National Council of Teachers of Mathematics. (2000). *Principles and standards for school mathematics.* Reston, VA: Author.

National Council of Teachers of Mathematics. (1995). *Principles and standards for school mathematics.* Reston, VA: Author.

National Research Council. (2001). *Adding it up: Helping children learn mathematics.* Washington, DC: National Academy Press.

National Research Council. (1989). *Everyday counts: A report to the nation on the future of mathematics education.* Washington, DC: National Academy Press.

Riccomini, P. J. (2005). Identification and remediation of systematic error patterns in subtraction. *Learning Disability Quarterly, 25,* 233–242.

Safer, N., & Fleishman, S. (2005). How student progress monitoring improves instruction. *Educational Leadership, 62,* 81–83,

Witzel, B. S., Ferguson, C. J., & Brown, D. (2007). Early numeracy skills for students with learning disabilities. *LDOnline Exclusive* [Available online at www.ldonline.com].

Woodward, J. (2004). Mathematics education in the United States: Past to present. *Journal of Learning Disabilities, 37*(1), 16–31.

Woodward, J., & Montague, M. (2002). Meeting the challenge of mathematics reform for students with LD. *The Journal of Special Education, 36* (2), 89–101.

12

Cases About Teaching Math Skills in Inclusive Classrooms

CASE 1

Not a Sweet Deal

Carri Webber handed out a worksheet with 15 word problems on it and told the students to read the first question to themselves. "Okay, now that you have had some time to review the first problem, let's discuss it," said Mrs. Webber. Dosha Kunkle had read the problem silently and quietly told herself how much she hated doing math problems, particularly math word problems. She followed that thought with a heavy sigh.

"Dosha, I want you to read the problem out loud and we'll work through it together," Mrs. Webber continued. As Mrs. Webber waited patiently at the board, Dosha's anxiety level had risen, and her face grimaced as she began to read the problem. "Tiasha had 12 bags of chocolate kisses and there are 42 kisses per bag. She opened up all the bags and put them on the table. When she did so, she found that four chocolate kisses were bad and had to be thrown out. Tiasha decided to pack the remaining kisses into bags, with 10 kisses per bag. How many bags of kisses did she make?" "Whew!" Dosha exclaimed. "That is one long problem." "Yes," remarked Mrs. Webber as she wrote parts of the problem on the board. She continued, "Okay, Dosha, let's look at the parts and solve this problem together. How many kisses were dumped on the table?" Dosha silently voiced parts of the problem and finally said, "Twelve bags times, however, many are in a bag." "Right," Mrs. Webber remarked and continued, "Now if there are 42 in a bag, how many are on the table?" Dosha tried to think through the problem, but by now she was completely lost. "Well, Dosha, how many?" Finally, after Mrs. Webber asked her a third time for the answer, Dosha said, "I don't know, and besides, I don't even like chocolate." Mrs. Webber said, "Alright let me do it, and you listen. Okay class, write this down." Mrs. Webber wrote *12 × 42 = 504*. As she looked around the room, all of her students were busy writing down the answer, except Dosha, who was staring out the window. Mrs. Webber, who was getting irritated with Dosha, shouted back to her, "Write it down!" Dosha, who wasn't paying attention, simply wrote down what was written on the board (failing to comprehend how her teacher derived the answer).

"Now you do the rest with me," she instructed the class, despite the fact that many students were already finished the problem and had moved on to the next one. As Mrs. Webber completed the problem on the board (*504 − 4 = 500, and 500/10 bags = 50 per bag*), she stopped everyone and made them respond in unison, "There are 50 kisses per bag."

It is not surprising than many of the students were working ahead because the class had been reviewing word problems for the past 3 weeks. However for Dosha, an inclusion student with learning disabilities (LD), completing math word problems is an excruciating task. In addition to her reading problems, she performs poorly in math, often failing to pick up concepts that other students easily understand. Over time, despite the quality of her math instruction, Dosha had grown to dislike math and often avoids anything related to it. For example, when Mrs. Webber informed students that they could complete one extra worksheet per week for bonus points, Dosha flatly refused, despite the fact that it could have raise her D grade to a C.

Perry Vascar, the LD resource teacher, is aware of Dosha's problems in math, and occasionally co-teaches with Mrs. Webber, but lately has been unable to co-teach because of other duties. In reviewing Dosha's most recent psychological evaluation on achievement, Mr. Vascar found the following scores:

Woodcock-Johnson III NU—Tests of Achievement

Subtest	Percentile Rank	Standard Score
Letter-Word Identification	53	101
Reading Fluency	37	92
Story Recall	27	62
Understanding Directions	12	29
Calculation	19	40
Math Fluency	17	34
Spelling	43	78
Writing Fluency	48	97
Passage Comprehension	37	95
Applied Problems	10	24
Writing Samples	42	97
Story Recall—Delay	34	76

"Huh," Mr. Vascar remarked to himself, "just what I thought. Dosha has some problems with calculation and application of math problems." As Mr. Vascar further reviewed her records, he noticed that someone at her previous school had also administered the *Test of Math Ability* (*TOMA*). The report reads, "Dosha performed 'average' on the subtest of vocabulary (percentile rank score = 50), 'below average' on the subtests of computation (percentile rank score = 9) and general information (percentile rank score = 16), and 'poor' on the subtest of story problems (percentile rank score = 2).

Discussion Questions

1. From the case, what skill(s) would you target for remediation? Or what skill(s) would you target for further assessment?
2. In the classroom, choose a skill area, and decide what modifications and/or supports could be used to help Dosha.
3. Outside of the inclusion class, choose a skill area, and decide what remedial technique(s) and/or strategy(ies) could be taught to her to strengthen a weak skill area(s).

4. If you taught this student a strategy or technique outside of the inclusion classroom, what could you do to ensure that it generalized to her classes or other settings?

5. How would you monitor progress on the skill(s)? Describe how and when you would monitor progress.

CASE 2

Let's Talk Math Skills

As the individualized educational plan (IEP) meeting began, Lance was the first to speak, "If I gotta learn math, I wanna learn stuff that can get me into college." "That's good thinking on your part, Lance, but you also have to consider that math skills can help you in everyday living," replied Henry Reath, Lance's special education math teacher. Sitting around the table were Lance's parents, Judy and Frances Kiko; Lance's 10th-grade math teacher, Latera Young; the assistant principal, Douglas Cox; and Lance's transition specialist, Pierre LaFranc. Most listened intently and patiently to Lance's request for more academic math classes that would earn him enough credits to graduate with a regular diploma and those that would allow him to enter Gordon Grey Community College. But everyone, except Lance's parents and Lance himself, knew that Lance had difficulty in math and probably needed more functional math skills such as those taught by Mr. Reath. As the discussion went back and forth with both sides eventually reaching a compromise on a mix between both types of IEP objectives, and therefore two different math classes, Mr. Reath left the room feeling as if he had his work cut out for him in trying to help Lance master math skills from many different levels.

Mr. Reath had been at Quigley High School for the past several years and had begun co-teaching math with Ms. Young for the past 2 years. Henry spends most of his day in collaborative math classes and spends one block of time teaching remedial math to 10th- and 11th-grade students such as Lance. Mr. Reath feels that his job is to teach these kids math skills that will help them in life. Lance, on the other hand, frequently has difficulty with even some of Mr. Reath's easiest problems. Having to experience Lance's math problems on a daily basis, Mr. Reath has a difficult time accepting the fact that Lance should be in the inclusion algebra class. When Lance complains that his remedial math is too difficult, Mr. Reath points out to Lance that he is doing only seventh- or eighth-grade math.

Lance has been in classes for students with LD since he was first identified as LD in fourth grade. Lance has a slightly higher-than-average IQ, yet his disabilities prevent him from fully reaching his true potential, particularly in math. In other subject areas, Lance performs average or above average. His math disability is the main reason he continues to receive special education services. For Lance, math is a constant struggle; he displays what his teacher calls "splinter skills" in math. In other words, Lance has mastered certain math skills, yet has not mastered and may never master other math skills. For instance, Lance still has difficulty with higher multiplication facts (e.g., eights and nines), yet he understands some higher level geometry and algebra concepts that other students did not master. Lance gets a lot of math. In addition to being tutored after school, Lance attends another math class on weekends at the local university. This college-level math class specializes in remedial math; it does not count toward college credit because it is remedial math.

In Lance's inclusion algebra class, he and another student with LD are learning Algebra I. Ms. Young and Mr. Reath co-teach this class. They take turns leading and supporting math lessons.

Usually, Mr. Reath completes the warm-up (i.e., a review of yesterday's lesson and homework) with students and Ms. Young takes over to teach the new concepts. Lance has been struggling in this class. He has difficulty learning many of the subjects and has earned some low scores on recent tests. Even though his tutor has retaught Lance much of the material, he still struggles. For example, during a recent lesson Ms. Young was teaching students how to use a formula to determine slope. Lance said he understood the formula, but then scored poorly on a weekly test. He missed the problems that involved determining the slope of a line. Incidents like these lead Mr. Reath to conclude that Lance belongs in his remedial math class on a full-time basis.

During a planning period, Ms. Young and Mr. Reath discussed Lance's problems on a recent test and possible accommodations that they could provide for him. "There goes our math genius," Mr. Reath said to Ms. Young as the students filed out of class. Ms. Young chuckled and replied that Mr. Reath "deserves a medal for the 'most patience' in math." Mr. Reath just smiled, knowing that his patience was slowly running out. "Well" he said, "what can we do for this kid besides providing math fact charts? Are there other accommodations that we should be providing?" "Or, for that matter, want to provide?" Ms. Young followed up. Both felt that the use of a calculator might be an accommodation at times, yet be an unfair advantage at other times. "I'm not for allowing unlimited use of a calculator," Henry blurted out. "Yes, I agree," said Ms. Young, "but if we don't, he'll probably fail most of the upcoming math tests. Let's face it; he missed most of the test problems because of his poor multiplication and division skills." "What else can we do?" asked Henry, knowing that Lance might be reaching his limits in the area of math.

Discussion Questions

1. From the case, what skill(s) would you target for remediation? Or what skill(s) would you target for further assessment?
2. In the classroom, choose a skill area and decide what modifications and/or supports could be used to help Lance. When does an accommodation become an unfair advantage or crutch for students in special education?
3. Outside of the inclusion class, choose a skill area and decide what remedial technique(s) and/or strategy(ies) could be taught to Lance to strengthen a weak skill area(s).
4. If you taught this student a strategy or technique outside of the inclusion classroom, what could you do to ensure that it generalized to other classes or settings?
5. How would you monitor progress on the skill(s)? Describe how and when you would monitor progress.

CASE 3

Two Wells Make a Dam

Allyson Wiath is a pleasant, happy fifth-grade child for most of the day, except during math class. During this time she often becomes frustrated, particularly with math word problems.

Allyson (or, "Ally," as she is called) receives special education services in the emotional disturbance (ED) program. Math is the only area that she receives special education services, and she receives these services in a collaborative math class. For Ally, math is a subject that has long tormented her, along with two other children in the class: Tasha Turner and Freda Wallace.

Yesterday's math word problems frustrated her to such an extent that she ended up throwing her books at the wall in a fit of rage and taking a swipe at her classroom nemesis, Tasha. The first problem that she encountered looked like this:

Question 1: The movie, *China's Population*, has a running time of 48 minutes. Mr. Glass wants to have a 25-minute discussion after the film and wants to finish the class by 2:10 p.m. What time should he start showing the movie?

"What do I care when the movie should begin," Ally quietly said to herself. Ally then wrote down *48 + 25 = 73*. She then added 73 minutes to 2:10 and came up with 3:83. When the fifth-grade collaborative teacher, Grace Cooke, came by, she exclaimed, "Ally, my dear, what have you done? How can you have a time of 3:83 p.m.?" Tasha, who was sitting next to her, giggled with joy when she overheard what Ally had done. "Shut up, or I'm gonna give it to you," was Ally's response to Tasha's chuckle. By the time Mrs. Cooke could tell Tasha to mind her own business, the two were yanking at each others' clothes and raising their hands ready to begin a full-fledged fight. "Stop it! Both of you!" bellowed Mrs. Cooke as she moved between the two girls. Tasha relaxed her grip on Ally, and Ally sat down. "Now girls, let's try to get along nicely," demanded Mrs. Cooke. After a deep sigh, Mrs. Cooke began explaining to Ally where she had made her mistake. Just as she finished, Silas Hillard, the ED collaborative teacher, walked in the room. "Sorry, sorry, sorry, I'm late but I have had a heck of a day," Mr. Hillard began explaining to Mrs. Cooke. "That's okay. We just almost had a problem, but it seems to be resolved," Mrs. Cooke replied. After a quick retell of the problem, Mr. Hillard moved next to Ally to help her with her math.

Ally wasn't the only one in the class who had a difficult time completing word problems. It seems that both Mrs. Cooke and Mr. Hillard were not very adept at teaching students how to solve word problems. For Mr. Hillard, math was actually his weakest subject area, and Mrs. Cooke was not much better.

No sooner had Mr. Hillard and Ally solved the first problem together when tensions arose again because of the second word problem:

Question 2: Sally spent $2.35 on lunch. Bert spent $.35 more than Sally. Gary spent $.20 less than Sally. What is the total amount that they spent?

"Great! Kids with lunch money," Ally said as she read the problem. "Now, now Ally," said an animated Mr. Hillard. "Let's see where we begin with this problem." As he stretched out his arms, rolled up his sleeves, and jotted down numbers on a piece of paper, Mr. Hillard actually looked as if he knew what he was doing. He then wrote down the answer and walked over to the teacher's guide only to find that he has done the problem incorrectly. "Well, well, let's see how to do this," he said to himself as he scratched his head and wet the tip of his pencil. "My grandmom says two wells make a dam," Tasha whispered to Freda as the two chuckled. Finally after his third attempt, Mr. Hillard came up with the correct answer. "Okay Ally, let's walk you through this one," said Mr. Hillard as he sat down next to her. "And you be quiet," he yelled over to Tasha when he saw the smirk on her face. As he began to explain to Ally, he stumbled a number of times when telling her what number to add to what. Finally, he showed her his paper and said, "Just copy this down. This problem is too hard for you anyhow." Between Ally's low frustration level and her teachers' poor teaching, it was no wonder that she continued to struggle in math until the end of the school year.

Discussion Questions

1. From the case, what skill(s) would you target for remediation? Or what skill(s) would you target for further assessment?

2. In the classroom, choose a skill area, and decide what modifications and/or supports could be used to help Ally.

3. Outside of the inclusion class, choose a skill area, and decide what remedial technique(s) and/or strategy(ies) could be taught to Ally to strengthen a weak skill area(s).

4. If you taught this student a strategy or technique outside of the inclusion/collaborative classroom, what could you do to ensure that it generalized to her classes or other settings?

5. How would you monitor progress on the skill(s)? Describe how and when you would monitor progress.

6. When teaching math word problems, what could you do to aid student understanding in this area?

CASE 4

Too Much Dividing at Once

Vladimir Sheshenski is a sixth-grade student at Colonial Ark Middle School (CAMS). CAMS takes in students from three area elementary schools and is one of the largest and most crowded middle schools in the state. As such, most new middle school students often feel lost once they enter the doors of CAMS. However, Vladimir, or Vlad for short, was a tough young guy from the urban streets and wasn't going to let anyone tell him what to do.

Vlad was identified as ED, although his elementary school teachers claimed that all of his problems were strictly behavioral. He had caused numerous behavioral problems for all of his past elementary school teachers, and his CAMS teachers had already been warned by his fifth-grade teacher, Julius Duncan. In fifth grade, Vlad has been in a number of fights with both teachers and other students. His academic skills were less than stellar, especially his grades in mathematics which was a subject that he hated the most. Often Vlad came to school angry and full of rage.

At CAMS, Swazi Perkins, the inclusion teacher and the sixth-grade teacher, Lizzy Snead, had worked together over the past 2 years. Mr. Perkins teaches three collaborative classes with Mrs. Snead and also works with students in small groups in his resource room. Besides Vlad, Mr. Perkins is responsible for seven other students with disabilities. All of his students spend all or most of their day in Mrs. Snead's collaborative classes. Typically, Mr. Perkins spends his mornings co-teaching and his afternoons working with students individually or in small groups in the resource room.

From Vlad's paperwork, Mr. Perkins was able to determine that Vlad was identified 4 years ago as ED because of excessive talking, fighting, and disrespect of teachers and other authority figures. He also found out that Vlad's slightly lower IQ of 87, along with the aggressive behavior, might be his biggest problems with school. Because of this, Mr. Perkins decided to break down tasks into small manageable parts so that Vlad would not become frustrated, and provide lots of practice with these parts and lots of reinforcement for working appropriately. Mr. Perkins also noticed that Vlad has a lot of difficulty when given too much work at once and that Vlad has to get his anger under control if he is to ever make it in the world.

In math, when Mrs. Snead and Mr. Perkins examined some work samples, they found that Vlad knew most of his math facts but had performed poorly on fifth- and sixth-grade math skills such as multiplying and dividing multi-digit numbers, adding and subtracting fractions, and multiplying and dividing decimals. In particular, when they examined Vlad's division problems, they found that he made numerous mistakes on long-division problems.

When they examined five problems, they found that he made these errors:

$$
\begin{array}{r}
222 \\
3\overline{)666} \\
-600 \\
\hline
66 \\
-60 \\
\hline
6 \\
-6 \\
\hline
0
\end{array}
\qquad
\begin{array}{r}
680 \\
3\overline{)258} \\
-240 \\
\hline
18 \\
-18 \\
\hline
0
\end{array}
\qquad
\begin{array}{r}
222 \\
4\overline{)888} \\
-800 \\
\hline
88 \\
-80 \\
\hline
8 \\
-8 \\
\hline
0
\end{array}
$$

$$
\begin{array}{r}
310 \\
5\overline{)515} \\
-500 \\
\hline
15 \\
-15 \\
\hline
0
\end{array}
\qquad
\begin{array}{r}
650 \\
6\overline{)336} \\
-300 \\
\hline
36 \\
-36 \\
\hline
0
\end{array}
$$

(1) $3\overline{)666}$ (2) $3\overline{)258}$ (3) $4\overline{)888}$ (4) $5\overline{)515}$ (5) $6\overline{)336}$

Discussion Questions

1. From the case, what skill(s) would you target for remediation? Or what skill(s) would you target for further assessment?
2. In the classroom, choose a skill area and decide what modifications and/or supports could be used to help Vlad. When does an accommodation become an unfair advantage or crutch for students in special education?
3. Outside of the inclusion class, choose a skill area, and decide what remedial technique(s) and/or strategy(ies) could be taught to Vlad to strengthen a weak skill area(s).
4. If you taught this student a strategy or technique outside of the inclusion classroom, what could you do to ensure that it generalized to his classes or other settings?
5. How would you monitor progress on the skill(s)? Describe how and when you would monitor progress.

CASE 5

No Time for Time

Ms. Jane Sawyer is the LD teacher who co-teaches with Harrison Keys, the second-grade teacher. On most days, they use parallel teaching when working on new concepts; they split the class in two, and each teaches the same content to their respective groups. They feel that working with each group enables them to teach concepts more thoroughly and provide immediate feedback during guided practice. Now in their third year of collaboration, the two work well together and play off each other's strengths. This week involves using miniature clocks to help students tell time.

As Wilma held the clock's minute hand down on the 1 and simultaneously moved the hour hand to the 3, she thought about how cool it was to have a clock that she could play with during math. "Wilma, what time does your clock say?" asked Ms. Sawyer. Ms. Sawyer was working with her group on math in the back of the room. "Ah, I think . . . I think . . . it say three O' one," responded Wilma in a less-than-certain tone. Wilma was one of her students with disabilities who always needed additional review or overlearning to learn concepts to mastery. "Three O' five is the correct answer," replied Ms. Sawyer. "Okay class, let's move the minute hand to the 7 and the hour hand between the 8 and the 9. Now what time is it?" asked Ms. Sawyer. Just then the bell rang, and Clark (another student with disabilities) blurted out, "It means it's time to go to lunch." The children around him giggled, and Ms. Sawyer glared at him as she repeated her question: "What time is it?" As the noise level grew louder and the anticipation of lunch came closer, Ms. Sawyer finally said, "Okay, it's 8:35. Now, you can go."

As the students raced out of the room, Mr. Keys quickly followed after them, yelling out the names of those who needed lunch tickets. As he exited the class, he said, "Lorna, don't go anywhere. I want to discuss math for tomorrow, okay?" Lorna nodded her head in agreement and let out a big smile because she knew that she could now have a minute or two of quiet time to herself. The aroma of battered fish and french fries wafted into the room from the cafeteria. "Mmm, smells edible today," she thought to herself.

Within minutes Mr. Keys returns. "Lorna, thanks for sticking around. I noticed that both groups are really having a tough time telling time. No pun intended," he said. Ms. Sawyer had also noticed that her two students with mild CI (cognitive impairments) and three students with LD were also having trouble with telling time by fives. "Yeah, the group in general is kinda not getting it . . . except Roger and Airsha [the two high achievers]," replied Ms. Sawyer. "I really don't know if I should go back to half-hour problems or spend more time counting by fives." Mr. Keys said. "Well, we need to do something because they just aren't getting it," Ms. Sawyer responded, "especially my students (with disabilities). I'll think about it over my lunch of fish and chips, or as the kids call it, 'farts and chips.'" "Yeah," said Mr. Keys, who was now lost in deep thought.

As Ms. Sawyer walked down the hall, she too had thought about a better way to teach telling time, but as of yet couldn't think of anything. She knew that her students needed to master this concept, or they would perform poorly on the annual state standards test. The problem with teaching with Mr. Keys was that he moved too quickly over concepts and relied too heavily on homework to make up for his poor teaching and insufficient time spent on concepts. She knew that she had only 1 more day to help students in the class because 2 days from now they would be moving on to a new concept—counting money. She thought to herself, "It's ironic that there's no *time* for teaching *time*." According to the skills-pacing chart in Mr. Keys's room, they should have completed "time" two weeks ago.

The next day when she returned to his class, Ms. Sawyer found that Mr. Keys had prepared materials for teaching students how to count money. "Let's try to finish up telling time in the first half of math and try to cover counting money in the second half," he told Ms. Sawyer as she entered the room. "Okay," she said, "but we really need to. . . ." Just then students began to file into the room. As she rushed to get them into their groups, she thought about how they needed more review and coverage on telling time. "Okay, my group, come back with your chairs to me," she yelled over student voices. When she began her lesson with them, she found most of them knew how to complete the worksheet with clock faces, but her two students, Wilma and Clark, did not know how to correctly solve the questions.

Before she could completely review the entire worksheet, she heard Mr. Keys say that it was time to move on to counting money. "What else could I have done to help them learn how to tell time?" she thought to herself.

Discussion Questions

1. From the case, what skill(s) would you target for remediation? Or what skill(s) would you target for further assessment?
2. In the classroom, choose a skill area, and decide what modifications and/or supports could be used to help Wilma.
3. Outside of the inclusion class, choose a skill area, and decide what remedial technique(s) and/or strategy(ies) could be taught to Wilma to strengthen a weak skill area(s).
4. If you taught a student a strategy or technique outside of the inclusion classroom, what could you do to ensure that it generalized to classes or other settings?
5. How would you monitor progress on the skill(s)? Describe how and when you would monitor progress.

13

Effective Techniques for Teaching in the Content Areas

Teachers charged with the responsibility of instructing students with and without disabilities in science and social studies are faced with many challenges and opportunities. The challenges lie in the difficulties many students face in mastering content, as well as with potential teacher preparation concerns; however, opportunities exist in the many techniques available to more efficiently implement instruction to meet student needs. To briefly review teacher preparation in both general and special education, teachers certified to teach in grades K–6 typically hold elementary-level certification. Their college/university coursework prepares them as generalists rather than content-area experts. Depending on the college program and state requirements for initial certification, teachers focusing on K–6 may have as few as one course preparing them to teach science and/or social studies and limited coursework in working with students with disabilities. On the other hand, teachers certified to teach in grades 7–12 hold either middle-grades certification, with "content-specific" certification in one or more areas, or, usually at the high school level, certification in a specific area of instruction such as science, history, math, English, and so on. Again, these teachers may receive little preparation for working with students with disabilities. On the other hand, teachers certified to teach students with mild disabilities in grades K–12 are prepared to instruct students across all subject areas but generally lack "content-specific" expertise (Dieker & Murawaski, 2003). As a result, special education teachers serve as "experts" in working with content-area specialists, assisting them in modifying materials, creating accommodations on assessments, and modifying instruction in order to meet the needs of students with mild disabilities.

These differences in teacher preparation programs between general K–6, content-specific 7–12, and K–12 special education affect the roles of teachers working to support the content area needs of students with mild disabilities (Dieker & Murawski, 2003). Additionally, the delivery model of instruction specified by each student's individualized education program (IEP) affects the role of the special education teacher in this support process. Depending on IEP recommendations, a student with mild disabilities may receive limited-to-no support from a special education teacher when in an inclusive content-area class. Conversely, another student with mild disabilities might receive extensive support from a special education teacher or paraprofessional when included in a content-area class or when receiving primary instruction from the special education teacher. Therefore, the role of general and special education teachers in delivering content-area instruction to students with mild disabilities is in many ways predicated on the IEP and varies accordingly (Dieker & Little, 2005). However, regardless of IEP requirements for service delivery, the challenges and needs of students with disabilities, as well as those who have limited English proficiency and those who may be at risk for failure, must be met.

This chapter focuses on some of the problems and concerns in working with students in the content areas, as well as on research and effective techniques for supporting students with mild disabilities.

PROBLEMS IN THE CONTENT AREAS

Many students with and without mild disabilities struggle with learning concepts, understanding content, and demonstrating knowledge in social studies and science (Grigg, Lauko, & Brockway, 2006; Lee & Weiss, 2007). These students' issues with learning and their troubles in demonstrating knowledge are compounded by difficulties in decoding, comprehension, memory, and text navigation, as well as in performance on tests (Lenz, Deshler, & Kissam, 2004; Scruggs, Mastropieri, & Okolo, 2008). In an effort to define students' mastery of curriculum and/or achievement, the U.S. Department of Education has gathered performance data on students in public and private school settings for more than 30 years (Grigg, Lauko, & Brockway, 2006). These data have been reported through *The Nation's Report Card* via the National Assessment of Educational Progress (NAEP). The NAEP reports three achievement levels, from lowest to highest:

1. *Basic*—denotes partial mastery of the knowledge and skills that are fundamental for proficient work at a given grade.
2. *Proficient*—represents solid academic performance. Students reaching this level have demonstrated competency over challenging subject matter.
3. *Advanced*—signifies superior performance. (Grigg, Lauko, & Brockway, 2006, p. 5)

Student skill sets and/or achievement at each level (e.g., basic, proficient, and advanced) and grade tested (e.g., 4th, 8th, and 12th) are also defined by the NAEP. For example, students in grade 4 who perform at a basic level in social studies/U.S. history would be described as being able to

> identify and describe a few of the most familiar people, places, events, ideas, and documents in American history. They should be able to explain the reasons for celebrating most national holidays, have some familiarity with the geography of their own state and the United States, and be able to express in writing a few ideas about a familiar theme in American history. (Lee & Weiss, 2007, p. 19)

Students in grade 4 who perform at a basic level in science would be described as being able to

> demonstrate some of the knowledge and reasoning required for understanding the Earth, physical, and life sciences at a level appropriate to grade 4. For example, they can carry out simple investigations and read uncomplicated graphs and diagrams. Students at this level also show a beginning understanding of classification, simple relationships, and energy. (Grigg, Lauko, & Brockway, 2006, p. 10)

According to *The Nation's Report Card*, student performance on the NAEP in U.S. history in 2006 improved for all grade levels measured and most subpopulations (Lee & Weiss, 2007). Data were reported differently for each grade level with regard to percentages at or above basic and at or above proficient. Seventy percent of 4th-grade students were reported to be at or above basic, 17% of 8th-grade students at or above proficient, and a scaled-score average of 12th-grade students at 290 (with the basic cut-off score being 294). These data reflect an issue with students achieving a minimum targeted performance at the proficient level at all grade levels in the area of U.S. history.

As per *The Nation's Report Card*, student performance on the NAEP in science in 2005 was mixed (Grigg, Lauko, & Brockway, 2006). In general, student performance in 4th-grade increased, in 8th-grade remained the same, and in 12th-grade declined. Sixty-eight percent of 4th-grade students performed at or above basic levels with only 29% performing at or above proficient levels. Fifty-nine percent of 8th-grade students performed at or above basic levels with only 29% performing at or above proficient levels. The results for middle school students with disabilities were even more sobering. Results from the 2005 NAEP in science found that only 27% scored at or above the basic level, with an astonishing 73% of these students scoring below basic. Similar trends are seen on state assessment tests for science, particularly for students from economically disadvantaged backgrounds and students with disabilities (Mastropieri et al., 2006). NAEP results for 12th-grade students showed that average scores declined from 1996 testing; 54% of students performed at or above basic levels, with only 18% performing at or above proficient levels (Grigg, Lauko, & Brockway, 2006).

Before more closely examining the skills students need to possess to perform adequately (i.e., at a proficient level or above on measures of knowledge), it is important to explore how social studies and science are typically taught at the elementary through high school levels in general education classrooms. In both social studies and science courses, textbooks and teachers tend to serve as primary sources of information for students (Scruggs, Mastropieri, & Okolo, 2008). In the early grades, teachers serve as primary conveyers of information; then, as students become more proficient in reading, they read texts for information (to learn). When this shift in instruction occurs, typically in fourth grade, students with mild disabilities, those learning English as a second language, and students at risk for academic failure tend to begin struggling in the content areas (Gunning, 2010). Furthermore, the depth and breadth of content that students are expected to learn increases exponentially by grade level. Once students enter middle and high school, content-area general education teachers approach instruction in a manner that matches the curriculum and/or scope and sequence of the courses taught, as well as their personal teaching preferences. These instructional methods may include lecture, cooperative learning activities, projects, labs, web-based activities, films, independent learning and/or reading of content, and so on (Scruggs, Mastropieri, & Okolo, 2008).

Students with mild disabilities and those at risk for academic failure in social studies and science share some common characteristics. Many have difficulty in literacy skills such as reading, language, and memory (e.g., decoding, interpreting visual information, comprehending written and spoken information, understanding and remembering the vast array of vocabulary); written language (e.g., taking notes, writing papers, responding to written test questions etc.); and relating content to personal lives (e.g., seeing the relevance of instruction) (Gunning, 2010; Lenz, Deshler, & Kissam, 2004; Scruggs, Mastropieri, & Okolo, 2008). In the areas of literacy and interpreting texts, students may face issues with discriminating between main ideas and supporting details, as well as with organizing information, screening relevant information, and remembering it. Furthermore, they may have difficulty expressing their knowledge concerning content through writing (Bulgren, Marquis, Lenz, Schumaker, & Deshler, 2009) due to deficits in written language skills (Gunning, 2010). Additionally, content area textbooks are heavily laden with vocabulary and information (Scruggs, Mastropieri, & Okolo, 2008), creating increased pressure on students already at risk for difficulty. Beyond these difficulties in classroom perform-ance measures, numerous research studies in the field of education (Anderman, 1998; Grigg, Lauko, & Brockway, 2006; Lee & Weiss, 2007; Mastropieri et al., 2006; Scruggs, Mastropieri, & Okolo, 2008) have demonstrated that students with mild disabilities and students who are at risk for academic failure are inclined to perform poorly on traditional measures of achievement in social studies and/or science. Thus, it is extremely important for general and special education teachers to work together to meet the needs of students with mild disabilities and students who are at risk of failure in the content areas.

STRATEGIES AND TECHNIQUES FOR CONTENT-AREA INSTRUCTION

The following sections present strategies and techniques that teachers may use to meet the needs of students served in inclusive content area classrooms. This information is not intended to cap-ture all of the strategies and techniques currently supported by the research, but rather to high-light a few for the reader.

Course Organizer

A group of researchers at the University of Kansas Center for Research and Learning created the *Course Organizer Routine* as part of the *Content Enhancement Series* (Lenz, Schumaker, Deshler, & Bulgren, 1998), published currently by Edge Enterprises, Inc. According to Lenz et al., "Content enhancement is an approach to planning instruction for and teaching content to diverse groups of students. It involves making decisions about what content to teach, manipulat-ing and translating that content into easy-to-understand formats, and presenting it in memorable ways" (1998, p. 1). The *Course Organizer Routine* may be used to organize course content that is typically provided over an extended period of time (e.g., a grading period, semester, and school year) and can be separated into units and lessons of instruction.

When using a Course Organizer, the teacher arranges the content and/or instruction into accessible segments. Course Organizers are broken into eight sections, with each section relating to a specific aspect of the course (Lenz, Schumaker, Deshler, & Bulgren, 1998). For example on page 1 of the Course Organizer shown in Figure 13.1, section 1 describes two forms of informa-tion (course title and course paraphrase). The course paraphrase is a summary statement of what the course is about and contains critical ideas that will be addressed. Section 2 lists a group of critical course questions that each student should be able to answer at the end of the course. The questions are designed to be broad in nature and to promote discussion. Course standards are listed in section 3. These standards describe the content of assignments and the processes used to demonstrate knowledge with respect to each with associated point values for each component. Section 3 also includes a course progress graph where students may graph their progress on each component measured by the standards.

On page 2 of the Course Organizer (see the sample course map in Figure 13.2), section 4 lists the critical concepts of the course in an oval. Directly below section 4, section 5 maps the content of the units in the course. The units are listed in the order of presentation. Section 6 includes community principles that illustrate the standards for learning and behavior of the group in the course. Section 7 lists the routines, or "rituals," that will be used to facilitate

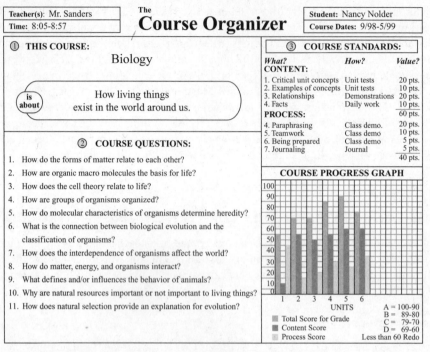

FIGURE 13.1 *Course Organizer Routine* Page 1 Sample

Source: Lenz, B. K., Schumaker, J. B., Deshler, D. D., & Bulgren, J. A. (1998). *The content enhancement series: The course organizer routine,* p. 73. Lawrence, KS: Edge Enterprises, Inc. Reprinted with permission.

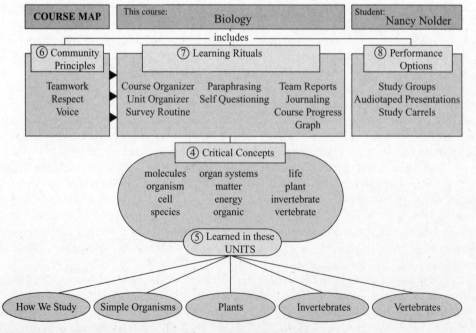

FIGURE 13.2 *Course Organizer Routine* Page 2 Course Map Sample

Source: Lenz, B. K., Schumaker, J. B., Deshler, D. D., & Bulgren, J. A. (1998). *The content enhancement series: The course organizer routine,* p. 74. Lawrence, KS: Edge Enterprises, Inc. Reprinted with permission.

learning during the course. And finally, section 8 lists the accommodations that will be available in the course to students to demonstrate mastery of information.

After general and special education teachers collaborate to develop drafts of both pages of the Course Organizer, they introduce the organizer to students. During this interactive process, teachers use the Linking Steps and Cue-Do-Review Sequence as part of the instructional routine. Because teachers must receive certification in content enhancement routines, including the *Course Organizer Routine,* interested teachers are referred to the University of Kansas at http://www.ku-crl.org/sim/content.shtml for more information on professional development opportunities in the use of the *Course Organizer Routine* and the *Content Enhancement Series.*

Unit Organizer

The *Unit Organizer Routine* is part of the *Content Enhancement Series* developed by researchers at the University of Kansas Center for Research on Learning. This particular routine was developed by Lenz, Bulgren, Schumaker, Deschler, and Boudah (1994) and is intended to supplement the *Course Organizer Routine* previously described. According to Lenz et al. (1994), "A unit is any 'chunk' of content that a teacher selects to organize information into lessons and that ends in some type of test or closure activity" (p. 2). Unit organizers are generally used in subject-area courses such as science, social studies, math, and so on.

As was the case with the Course Organizer, the Unit Organizer is also broken into sections (see Figure 13.3; Lenz et al., 1994). On page 1, section 1 lists the current unit and title name.

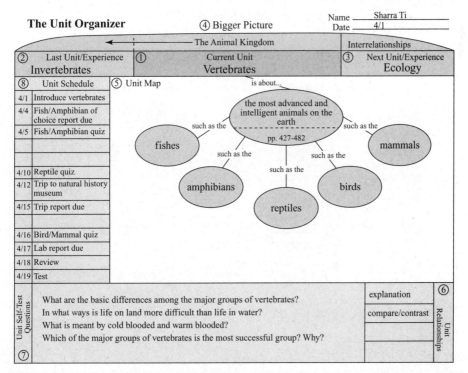

FIGURE 13.3 *Unit Organizer Routine* Page 1 Sample

Source: Lenz, B. K., Bulgren, J. A., Schumaker, J. B., Deshler, D. D., & Boudah, D. A. (1994). *The content enhancement series: The unit organizer routine,* p. 20. Lawrence, KS: Edge Enterprises, Inc. Reprinted with permission.

Section 2 lists the last unit or experience students had prior to the introduction of this particular unit. Section 3 lists the subsequent unit or experience that will follow. Section 4, the Bigger Picture, lists the main idea or theme that binds the units to each other. Section 5 contains a unit map graphic organizer with the unit paraphrase written in an oval, with corresponding page numbers from texts listed inside the oval as a reference. Content maps are then graphed below the oval describing or supporting how the unit content is organized. Transition and/or relational words are written on the lines leading from/to the main idea to the supporting detail sections. These words are critical elements designed to assist students in understanding the relationships between concepts included in the unit. Lenz et al. (1994) suggest that no more than seven subsections of the main topic be listed on the graphic organizer. Section 6 contains a brief list of unit relationships that may be investigated. Section 7 includes self-test questions that students should be able to answer at the conclusion of the unit. Section 8 provides a schedule for reference.

The second page (see Figure 13.4) contains two sections: an expanded unit map and new self-test questions.

After teachers develop drafts of both pages of the Unit Organizer, they introduce the organizer to students. During this interactive process, teachers should use the Linking Steps and Cue-Do-Review Sequence as part of the instructional routine, as was the case for the *Course Organizer Routine*.

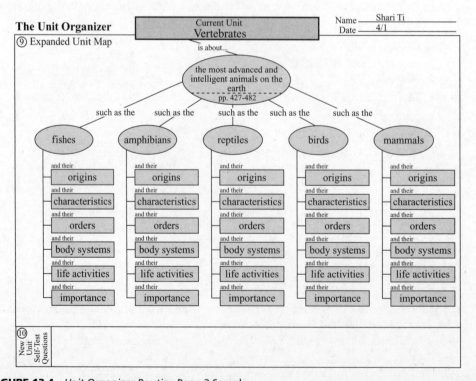

FIGURE 13.4 *Unit Organizer Routine* Page 2 Sample

Source: Lenz, B. K., Bulgren, J. A., Schumaker, J. B., Deshler, D. D., & Boudah, D. A. (1994). *The content enhancement series: The unit organizer routine*, p. 26. Lawrence, KS: Edge Enterprises, Inc. Reprinted with permission.

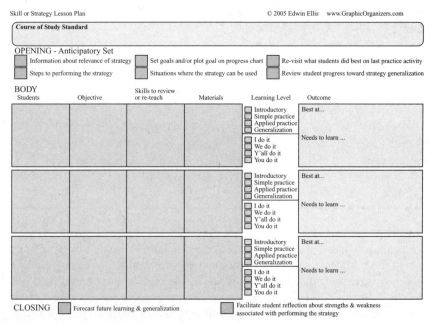

FIGURE 13.5   Makes Sense Strategy Sample Organizer

Source: Ellis, E. (2005). *Skill or strategy lesson plan.* http://www.GraphicOrganizers.com. Reprinted with permission.

Makes Sense Strategies

Developed by Edwin Ellis and Marcia Rock (2001), Makes Sense Strategies™ (MSS) are research-based procedures and instructional resources intended to enhance rather than "water-down" the curriculum. These strategies include a vast array of graphic organizers and methods that teachers can use to assist students in significantly increasing their academic performance across multiple content areas. According to Ellis (2008), MSS

- is based on principles of brain-based learning and universal instruction,
- features the use of cognitive elaboration strategies and higher order thinking skills,
- focuses on essential understandings of big ideas rather than memorization of trivia, and
- is used when teaching
- critical and analytical thinking;
  reading and listening comprehension;
  process writing and abstract concepts;
  social studies, science, and math; and
  social skills and character education. (p. 1)

Figure 13.5 illustrates one of the graphic organizers available from MSS. This particular organizer represents a skill or lesson plan teachers can follow.

   For further information on MSS, see http://www.GraphicOrganizers.com.

Supporting Reading and Writing in Content Area Instruction

Before moving into a discussion of content-specific strategies, we will next examine some methods that can be used to support reading and writing across content areas.

TABLE 13.1 Content-Area Textbook Characteristics

General Features	Specific Features
Table of contents	Use of bold print
Chapter introduction	Use of italics
Goals and/or learning objectives	Graphic organizers
Chapter conclusion	Charts, tables, graphs
Chapter questions	Illustrations and captions
Glossary	Textboxes and/or section summaries
Index	Vocabulary
Appendix	Amount of text

TEXT STRUCTURE. Textbooks are frequently used as the primary source of information in content-area classes (Conderman, Bresnahan, & Pedersen, 2009; Vaughn, Bos, & Schumm, 2007). Unfortunately, many students with and without disabilities have difficulty reading, comprehending, and navigating these texts. Difficulties at the middle and secondary level have come to be known as the "quiet crisis" (Gunning, 2010). Content area teachers and special education teachers supporting content instruction may need to explicitly teach students how to navigate and read texts (e.g., look at headings, make note of words that are in bold print). To do this, Vaughn, Bos, and Schumm (2007) recommend that teachers first familiarize themselves with the texts they plan to use by examining subject matter and social content, instructional design, readability, and friendliness level. Once these factors are determined, teachers should design instruction that leads students toward independent and/or supported navigation and reading of their texts. Table 13.1 briefly lists some textbook characteristics that teachers may wish to address during this evaluation.

WRITING IN THE CONTENT AREA. Smith, Rook, and Smith (2007) explored the use of metacognitive writing strategies paired with affective questioning techniques to increase engagement and student performance in ninth-grade world history. Specifically, they compared the use of structured journal writing with and without metacognitive and affective questions. They found that students who responded to metacognitive and affective questions while completing structured journal entries outperformed on end-of-the-semester-grades compared with students not using this technique. The results suggest that teachers who incorporate metacognitive and affective questioning techniques while using structured journal writing in content-area classrooms may increase student performance and learning. Bulgren, Marquis, Lenz, Schumaker, and Deshler (2009) investigated the effectiveness of question exploration techniques for increasing student comprehension and knowledge in inclusive content-area courses. Specifically, they explored the impact of content enhancement routines using Question Exploration Guides with their respective Question Exploration Routines to determine the impact on learning and comprehension. Additionally, they investigated the impact of these routines on students' writing about content. Bulgren et al. found that these interventions demonstrated significant results for students with and without learning disabilities.

STRATEGIC NOTE-TAKING SKILLS. Teaching students to take strategic notes during content-area classes has proven effective as a mechanism for increasing comprehension and future recall of information (Boyle, 2001, 2007, in press; Boyle & Weishaar, 2001). Simply described, strategic note taking involves students being taught to complete a strategic note-taking form. Initial instruction is direct and explicit (modeled using "think alouds"), and then moves into a guided practice phase, and then to an independent practice phase of the targeted skill.

Throughout the lecture, listen for CUES by using the following components:

C—Cluster: Cluster together three to six main points of the lecture.

U—Use: Use teacher cues to record ideas.
  Number cues—e.g., "There are six parts to the cell."
  Importance cues—e.g., "This is really important to remember."

E—Enter: Enter important vocabulary.

S—Summarize: Summarize quickly and whenever possible.

FIGURE 13.6   CUES to Strategic Note Taking

According to Boyle (2007), note taking should be viewed as a process that begins prior to the lecture and ends after students review their notes. Before the lecture, students should prepare themselves for the process of learning. During the lecture, students should strategically take notes. Following the lecture, students should review their notes by completing or filling in any missing information, clarifying information to enhance comprehension and, finally, reading the information several times to ensure recall. The CUES strategy (see Figure 13.6) was developed to assist students as they take notes using the strategic note-taking paper (see Figure 13.7).

Strategic Note-Taking Paper

Page 1

What is today's topic?
Describe what you know about the topic.
(Fill in this information before the lecture begins.)

When the lecture begins, use these pages to take notes.

Today's topic?
Name three to six main points with details of today's topic as they are being discussed.
Summary—Quickly describe how the ideas are related.
New vocabulary or terms:

Page 2

Name three to six **new** main points with details as they are being discussed.
New vocabulary or terms:
Summary—Quickly describe how the ideas are related.

Page X

Name three to six **new** main points with details as they are being discussed.
New vocabulary or terms:
Summary—Quickly describe how the ideas are related.

Last Page

At End of Lecture

Write five important lecture points and describe the details of each:

FIGURE 13.7   Strategic Note-Taking Paper (Abbreviated Version)

Source: From "The effects of a strategic note-taking technique on the comprehension and long term recall of lecture information for high school students with LD," by J. R. Boyle & M. K. Weishaar, 2001, *Learning Disabilities Research and Practice, 16*(3), p. 136.

Teachers can assist students in all of these phases by providing information in a logical and organized fashion.

GUIDED NOTES.   Guided note-taking procedures are supported in the research literature as a tool for increasing the academic performance of students with and without disabilities (Boyle, 2001; Konrad, Joseph, & Eveleigh, 2009; Lazarus, 1991). Generally defined, guided notes are typically formatted as outlines with blank spaces provided as areas for students to fill in information gained through lectures (listening and viewing) and reading (Boyle, 2001). Konrad, Joseph, and Eveleigh (2009) conducted a meta-analysis of the research concerning guided notes. They found that research indicates using guided notes is ". . . an effective and socially valid method for increasing note-taking accuracy and improving academic performance, particularly for school-age students" (p. 421). The authors also offered suggestions based on research by Heward (2001) for teachers wishing to implement this procedure:

> Guided notes are a low-cost and efficient way to help teachers promote active engagement during their lectures. Heward (2001) recommends the following steps for creating guided notes. First, teachers should create an outline of the lecture to be presented to students, focusing on the most salient concepts that students need to master. This outline can be created using presentation software (e.g., PowerPoint) or overhead transparencies, which the teacher will use to guide the lecture. Next, teachers should create a handout for the students, strategically omitting important information from the outline, leaving blanks for students to fill in as they listen to the lecture. Though students should not need to write lengthy responses, an adequate number of blanks must be distributed throughout the handout to encourage active attending and engagement. Also, there should enough space at each blank so students can record all information provided during the lecture. One way to identify which information to delete is to determine which content will be included on the follow-up assessments. (pp. 440–441)

The strategies and techniques noted in this section serve as models for ways in which teachers can generally assist struggling learners in content area classrooms. The following sections also offer strategies that can be implemented across content areas but, for the purposes of this chapter, have been separated into science or social studies instruction.

STRATEGIES AND TECHNIQUES FOR SCIENCE INSTRUCTION

Extensive research has been conducted over the last 15 years concerning strategies and techniques for supporting academic instruction and performance of students with learning disabilities in the area of science. The following sections highlight some of the strategies and techniques that have proven effective.

Mnemonic Instruction

Mnemonic techniques differ in their intricacy and their cognitive demands (Wood, Woloshyn, & Willoughby, 1995). Some techniques include one or two steps, such as seen in rote memorization through verbalization, whereas others involve more complex sequences such as those used in visual imagery and memorization. Wood, Woloshyn, and Willoughby noted that, "Imagery is an important component of many mnemonic strategies because the process of creating unique mental pictures to represent new information makes that material more *distinctive* and, therefore, more memorable" (p. 6).

There are five types of mnemonic strategies: rhymes, first-letter mnemonics, method of loci, pegwords, and keywords. Rhymes can be used as cues to assist individuals with recalling words, phrases, or important information. For example, the rhyme: "Red sky at night, sailor's delight; Red sky at morning, sailors take warning" helps students remember that a colorful sunset usually means nice weather is coming, whereas a colorful sunrise means there might be a storm. Teachers may choose to directly teach students rhymes to aid in recall of information or guide students through the process of creating their own rhymes (Wood, Woloshyn, & Willoughby, 1995).

First-letter mnemonics are words, acronyms, or acrostics that may be used to remember lists of words or phrases. For example, the words *Roy G. Biv* may be used to help students remember the colors of the rainbow (red, orange, yellow, green, blue, indigo, and violet). Additionally, the acronym PEMDAS might be used to represent the phrase *Please Excuse My Dear Aunt Sally* to aid students in remembering the order of operations in mathematics (Parentheses/Exponents/Multiplication and Division/Addition and Subtraction).

The method of loci is reported to be the oldest mnemonic system, dating back to the ancient Greeks. This system involves visualizing a series of well-known locations and then ordering items or concepts in these locations as a cue for remembering in sequence. While in the remembering/retrieval stage, the individual "walks" though each location, recalling information in succession. Wood, Woloshyn, and Willoughby (1995) noted that individuals using this strategy must construct a connection and/or interaction between items and their corresponding locations.

Pegwords are sets of rhyming words used to symbolize numbers. This strategy is used to help individuals remember information concerning numbers or other information in a specific sequence. Here again, individuals need to use imagery in order to remember and associate the number with the rhyming pegword. Table 13.2 illustrates a common list of pegwords used for the numbers one through eight.

The final mnemonic strategy is the key word. Key words require individuals to not only make a visual image, but also an auditory link (associate the word with a word or part of a word that sounds the same). For example, an individual wishes to learn and remember the Mohs scale

TABLE 13.2 Common List of Pegwords Used for Numbers One Through Eight

Number	Peg
one	bun
two	shoe
three	tree
four	door
five	hive
six	sticks
seven	heaven
eight	gate

Word	Image of Word	Keyword	Image of Keyword
talc		talcum	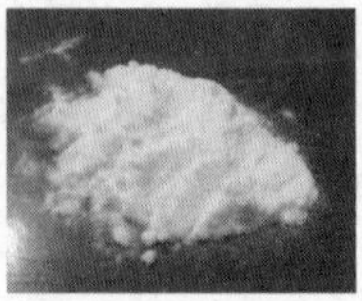
gypsum		gypsy	

FIGURE 13.8 Key Words and Images for the Mohs Scale of Mineral Hardness

of mineral hardness (talc, gypsum, calcite, fluorite, apatite, orthoclase feldspar, quartz, topaz, corundum, diamond). He/she associates the word *talc* with the word *talcum* and then visualizes powder. The word *gypsum* is associated with *gypsy,* and then a gypsy is visualized, and so on. Figure 13.8 illustrates these examples.

Several research studies have demonstrated the effectiveness of teaching mnemonic strategies to students with mild disabilities for learning science-related vocabulary and content (Mastropieri, Scruggs, & Graetz, 2005; Scruggs & Mastropieri, 1992; Scruggs & Mastropieri, 2000; Scruggs, Mastropieri, & Okolo, 2008). For more information concerning mnemonic and/or cognitive strategy instruction, see the sources Babkie and Provost (2002); Pressley et al. (1995); and Wood, Woloshyn, and Willoughby (1995), to name a few.

Effective Techniques for Science Text Comprehension

Summarization strategies to facilitate comprehension of science-based texts have proven effective for students with mild disabilities, students at risk for academic failure, and students learning English as a second language (Honnert & Bozan, 2005; Scruggs, Mastropieri, & Okolo, 2008). Honnert and Bozan (2005) found that, for teaching students served in special education programs who were also learning English as a second language, summarization strategies as part of reading science-related texts increased student ability to attain, comprehend, and use information. Furthermore, they found that teaching students to use summary frames improved their subsequent ability to apply learned information to class discussions, hands-on assignments, and other activities. One such strategy includes summary frames in which teachers provide a list of questions for students. Students are directed to answer these questions, then summarize their responses into paragraph form. Scruggs, Mastropieri, and Okolo (2008) noted that multiple research studies show positive results for students with learning disabilities when taught summarization strategies for comprehending the main idea and supporting details, evaluating text structure, and studying expository texts.

Classwide peer tutoring is another technique supported by the research literature for enhancing science instruction for students with mild disabilities and for English language learners (Mastropieri et al., 2006). Although there are multiple models of classwide peer tutoring, only one is described here. This example focuses on differentiated instruction designed to meet the diverse needs of learners. Tutors and tutees then take turns in each role and support each other in learning content. The Mastropieri et al. (2006) study showed that classwide peer tutoring, when paired with differentiated instruction, facilitated increased student performance on content-area summative tests, as well as on high-stakes assessments.

Lab-based and/or hands-on science instruction is an additional procedure proven effective for increasing the science-based knowledge of students with and without disabilities (Kirch, Bargerhuff, Turner, & Wheatly, 2005; Lee, Lewis, Adamson, Maerten-Rivera, & Secada, 2007; Scruggs, Mastropieri, & Okolo, 2008). Multiple studies have demonstrated the positive effects of these methods for learning content, ranging anywhere from the knowledge of rocks to understanding magnetism to the differences in ecosystems to the intricacies of high school chemistry (Mastropieri et al., 2005; Scruggs, Mastropieri, & Okolo, 2008). Lab-based and/or hands-on science activities provide students with opportunities to interact with concrete examples of the content they are responsible for learning and remembering.

Coached elaboration and guided inquiry are further procedures that have been found to support science learning of students with mild disabilities. When instruction is delivered in highly structured and supportive learning environments, students with mild disabilities profit from guided inquiry procedures using higher order questioning techniques. Additionally, coached elaboration is also beneficial for this population in both laboratory-like and classroom-based settings (Scruggs, Mastropieri, & Okolo, 2008).

As noted by Scruggs, Mastropieri, and Okolo (2008) concerning conclusions made by Scruggs and Mastropieri, supporting successful science education in inclusive classrooms requires not only the various techniques reviewed in this section, but also:

1. An open, accepting classroom environment.
2. Administrative support for inclusion.
3. Effective teaching skills on the part of the general education teacher.
4. Special education support in the form of consultation or direct assistance.
5. Peer mediation in the form of classroom assistance or cooperative learning.
6. Appropriate curriculum (supporting a hands-on approach to science learning).
7. Teaching skills specific to particular disability or need areas. (p. 7)

STRATEGIES AND TECHNIQUES FOR SOCIAL STUDIES INSTRUCTION

A number of studies have been conducted on effective strategies and instructional techniques in social studies instruction for students with mild disabilities, students at risk for academic failure, and students learning English as a second language (e.g., Brown, 2007; Bulgren, 2006; Bulgren, Deshler, & Lenz, 2007; Mastropieri et al., 2005; Scruggs, Mastropieri, & Okolo, 2008; Weisman & Hansen, 2007). Brown (2007) noted several characteristics of students learning English as a second language, which are similar to those seen in students with mild disabilities. These include limited background knowledge and vocabulary as related to social studies content, difficulty navigating text discourse, and struggles with comprehension. In order for students to learn social studies content, they must acquire a theoretical understanding of historical events, geographical locations, and social stances as they relate to each other and to the information presented in textbooks, lectures, and instructional materials. Research suggests that teachers providing social studies instruction incorporate and expand upon student background knowledge in an effort to make abstract concepts more concrete (Brown, 2007; Scruggs, Mastropieri, & Okolo, 2008). Additionally, teachers should scaffold instruction and provide multiple means for students to demonstrate the comprehension of content. By incorporating a universal design for learning, students who typically struggle with learning social studies content will have more opportunities for success (Meo, 2008). Examples of specific intervention techniques are presented in the following pages.

Content Enhancement Routines

Content enhancement routines have been used to assist teachers in organizing social studies content and instruction for students with and without disabilities. Bulgren (2006) and Bulgren, Deshler, and Lenz (2007) have advanced the research base supporting content enhancement routines for students with and without mild disabilities in learning social studies content. Their research, combined with the research from the University of Kansas Center for Research on Learning, demonstrates the effectiveness of this model for course, unit, and lesson organization.

Levels of Learning and Associated Instructional Techniques

According to Scruggs, Mastropieri, and Okolo (2008), social studies instruction can be visualized as working on four distinct levels: factual, conceptual, procedural, and investigative. Factual learning involves expanding knowledge concerning vocabulary, individuals, distinct events, and dates. Conceptual learning expands factual learning through an understanding of the primary features of objects, events, ideas, and the attributes that categorize and classify each. Procedural learning requires an understanding of the process used to execute a task or assignment. Investigative learning involves inquiry and the exploration of concepts in an integrated fashion. Each of these levels of learning, with associated techniques for enhancing instruction, have been explored by researchers interested in the learning of students with mild disabilities.

In the area of factual learning, teaching vocabulary associations through previewing, multiple opportunities for practice, and linking to background knowledge have been demonstrated as effective instructional techniques (Scruggs, Mastropieri, & Okolo, 2008). Other effective techniques include reviewing prior information, guided note taking, providing outlines, and using questioning and/or summarizing techniques during lectures.

In the area of conceptual learning, vocabulary instruction using mnemonic strategies to enhance a deeper understanding of meaning and generalization of words has proven successful (Scruggs, Mastropieri, & Okolo, 2008). Course and/or content organizational routines, such as the content enhancement routines mentioned previously, as well as focusing on main ideas, aid students in conceptual learning. Graphic organizers also support conceptual learning by assisting students in describing facts, concepts, and associations among and/or between ideas. Scruggs, Mastropieri, and Okolo (2008) cite research conducted by Gallavan and Kottler (2007) describing four categories of graphic organizers appropriate for social studies instruction: "*Assume and anticipate graphic organizers*, such as K-W-L . . ." (p. 13); "*Position and pattern organizers,* such as a timeline . . ." (p. 13); "*Group and organize organizers,* such as concept maps . . ." (p. 13); and "*Compare and contrast organizers,* such as Venn diagrams . . ." (p. 13). Finally, personalizations of content and classroom discussions represent two other methods supported by research as facilitating conceptual learning.

In the area of procedural learning, cognitive strategy instruction has received wide attention and support by the research community (Babkie & Provost, 2002; Scruggs, Mastropieri, & Okolo, 2008; Wood, Woloshyn, & Willoughby, 1995). Cognitive strategy instruction not only teaches students a process for learning, but also concepts related to instruction (e.g., vocabulary and content). In the area of social studies, numerous cognitive strategies have been created and evaluated. These strategies include, but are not limited to, the keyword method, literacy strategies, question-generation strategies, and so on. Additionally, the use of Collaborative Strategic Reading (CSR) and reciprocal teaching has improved student academic performance in social studies.

The research base concerning effective practices for students with mild disabilities in the area of investigative learning is just beginning. Scruggs, Mastropieri, and Okolo (2008) describe a few curricular programs and interventions that have been used with this population of learners, including those that are paper-based and those that are web-based. Of the programs with positive results, one included the use of "anchor" videos to promote the learning of social studies content. Specifically, these programs used *To Kill a Mockingbird* or *Eyes on the Prize* to facilitate comprehension, discussions, and investigations. The data showed that student performance increased with respect to understanding, reasoning, and motivation for learning. Another program with positive results included the use of a project-based learning approach involving cooperative learning groups. These projects investigated controversial topics in social studies structured around one or more main ideas and incorporated analyses of primary and secondary sources of information. Results showed that project-based learning approaches were beneficial to students with mild disabilities as long as teachers practiced effective classroom management skills. The World Wide Web is another resource that teachers and students may access for information relating to social studies content. Additionally, Scruggs, Mastropieri, and Okolo (2008) created a virtual web-based learning environment, the Virtual History Museum (VHM), for teachers and students to use. Please see http://vhm.msu.edu for more information.

Conclusion

Teachers providing instruction to students with mild disabilities in the content areas have a wide array of resources and research-based methods to facilitate this process. Whether the teacher serves as the content area expert or the accommodation expert, he/she is encouraged to use one or more of the instructional techniques presented in this chapter. Furthermore, we encourage our readers to actively use the methods included in the universal design for learning. Given that research strongly supports the inclusion of students with mild disabilities and those with diverse learning needs in content area classrooms, both general and special education teachers must focus on ways in which all learners can master content area knowledge in order to achieve academic success.

References

Anderman, E. M. (1998). The middle school experience: Effects on the math and science achievement of adolescents with LD. *Journal of Learning Disabilities, 31,* 128–138.

Babkie, A. M., & Provost, M. C. (2002). Select, write and use metacognitive strategies in the classroom. *Intervention in School and Clinic, 37*(3), 173–177.

Boyle, J. R. (2001). Enhancing the note-taking skills of students with mild disabilities. *Intervention in School and Clinic, 36*(4), 221–224.

Boyle, J. R. (2007, May/June). The process of note taking: Implications for students with mild disabilities. *The Clearinghouse, 80*(5), 227–230.

Boyle, J. R. (in press). Strategic note-taking for middle school students with learning disabilities in science classrooms. *Learning Disability Quarterly.*

Boyle, J. R., & Weishaar, M. (2001). The effects of strategic notetaking on the recall and comprehension of lecture information for high school students with learning disabilities. *Learning Disabilities Research & Practice, 16*(3), 133–141.

Brown, C. L. (2007, September/October). Strategies for making social studies texts more comprehensible for English-language learners. *The Social Studies, 98*(5), 185–188.

Bulgren, J. A. (2006). Integrated content enhancement routines: Responding to the needs of adolescents with disabilities in rigorous inclusive secondary content classes. *Teaching Exceptional Children, 38*(6), 54–58.

Bulgren, J. A., Deshler, D. D., & Lenz, B. K. (2007). Engaging adolescents with learning disabilities in higher-order thinking about history concepts using integrated content enhancement routines. *Journal of Learning Disabilities, 40,* 121–133.

Bulgren, J. A., Marquis, J. G., Lenz, B. K., Schumaker, J. B., & Deshler, D. D. (2009). Effectiveness of question exploration to enhance students' written expression of content knowledge and comprehension. *Reading & Writing Quarterly, 25*(4), 271–289.

Conderman, G., Bresnahan, V., & Pedersen, T. (2009). *Purposeful co-teaching: Real cases and effective strategies.* Thousand Oaks, CA: Corwin Press.

Dieker, L. A., & Little, M. (2005). Secondary reading: Not just for reading teachers anymore. *Intervention in School and Clinic, 40*(5), 276–283.

Dieker, L. A., & Murawski, W. W. (2003, April/May). Co-teaching at the secondary level: Unique issues, current trends, and suggestions for success. *The High School Journal, 86*(4), 1–13.

Ellis, E. (2008). Makes Sense Strategies. Northport, AL: GraphicOrganizers.com.

Ellis, E. S., & Rock, M. L. (2001). *Makes sense strategies: Connecting teaching, learning and assessment.* Tuscaloosa, AL: Masterminds.

Grigg, W., Lauko, M., & Brockway, D. (2006). *The nation's report card: Science 2005* (NCES 2006-466). U.S. Department of Education, National Center for Education Statistics. Washington, DC: U.S. Government Printing Office.

Gunning, T. G. (2010). *Assessing and correcting reading and writing difficulties* (4th ed.). Boston: Allyn & Bacon.

Honnert, A. M., & Bozan, S. E. (2005). Summary frames: Language acquisition for special education and ELL students. *Science Activities, 42*(2), 19–29.

Kirch, S. A., Bargerhuff, M. E., Turner, H., & Wheatly, M. (2005). Inclusive science education: Classroom teacher and science educator experiences in CLASS workshops. *School Science and Mathematics, 105*(4), 175–196.

Konrad, M., Joseph, L. M., & Eveleigh, E. (2009). A meta-analytic review of guided notes. *Education and Treatment of Children, 32*(3), 421–444.

Lazarus, B. D. (1991). Guided notes, review, and achievement of secondary students with learning disabilities in mainstream content courses. *Education and Treatment of Children, 14*(2), 112–127.

Lee, J., & Weiss, A. (2007). *The nation's report card: U.S. history 2006* (NCES 2007–474). U.S. Department of Education, National Center for Education Statistics. Washington, DC: U.S. Government Printing Office.

Lee, O., Lewis, S., Adamson, K., Maerten-Rivera, J., & Secada, W. G. (2007). Urban elementary school teachers' knowledge and practices in teaching science to English language learners. *Science Teacher Education, 92*(4), 733–758.

Lenz, B. K., Bulgren, J. A., Schumaker, J. B., Deshler, D. D., & Boudah, D. A. (1994). *The content enhancement series: The unit organizer routine.* Lawrence, KS: Edge Enterprises, Inc.

Lenz, B. K., Deshler, D. D., & Kissam, B. R. (2004). *Teaching content to all: Evidence-based inclusive practices in middle and secondary schools.* Boston: Pearson, Allyn & Bacon Pearson/Allyn & Bacon.

Lenz, B. K., Schumaker, J. B., Deshler, D. D., & Bulgren, J. A. (1998). *The content enhancement series: The course organizer routine.* Lawrence, KS: Edge Enterprises, Inc.

Mastropieri, M. A., Scruggs, T. E., & Graetz, J. (2005). Cognition and learning in inclusive high school chemistry classes. In T. E. Scruggs & M. A. Mastropieri (Eds.), *Advances in learning and behavioral disabilities: Vol. 18. Cognition and learning in diverse settings* (pp. 107–118). Oxford, U.K./Elsevier.

Mastropieri, M. A., Scruggs, T. E., Graetz, J., Norland, J., Gardizi, W., & McDuffie, K. (2005). Case studies in co-teaching in the content areas: Successes, failures and challenges. *Intervention in School and Clinic, 40*(5), 260–270.

Mastropieri, M. A., Scruggs, T. E., Norland, J. J., Berkeley, S., McDuffie, K., Tornquist, E. H., & Connors, N. (2006). Differentiated curriculum enhancement in inclusive middle school Science: Effects on classroom and high-stakes tests. *The Journal of Special Education, 40*(3), 130–137.

Meo, G. (2008). Curriculum planning for all learners: Applying universal design for learning (UDL) to a high school reading comprehension program. *Preventing School Failure, 52*(2), 21–30.

Pressley, M., Woloshyn, V., Burkell, J., Cariglia-Bull, T., Lysynchuk, L., McGoldrick, J. A., Schneider, B., Snyder, B. L., & Symons, S. (1995). *Cognitive strategy instruction that REALLY improves children's academic performance.* Cambridge, MA: Brookline Books.

Scruggs, T. E., & Mastropieri, M. A. (1992). Classroom applications of mnemonic instruction: Acquisition, maintenance, and generalization. *Exceptional Children, 58,* 219–229.

Scruggs, T. E., & Mastropieri, M. A. (2000). The effectiveness of mnemonic instruction for students with learning and behavior problems: An update and research synthesis. *Journal of Behavioral Education, 10,* 163–173.

Scruggs, T. E., Mastropieri, M. A., & Okolo, C. M. (2008). Science and social studies for students with disabilities. *Focus on Exceptional Children, 41,* 1–24. Retrieved May 29, 2009, from Academic Search Premier database.

Smith, K. S., Rook, J. E., & Smith, T. W. (2007). Increasing student engagement using effective and metacognitive writing strategies in content areas. *Preventing School Failure, 51*(3), 43–48.

Vaughn, S., Bos, C. S., & Schumm, J. S. (2007). *Teaching students who are exceptional, diverse, and at risk in the general education classroom* (4th ed.). Boston: Pearson/Allyn & Bacon.

Weisman, E. M., & Hansen, L. E. (2007, September/October). Strategies for teaching social studies to English-language learners at the elementary level. *The Social Studies, 98*(5), 180–184.

Wood, E., Woloshyn, V. E., & Willoughby, T. (1995). *Cognitive strategy instruction for middle and high schools.* Cambridge, MA: Brookline Books.

14

Cases About Teaching Content and Study Skills in Inclusive Classrooms

CASE 1

Inclusion and Behavior Issues in a Content-Area Classroom

Jason is a 10-year-old student with severe autism. In addition to autism, Jason is nonverbal (he does not sign, but is able to lead individuals to what he wants), exhibits frequent episodes of self-abuse (head slapping, hand biting, attempting to remove his g-tube), aggression to people (hitting, kicking, pushing, head-butting) and property (throwing objects), and flight behavior (running from the classroom or area). He receives liquids and food through a g-tube four times daily while at school, wears diapers because he is not toilet trained, and sits for limited periods of time (2 to 3 minutes or less). He enjoys watching videos on television while standing, walking outside, and limited one-on-one attention from preferred individuals. Jason dislikes having to sit and attend to tasks, having the staff block his attempts to self-abuse, being fed through his g-tube, having his mouth wiped and/or teeth cleaned, and waiting.

Jason receives educational services for the majority of the school day in a self-contained classroom for students with severe and multiple disabilities. He is included in general education classes for art, physical education, and music. He has a one-on-one paraprofessional who provides his feedings and meets his toileting needs. He receives services from a speech-language pathologist (SLP) in the area of communication. Presently, he is working on using a communication board with icons and voice activation software to express his wants and needs. He receives support services from a school district nurse to monitor the care of his g-tube. Jason receives 60 minutes per week of service from the occupational therapist (OT) to enhance his fine-motor skills. Additionally, he receives intermittent support services from a school district behavior specialist to address his self-abusive behavior and behavior management plan. When not in the self-contained classroom, Jason is supported by his paraprofessional and receives consultative support from his special education teacher.

The individualized education plan (IEP) team, with the input of the school district behavior specialist, developed the following plan to address Jason's behavior. To complete this plan, the team initially identified the maladaptive behaviors targeted for change: self-injurious behavior (SIB), aggression to people, aggression to property, and running from the classroom. Next, the team identified the adaptive behaviors targeted for change: use of communication board to express wants and needs, compliance to individual requests, and increased wait time (ability to wait for desired object or activity). The team completed a functional behavior analysis of Jason's behavior and found that his maladaptive behaviors served several needs that included escape, power, and communication. The team then agreed that when he exhibits self-abuse, aggression, or flight behaviors, they will provide a verbal cue to stop the behavior. If the verbal cue is unsuccessful as a desist, physical blocking will be used. If the behavior continues to escalate, then physical restraint in the form of gentle holding will be employed until Jason appears to be calm (no attempts at SIB, aggression, and/or flight). In order to increase his adaptive behaviors, the team designed a reinforcement schedule that reinforces each instance of a targeted adaptive behavior. As the episodes of maladaptive behaviors decrease to an acceptable level (fewer than 10 per day), a variable reinforcement schedule will be used.

Jason's educational needs are met for the majority of the school day in a self-contained special education classroom in a public school setting. The classroom has a total of eight students with severe and multiple disabilities, all of whom are assigned to the fourth or fifth grade. The classroom is lead by a special education teacher and has the support of three paraprofessionals; two of whom are assigned as one-on-one aides. The paraprofessional who is not assigned as a one-on-one aide has responsibilities outside of the classroom such as cafeteria duty and working in the school's copy room. She is in the special education classroom for 3.5 hours out of the 6-hour school day.

The students in this classroom have multiple needs and disabilities. Some are in wheelchairs because they are nonambulatory. Some have status seizure activity as well as feeding problems (e.g., g-tubes, pacing, food-stealing, allergies). The majority of the students receive services from the SLP, OT, and physical therapist (PT). Two of the students, including Jason, receive support services from a school district nurse for medical care (g-tube feedings and seizures).

School begins at East Park Elementary School at 8:00 a.m. The day begins earlier for students in Ms. Parks's classroom though. Her students arrive at school between 7:30 and 7:45 a.m. After arrival, students either go to the cafeteria for breakfast or to the classroom for toileting/feeding. For those students who go to the classroom prior to 8:00 a.m., they get to select free-time activities after toileting and until school begins at 8:00 a.m. When school begins, Ms. Parks conducts a circle-time activity every morning that incorporates a read-aloud, calendar activity, and plan for the day. She incorporates a visual schedule for her students and uses a total communication approach (e.g., sign, communication board, gestures) when providing this information to her students. Beginning at 8:30 a.m., Ms. Parks breaks her students into groups for communication instruction. She provides functional communication activities and encourages social skills with the support of her classroom paraprofessionals. Activities include, but are not limited to, sign language, picture identification and/or recognition, the use of communication boards, and switch activation. Starting at about 9:15 a.m., Ms. Parks initiates a functional theme (e.g., friendship). She leads a discussion on the theme and then provides activities (e.g., "What do you do to show friendship?" "How do you communicate with a friend?") that reinforce the theme of the week or month. After this lesson, the students have time for toileting/feeding, snack, and free time. Beginning at 10:15 a.m., students return in a whole group format for information on the next functional activity or lesson. These lessons may include, but are not limited to, fine/gross motor activities, communication, and academic instruction. Following this lesson, students are toileted/diapers are changed, grooming is completed, and feedings via g-tube are conducted. Students not engaged in these activities are allowed to have "center time." Beginning at about 11:30 A.M., students are taken outside for a walk and structured recess for 20 minutes. Students who eat lunch in the cafeteria then go to lunch and students who receive g-tube feedings return to the classroom. At noon, all students have a bathroom break and perform grooming activities. Then students go to specials (fine arts, physical education, and the media center—days rotate weekly) for 45 minutes. Following specials, students return to the classroom for final feedings/toileting, and an end-of-the-day circle-time activity.

The students in Ms. Parks's classroom attend specials with a fourth-grade general education class. When they go to specials, they are escorted and supported by all of her paraprofessionals. Mrs. Shultz is the music teacher. She has an undergraduate degree in music education and is working on a master's degree in special education. Mrs. Shultz works hard to create lessons that meet the needs of all of the students served in her music classes.

When the students arrive at the music class, soft music is playing in the room. Students are seated either in foldout chairs or on carpet squares. After everyone is settled, Mrs. Shultz provides an overview of the lesson for the day using picture cues for the students receiving special education services. Because fourth-grade students are expected to learn to play a recorder during this year of school, Mrs. Shultz provides instruction in this area. Unfortunately, many of the students from Ms. Parks's class have issues learning how to play this instrument so she incorporates other instrument choices (e.g., tambourines, bongo drums, maracas) for them. Mrs. Shultz incorporates cooperative grouping, mixing students with and without special needs in each group. She sets firm guidelines for each member of a group and rotates between each group to ensure compliance. She provides guidance to the special education paraprofessionals working one-on-one with selected students. She also supports the paraprofessionals when behavior issues arise. Generally speaking, the majority of her students successfully learn her classroom expectations and meet the state standards for fourth-grade music education.

The following three paragraphs provide a picture of one class period in music with Jason. Mrs. Shultz stands at the doorway to the music room to greet students as they arrive (soft music is playing). The students from Ms. Parks's class arrive with their paraprofessionals and go to their assigned areas. Next, the students from the fourth-grade general education class arrive and get settled in their areas. Students who are learning to play a recorder take them out and students learning other instruments find these at their seats. Mrs. Shultz provides an overview of the day's instruction while the paraprofessionals support her by showing an accompanying picture schedule for the class.

Mrs. Young, a special education paraprofessional, shows Jason the picture schedule and verbally prompts him to stay in his area. Jason is already getting restless, which is evident from his standing up, pacing, making noises, and hand flapping. Jason sits down and continues to make noises and hand flap.

Mrs. Shultz turns off the background music and then models the scales that students will be practicing today on their recorders. She repeats this process several times and provides picture cues to students as to finger placement on the recorder. After modeling, she directs students who are working on this skill to practice in their small groups. Next, she models how to play the bongo drum. After modeling, she directs students to practice in their small groups. She circulates between the groups and offers individual support. The room is beginning to get pretty noisy.

Jason hits the bongo drum a few times with verbal and physical prompting from Mrs. Young. After about 10 trials, he jumps up from his seat and begins head slapping. Mrs. Young verbally prompts him to stop. Jason continues to head slap. Mrs. Young attempts to block his behavior and then gently holds Jason's hands down to his sides and speaks in a very quiet voice to him, telling him that he is okay. Jason calms down and returns to his seat. Jason hits the bongo drum a few more times and then jumps up from his seat again. He starts running around the room, head slapping, and hitting other students. It looks like he's had enough of music for the day. Mrs. Young, with the assistance of Mrs. Shultz, stops Jason from hitting himself and his peers. Jason continues to escalate and attempts to head butt Mrs. Young while she is holding his hands to his sides. Mrs. Young and Mrs. Shultz decide that Jason needs to go on a walk to calm down. Mrs. Young takes Jason for a walk around the school. When they get back to music class, Jason begins to get agitated, so Mrs. Young takes Jason back to the special education classroom.

Discussion Questions

1. Jason has several maladaptive behaviors that he exhibits at school. Do you believe that his behavior intervention plan is appropriate for the school setting? Why? If not, what would you change?

2. Do you feel that it is appropriate to include Jason in special areas? Why? What other supports do you believe may be necessary for him to be successful in these classes?

3. Mrs. Shultz employs many strategies in her music class designed to enhance student success. What other strategies might she use?

4. When Jason became upset during music class, Mrs. Young and Mrs. Shultz worked together to address his behavior. What would you have done under the circumstances described? Do you believe that they may have inadvertently reinforced his maladaptive behavior? Why or why not?

5. In examining the instructional routine that Ms. Parks employs in her classroom, what modifications might you make? Why?

6. Based on the information provided in this case study, what functional activities and/or lessons would you teach? Why?

CASE 2

Inclusion and Instruction in the Content Areas

Georgia is a 15-year-old student with cerebral palsy, a mild intellectual disability, a seizure disorder, and a speech disorder (articulation). She has limited mobility due to her cerebral palsy and uses an electric wheelchair (self-directed). Georgia's seizures are partially controlled with medication. She averages between one to three seizures per month at school. Her speech is difficult to understand unless the person listening has known Georgia for an extended period of time. She receives special education services through programs designed for students with orthopedic impairments, other health impairments, and speech impairments. She receives related services from an OT, PT, and assistive technology. Georgia also has a one-on-one paraprofessional who helps her meet her personal care needs as well as access the general ninth-grade curriculum.

Georgia enjoys attending school. She strives to become an office assistant upon graduation from high school. Her range of motion allows her to use a computer successfully, although her typing speed is slow (20 words per minute). Georgia uses adaptive equipment for computer processing. Because Georgia's articulation is an issue, voice activation software for data entry/word processing is not appropriate at this time. During school, Georgia exhibits no incidents of maladaptive behavior. She is eager to learn and participate in all classroom activities and lessons. Georgia participates in a self-contained model of instruction for reading, writing, math, and community-based instruction. She is included for science and social studies. While in the general education classroom, Georgia is assisted by a one-on-one paraprofessional (Ms. Sparks).

The IEP team, with the input of the school district nurse and special education teacher (case manager), developed the following plan to address Georgia's seizures and personal hygiene needs. When Georgia experiences a seizure (generalized form—tonic-clonic) at school, Ms. Sparks, or the school staff present at the time, ensure her safety. Because Georgia is typically in her wheelchair and secured by a lap belt with shoulder straps, she is at a low risk for injury. During a seizure, Georgia typically loses consciousness for 90 to 120 seconds. She is not incontinent. After a seizure, Georgia tends to need to take a short nap (30 minutes in duration) in the school clinic and then is able to return to regular activity. If Georgia happens to be out of her chair when the seizure occurs, Ms. Sparks or the school staff present lower her to the floor or to a mat for her safety. After the seizure, Georgia is returned to her wheelchair and is then taken to the school clinic to rest. All seizure activity is documented, including the duration, time of occurrence, and date. The parent is notified of all seizure activity in writing. If Georgia experiences more than two seizures in one school day, the parent is notified by telephone because this may be a signal that she is becoming ill or requires an adjustment in her seizure medication. If Georgia experiences a seizure while in the community, she is made as comfortable as possible until her mother is able to pick her up and take her home for the remainder of the school day.

Georgia requires personal assistance in meeting her toileting needs. She is physically able to assist others in the transfer from her wheelchair to the toilet. She is able to balance independently on the toilet (with grab bars present). Georgia needs assistance with lowering and raising undergarments and external clothing; she is able to wipe herself independently. She needs assistance with feminine hygiene products during her menstrual cycle. Georgia is directly supervised in the bathroom while out of her wheelchair due to possible seizure activity.

Georgia's educational needs are met for the majority of the school day in a self-contained special education classroom in a public high school setting. The classroom has a total of 10 students with severe and/or multiple disabilities, all of whom are assigned to the 9th or 10th grade. The classroom is lead by a special education teacher and has the support of four paraprofessionals; three of whom are assigned as one-on-one aides. The paraprofessional not assigned as a one-on-one serves as a floater and assists the special education teacher and other paraprofessionals as necessary in the classroom and in the community.

The students in this classroom have multiple needs and disabilities. Four are in wheelchairs because they are nonambulatory. Some have seizure activity, feeding problems (e.g., need to be fed by another, g-tubes, food allergies), as well as behavioral issues. The majority of the students receive services from the SLP, OT, and the PT. Six of the students in this class, including Georgia, receive support services from a school district nurse for medical care (seizures and/or g-tube feedings).

School begins at Crestview High School at 7:15 a.m. The day begins earlier for students in Ms. Johnson's classroom. Her students arrive between 6:45 a.m. and 7:00 a.m. After arrival, students either go to the cafeteria for breakfast or to the classroom for toileting/feeding. Students who arrive at the classroom early select free-time activities until school begins at 7:15 a.m. When school begins, Ms. Johnson conducts an overview of the day, takes attendance and lunch orders, and completes a read-aloud. She incorporates a visual schedule for her students and uses a total communication approach (e.g., sign, communication board, gestures) when providing this information to her students. Beginning at 7:45 a.m., the students in Ms. Johnson's class travel to their mainstream general education classrooms for either science or social studies instruction.

Following science and/or social studies class, all of Ms. Johnson's students return to the special education classroom for instruction. Ms. Johnson provides small-group instruction in language arts, reading, and communication for the next hour. During this time, she emphasizes functional skills and encourages social skills with the support of her classroom paraprofessionals and the SLP. Activities include, but are not limited to, reading fiction and nonfiction texts, reading functional words, writing, completing job applications, sign language, picture identification and recognition, use of communication boards, switch activation, and so on. Starting at about 10:30 a.m., students separate into different groups based on their medical needs and IEP goals. Some receive occupational and physical therapy; others receive math instruction or have their personal care needs met. After this period, the students return in a whole-group format for information on the next functional activity/lesson. These lessons may include, but not be limited to, fine/gross motor activities, communication, and further academic instruction. Beginning at about 11:30 a.m., students who eat lunch in the cafeteria then go to lunch, and students who receive g-tube feedings remain in the classroom. At noon, all students have a bathroom break and perform grooming activities. Next, students prepare to depart for community-based instruction. The students in Ms. Johnson's class have the opportunity to work at one of two job sites (small business office or the laundry room at a local hotel). The classroom paraprofessionals, employees at the job sites, and Ms. Johnson support all the students in the community. Students spend approximately 90 minutes per day at the respective job sites and then return to school to prepare for their transportation home.

The students in Ms. Johnson's classroom attend science and social studies classes with their grade-level peers. When they go to these classes, they are escorted and supported by all of her paraprofessionals. Mr. Stevens is the 9th- and 10th-grade science teacher at Crestview. He has an undergraduate degree in science and a master's degree in science education. Mr. Stevens works collaboratively with Ms. Johnson to create lessons that meet the needs of all of the students served in his science classes. Ms. Johnson makes a point of being in his class at least once a week so that they have a chance to co-teach and she has the opportunity to observe her students' performance.

Mr. Stevens's science class is housed in a lab-type setting. The room has large, raised tables with bar-stool type chairs. Each table has a sink at the center of it. The tables are positioned in such a way that wheelchair access is a little tricky. The tables are too high for most students who must sit in their wheelchairs, and the stools are not safe alternatives. Thus, students who must sit in their wheelchairs are grouped at a different table at the back of the classroom.

When the students arrive, they are met at the door by Mr. Stevens. He greets each student, and they proceed to their assigned seats. After everyone is settled, Mr. Stevens provides an overview of the lesson for the day using visual cues for the students receiving special education services. Ninth-grade students take the earth science class. They learn content ranging from earth history to rock formations to topographical maps. Some of the content presented in this class is too difficult for Ms. Johnson's students to comprehend, so many of the assignments and activities are modified to meet their individual needs. Mr. Stevens works closely with the special education paraprofessionals so that they understand his expectations. He also provides direct instruction and support to his "special" students.

The next four paragraphs describe a lesson in Mr. Stevens's classroom. Students enter the science class and go to their assigned seats. The special education paraprofessionals sit with their students who need extra assistance. Mr. Stevens provides an overview of the lesson for the day and a brief lecture on the properties of minerals. He defines crystal forms, cleavage planes, fracture surfaces, striations, tenacity, hardness, color, streak, and luster. He uses multiple concrete examples while introducing these definitions. He tells students that today they will explore different minerals and rocks that represent these forms. Students will work in groups in order to classify and categorize a variety of rocks and minerals. The first step in the process will be for students to separate metallic from nonmetallic minerals. He tells them that "if they are unsure about a mineral's luster, then it is probably nonmetallic." The next step for the metallic minerals is to determine hardness, color, cleavage qualities, and streak. The final step for the nonmetallic minerals is to separate light from dark colors, determine hardness, cleavage qualities, and streak. Mr. Stevens then distributes samples to student groups to explore. He walks around the classroom providing direction as necessary.

While Mr. Stevens conducts the opening of the lesson, Ms. Johnson listens to his presentation. She makes notes to herself as to any content that her students may find difficult (that she hadn't already considered in their planning meeting) and determines strategies to address these challenges. Even though direct knowledge of mineral forms may not be essential for many of her students, she knows that the ability to classify objects based on physical form is an important skill.

After Mr. Stevens distributes the samples to each student group, Ms. Johnson speaks to him. She tells him that the students receiving special education services will probably need to focus on one attribute of a mineral at a time. When they were planning this lesson, she didn't realize how many attributes would be covered in the lesson and wants her students to succeed. Mr. Stevens considers her input and then tells the class that he wants everyone to first focus on separating metallic from nonmetallic minerals. He holds up an example of each and walks around the room to make sure that all the students can see the examples.

Georgia works at the "special" table with a group of five other students. Two students without special needs are included in the group. Each student takes turns picking up a mineral and then determining whether it is metallic or nonmetallic. When the group reaches consensus on the determination, the mineral is placed on a mat labeled by category with a visual example at the top. Ms. Johnson and Ms. Sparks are careful to offer assistance only as necessary. After about 15 minutes, this group successfully completes the first phase of the lab. Mr. Stevens notices that they are ready to move on to the next phase and demonstrates how to determine hardness for metallic minerals. Georgia and the students in her group begin on this task. It appears that they are all being successful.

Five minutes prior to the end of science class, Mr. Stevens conducts an ending review of the day's activities. He congratulates the students for successfully working together and informs them that the lab will continue when they return for their next class.

Discussion Questions

1. Georgia is included for science and social studies at Crestview High School. Do you believe that this is appropriate? Why or why not?
2. When examining the layout of Mr. Stevens's science classroom, what modifications would you make, if any? Why?
3. Do you feel that it is appropriate and/or functional for Georgia to learn about mineral forms? Why or why not?
4. What steps do you believe Ms. Johnson and Mr. Stevens should use to make their planning time more successful?

5. When Georgia experiences a seizure at school, she misses instructional time. How would you ensure that she gets the content she missed?

6. Currently, the community plan addressing Georgia's seizures is for her to go home after a seizure. Do you feel this is appropriate? Why? How would you modify this plan?

CASE 3

Cooperative Learning—Is It "Right" for All Students with Disabilities?

Ethan is an 8-year-old student with an identified learning disability in reading. He was found eligible for special education services while in the second grade after repeating the grade. Ethan possesses above-average intelligence as measured by the Wechsler Intelligence Scale for Children—4th Edition. He receives special education services through programs designed for students with learning disabilities in an inclusion setting. He receives no related services. He has difficulty with phonemic awareness, sight word vocabulary, phonics, and reading comprehension. Because of his reading difficulties, he experiences trouble in math (word problems) and content-area instruction that requires reading.

Ethan is frustrated in school. He does not like feeling "stupid" around his friends who are able to read. He does not like participating in class and prefers to complete independent activities/lessons where no one but the teacher knows his performance. Ethan is interested in science and social studies. His father is a college professor who teaches undergraduate and graduate students content in multiple science areas. Ethan's mother is in the field of international banking and finance. He is pleased with her ability in this area and thinks that he might want to go into science or international banking when he gets out of school, although he knows he will need to overcome his reading problems. Ethan likes the fact that his parent's combined income is more than $300,000 per year (although his mom makes a lot more money than his dad)!

Ethan is beginning third grade in the fall. He is assigned to be in George Winston's class and will have Kim Akin as his special education inclusion teacher for a portion of the school day. George and Kim have co-taught together for 2 years and have a great working relationship. Unfortunately, Kim has other responsibilities besides teaching. She is also the special education coordinator for her school and frequently is called away from classroom instruction to facilitate meetings and to provide behavioral support to students in other classrooms. Even so, George is thrilled to have the opportunity to work with Kim for another year. If the last 2 years are any indication, this should be another fantastic year.

Kim typically supports George in his classroom during the language arts block of instruction. At times, she is able to pop in to assist him with science and social studies instruction. During language arts, they use dynamic grouping for the Reading and Writing Workshop. In math, George has the assistance of a paraprofessional so that he can meet the needs of all of his students. For science and social studies, George tends to teach whole group and then incorporates cooperative learning activities. This year, George and Kim will have students from diverse backgrounds in their third-grade classroom. Thus, they have decided to use a read-aloud story, *Roots of Peace, Seeds of Hope: A Journey for Peacemakers*, to jump-start their instruction in language arts and social studies. In order to ensure that their students grasp the third-grade social studies standards concerning Native American history, George and Kim decide to give their students a few choices to demonstrate their comprehension of life in America today as compared to the past. After doing some research, they settle on having the students select one of the following activities: write a research paper, complete a web quest, interview a local Native American and write a paper summarizing the interview, or create a photographic documentary (using Photo Story and Audacity software) comparing Native American life of the past to the present. George agrees to create the web quest, and Kim will talk to their school's instructional technology person to get help in supporting students who wish to complete the photographic documentary.

School begins and George's class is a little larger than he expected. He has 28 students, 7 with special needs. Due to his numbers, he knows that he may lose a few after the 10-day count, but realizes that he will keep all of his students receiving special education support services. His is the only third-grade class with inclusive services this year.

George and Kim experience a good school beginning, even with their numbers. Ethan, on the other hand, has some difficulty. He is still hesitant to work in a group. The social studies project—the photographic documentary—may be an issue. George has put the students who made this choice in groups of two to select and download photographs. Ethan's partner, Shelby, is a computer wiz and Ethan is not. He doesn't like working with a girl much to begin with and definitely not a girl who is better at navigating web sites for photographs. Shelby is also a better writer than Ethan, which really irritates him. The other students who chose to complete this assignment are also girls. One of the girls is very quiet and has a mild intellectual/cognitive disability. Maybe George should group Ethan with her? He wants all of his students to be successful with the assignment and is not sure if this will work. George doesn't have much assistance during social studies from Kim and is not sure of how to proceed. Ethan is beginning to refuse to work and has started acting out in class. George needs to talk to Kim and see what ideas she has to address Ethan's behavior.

Discussion Questions

1. Based on the information provided in this case study, do you feel that Ethan is appropriately placed in an inclusion model? Why or why not?
2. George and Kim reportedly have a very good working relationship, although Kim is occasionally absent from George's classroom. Do you believe that a different teacher, who might be a consistent presence in the classroom, would be a better match for this inclusion model? Why or why not?
3. George and Kim decided to link a read-aloud with a unit of study in social studies. Do you feel that this is appropriate? What is your impression of the extension activities that they developed to show comprehension of content? What recommendations would you make for change, if any?
4. The case study depicts Ethan as a bright young boy with a mild learning disability. Do you believe that his behavior is typical of students with mild learning disabilities in the third grade?
5. If you were Kim, what would you recommend to George to address Ethan's learning situation? Support your answer with your knowledge of the characteristics of students with learning disabilities and inclusive practices.

CASE 4

Study Skills—Who Needs Them?

Laurie Beacon is a special education teacher who works at a magnet middle school in a large school district. She provides inclusive services to students in sixth grade as well as teaches learning strategies in a stand-alone course. Her school, the School of Arts and Science, has the highest test scores of any school in her district. Laurie loves teaching sixth grade and plans to do so until she retires from teaching at the age of 55 (after 30 years of service). She is now 46 years old.

Laurie works with three other sixth-grade teachers. She has a range of relationships with each. Carla Fish is a science teacher, Jacob Walsh is a social studies teacher, and Connie Bryant is an English language arts (ELA) teacher. She has a fair relationship with Carla, a good relationship with Jacob, and an excellent relationship with Connie. Laurie has worked with Jacob the longest and with Connie for the shortest amount of time. Each teacher was recruited by Laurie's school district from out of state, so their educational programs at college differed from hers. Connie's college program emphasized inclusive practices for students with disabilities. The other teachers had one course in exceptionalities and, according to Laurie, have no idea what these students need to be successful in the general curriculum.

This year, Laurie has decided that she needs to incorporate study skills into each class that she supports. She plans to teach the Test-Taking Strategy and the Self-Questioning Strategy, developed at the Center for Research and Learning at the University of Kansas, in her strategy class and then support their use in science, social studies and ELA. Laurie realizes that these strategies take a long time to teach, but feels it is worth the effort if the teachers will support their use in their classes.

Laurie sets up a meeting with her sixth-grade team to discuss her ideas. She wants to make sure that she has everyone's support prior to teaching the strategies she has selected to teach first. Laurie knows that learning a strategy in isolation does not promote maintenance and generalization of the skill, so she has to get buy-in from the other teachers on her team. Laurie meets with the group, and they agree to support the use of the strategies in their classes. The group decides that Laurie should teach the Self-Questioning Strategy first. After hearing Laurie's explanation of the strategy, they believe that this strategy might be good for all of their students to learn and use. The group does not come to a consensus on the Test-Taking Strategy, so Laurie decides to fight that battle later. If she is able to demonstrate through student performance that the Self-Questioning Strategy works, she hopes that the teachers will support her teaching the other strategy later.

In preparing to teach the Self-Questioning Strategy, Laurie first prepares student folders. She decides that her students will use the folders in her classroom first while learning the strategy, and then later they may carry an extra folder with them to their content-area classes. Laurie also prepares extra folders for the teachers on her sixth-grade team so that they will have a better idea of what the students will be working with. She expects that after the students learn the strategy and are able to use it comfortably in her strategy class, they will then be able to use it in their other classes with her support. Eventually, Laurie plans to teach the strategy to all the students of her sixth-grade team, but she is going to start first with her special education group. This will give them a head start and possibly allow them to be "experts" on the strategy. Ultimately, she wants Carla, Jacob, and Connie to promote the use of the strategy, too, with all of their students.

After about 3 weeks of instruction in strategies class, Laurie believes that her students are ready to begin practicing use of the Self-Questioning Strategy in their content area classes. She informs her sixth-grade team, and they agree to have her take a portion of each of their classes to teach all of the students the Self-Questioning Strategy. After a few weeks, most of the students have mastered the strategy. Some of the students receiving special education services still need prompting to use the strategy while reading and studying, but overall everyone has done well. Laurie is ready to broach the subject of teaching the Test-Taking Strategy again.

Laurie sets up another meeting with her sixth-grade team members. She talks about the success of the first strategy and provides a detailed rationale for teaching the second one. Carla and Connie are all for it, but Jacob doesn't want to "waste" instructional time in his class to teach everyone the strategy. The team compromises and Laurie teaches the Test-Taking Strategy in strategies class, and then individually supports its use in the content area classes. She hopes that "her" students will prove to the group that the time was worth the effort, and that maybe next year they will agree to have her teach all of their students this strategy.

Discussion Questions

1. If you were Laurie, how would you work to increase Carla and Jacob's knowledge of students with disabilities?
2. Laurie first instructed the students with disabilities in strategy use and then taught all of the students in science, social studies, and ELA. Do you agree with this decision? Why or why not?
3. By teaching all of the sixth-grade students in her team's classes the Self-Questioning Strategy, she also indirectly taught the teachers. How do you believe this may have supported the use of the strategy for all students?
4. Laurie did not receive consensus from her team to teach the Test-Taking Strategy in their classes due to the time involved. Would you have forced the matter? Why or why not?
5. If you were the special education teacher working with this group of teachers, what would you do to promote instruction in study skills for all students?

CASE 5

Are You Ready to Teach Biology?

Bill Gillespie is a 10th-grade biology teacher at a large high school in a growing school district. He has taught biology for 6 years and enjoys it. Teaching is Bill's second career. Previously, he worked as a researcher for a large biomedical company. After retiring from that job, he decided to try his hand at teaching. Because high school science is a critical area in his state, he did not have to obtain regular certification to teach. Even so, Bill seems to be a natural teacher. He works hard to not talk at his students, but to involve them in a variety of learning experiences.

Eve Dimple is a special education teacher assigned to support 10th-grade inclusion students. This is her second year at this school and her first year working with 10th-grade content-area teachers. Eve is a little nervous about the upcoming year. She is confident in her ability to support her students in all of their subjects except biology. Biology was her worst subject in high school and college. She especially dislikes anything having to do with dissecting animals and hopes that she won't have to be in the room before, during, or after this is completed. Eve thinks that she should probably share these feelings with Bill now rather than later, when she might either vomit or faint.

Bill and Eve meet with the school guidance counselor, Abigail Ryan, before school begins to see how many students with disabilities will need inclusive support in 10th-grade biology. Abigail tells them that there will be six students with IEPs in biology. Eve knows all but one of the students; the student she doesn't know is new to their school. Bill doesn't know any of them. Abigail gives Bill and Eve copies of each student's IEP and answers any questions they have. Eve shares her impressions of the students that she knows from teaching them last year. Five of the students they will work with have learning disabilities and one student has very high-functioning Asperger syndrome. Bill asks good questions and gives the impression that he is happy to have all of these students in his class. Eve is beginning to like Bill. He reminds her a little of her father. He is kind, asks good questions, and seems like he will be easy to work with. Eve thinks, "Maybe biology class won't be so bad."

After the meeting with Abigail, Eve and Bill meet individually to discuss the scope and sequence of the biology course. Bill briefly reviews how he structures the course and the learning activities he uses. During their meeting, Eve is relieved to discover that Bill doesn't use real animals in his labs. Virtual technology has eliminated this need in high school. Eve shares with Bill that her content knowledge of biology is rather weak and that she is nervous about supporting the students with it. Bill assures her that after this year, she will have a better grasp on biology. He gives her a copy of the teacher edition that they will use for the class and tells her what content they will cover first. They agree that Eve will read the content included in the text and develop questions to ask him before beginning each study unit. Bill will act as lead instructor, and Eve will support any student who needs assistance. If Eve has difficulty, Bill will help her.

The first unit of instruction in biology covers the characteristics of living organisms and includes numerous definitions. Bill introduces the terms: order, metabolism, motility, responsiveness, reproduction, development, heredity, evolution, and adaptations. With Eve's assistance, he promotes guided note taking and elicits definitions and examples from the students. He uses visual representations for many of the terms and provides multiple examples. Bill next divides the students into groups and has them supplement their notes with information from the text. Bill and Eve circulate throughout the classroom, providing students with assistance as necessary. After about 20 minutes, Bill prompts the students to stop where they are and to watch a short film that reinforces the content covered in the day's lesson. He directs students to write down any questions that they may have while viewing the film. After the film, the students are given the opportunity to ask questions and receive answers. Finally, Bill ends the class with a review of the content learned and an overview of what the students can expect to learn tomorrow.

At the end of the school day, Bill and Eve meet to discuss how the class went. Eve confides in Bill that she is still not as comfortable with the content as she'd like, but she thinks that she will get better as time goes on. Bill asks Eve what other supports he might use to assist her as well as their students. Eve is not sure of what to say at this point. She thinks that multiple examples and opportunities for practice with the content will help both her and her students. She tells Bill that his enthusiasm for the content and his teaching manner make the learning situation bearable. They both laugh! Bill thinks that with enough time, he might be able to get Eve to like biology.

Discussion Questions

1. As a special education teacher supporting inclusion, what steps would you take to teach and support the learning of content that you are not familiar with?
2. If you were Bill, what suggestions would you give to Eve to make her more comfortable with biology?
3. Analyze the lesson described in the case study. Do you have any suggestions for change? If so, what? If not, why not?
4. Bill is the biology teacher and therefore takes the lead on content-area instruction. In order for Bill and Eve to co-teach, what steps will Eve have to take?
5. At this point in the case study, we see a very supportive relationship between the two teachers. What does Eve need to do to maintain this relationship?

INDEX

Page numbers followed by *f* and *b* indicate figure and boxes respectively.